YUGOSLAVIA—A MULTINATIONAL STATE

Regional Difference and Administrative Response

*Chandler Publications in
Political Science*
Victor Jones, Editor

Yugoslavia— A Multinational State

Regional Difference and Administrative Response

JACK C. FISHER
Cornell University

CHANDLER PUBLISHING COMPANY
124 Spear Street, San Francisco, California 94105

To Kit

Contents

Tables

Tables

Figures

Figures

Foreword

Yugoslavia was created in 1918. The new state was composed of areas which had never enjoyed a common government, and which had been under the domination of different foreign powers for centuries. The interwar period was marked by bitter conflict between the Serbian-dominated government and the Croatians and other ethnic groups. The distinguishing characteristic of the post-1950 administrative system was the government's political response to this situation and the unique attempt to create a politically and economically integrated state out of the country's multinational and divergent structure. Thus political response to regional variation produced an administrative reorganization, which increased the authority of local institutions under formally indirect federal supervision and control, thereby providing a microregional approach to development.

The present study was undertaken to examine the effects of the uniform system of local administration which was superimposed over the country's heterogeneous cultural and economic matrix after World War II. An

investigation of the differences and similarities among the cities and
communes of Yugoslavia was conducted in order to obtain quantitative
expression of existing regional variation. This analysis and the approach
utilized provide insights into Yugoslavia's unique historical evolution and
the functioning of its contemporary administrative system. The evolution
of the local administrative system, the communal system, is described in
detail. Particular functions, such as city planning and housing administration and development, which were delegated to local authorities, are
examined.

A further objective of this book is to present a statistical and carto-
graphical source of information on Yugoslavia. Since readily available and
accurate maps are generally not available in English sources, much time
and effort was expended to overcome this deficiency. At the present time,
there are few studies in the important field of local administration and
planning in Eastern Europe. It is hoped that this volume will help to
stimulate further work in this area.

Acknowledgments

This study could never have been completed without a long period of residence in Yugoslavia and the help of Yugoslavs willing and able to supply information and guidance. The Ford Foundation made this possible originally through a Foreign Area Fellowship Grant in 1960 and subsequently by a Travel-and-Study Grant in 1963. These grants provided the opportunity to remain in the country long enough to gain insight into the complex forces, both past and present, operating to create that unique socioeconomic and political setting that is Yugoslavia.

During both periods of residence in Yugoslavia, I was given every opportunity to pursue my research interests with the help of official governmental agencies. In 1963, the Federal Office for Town Planning, Housing, and Communal Affairs scheduled my visit throughout the various republics. I am greatly indebted to them for the time and energy they expended on my behalf. Each of the republics and the various republic and municipal agencies were most helpful in providing information and guidance. There were no barriers put in my way, no obstacles, artificial or real, to hinder inquiry. This book is intended as a tribute to my Yugoslav colleagues at all levels and as a confirmation of the success of their policy of true and unrestricted cultural exchange between our two countries.

I would like to use this occasion to thank a few of my Yugoslav friends: in Belgrade, Sreten Bjeličić, Stanko Grozdanić, Stjepan Han, Branko Horvat, Petar Ivičević, Miloš Macura, Miladin Šakić, Jakov Sirotković, Radomir Urošević, Anton Vratuša, and Iztok Žagar; in Zagreb, Boris Bakrač, Rudolf Bičanić, Zdenko Kolacio, Veljko Rogić, Josip Roglić, and Stanko Žuljić; and in Ljubljana, Marko Šlajmer and Jako Štular. These people not only contributed directly or indirectly to my professional work but in many ways helped my wife and me during our stay, thereby adding to the pleasure of our period of residence. I hope that my respect for Yugoslavia, and for the pragmatic character of her peoples and their willingness to discuss problems as well as successes is clearly evident in the pages that follow.

Appreciation is extended to my colleagues in the Department of City and Regional Planning at Cornell, who gave much support and necessary criticism. The Center for International Studies, which has been a principal source of help ever since my arrival at Cornell, provided a summer grant to cover the cost of card punching and the initial programming. The Cornell Computing Center gave computer time for the factor analysis and multiple regression runs.

Various portions of the original draft were read by Brian J. L. Berry, Cyril Black, Branko Horvat, Harvey Perloff, and Silva Škerlak. Special appreciation is extended to Stanko Žuljić and his assistant Jakov Jelić for their over-all help and their special contribution to the preparation of many of the maps. Cornell colleagues Douglas Ashford, Allan Feldt, John Lewis, George Myers, and Seymour Smidt made many useful suggestions and criticisms of the manuscript. Douglas Lee and Richard Ragatz, graduate students in the Department of City and Regional Planning, also provided some assistance. None of these people, however, bear any of the responsibility for the material contained herein. Special appreciation must be given to Alison Bishop for her effective editorial assistance during the final phase of manuscript preparation. Finally, I am indebted to Professor Victor Jones for his encouragement.

Use of the statistical techniques employed here is the result of the encouragement (and criticism) of my colleagues in the field of geography. I was given the opportunity to attend two Quantitative Institutes sponsored by the National Science Foundation, in 1962 at Northwestern University and in 1964 at the University of California at Berkeley. These were a most useful and important addition to my education.

JACK C. FISHER

Ithaca, New York
May, 1965

YUGOSLAVIA—A MULTINATIONAL STATE

Regional Difference and Administrative Response

Introduction

Yugoslav society has undergone an impressive transformation since 1945 as a result of policies designed to accelerate the country's economic progress. New industrial complexes have been created and traditional urban settlements have emerged as postwar centers of administration and economic advancement in the backward wastelands of central and southern Yugoslavia. The over-all purpose of this study is to place the well-known diversity of the country into a sharper spatial focus—to compare various areas in relation to their past and present-day interdependence—and in essence, to appraise Yugoslavia's attempt to advance as rapidly as possible. The postwar government's response to the sharp regional variations within the structure of a multinational state establishes the basic framework. Since political power was sensitive to local pressure, special attention is given to the evolution of local administration, including both housing and planning policies.

Yugoslavia has made remarkable strides in the last decade or so.

In the 1948–52 period the rate of [economic] growth remained at the prewar level of 1.9 percent; in the 1953–56 period it increased to 8.4 percent; and in the period of the Third Five Year Plan, 1957–60, it reached 13 percent. The average rate of growth in the postwar period as a whole is 7.2 percent. This is one of the highest rates of growth in the world for that period.[1]

Striking as these statistics are, they reveal little of the internal development patterns which characterized Yugoslav society during this period. A real understanding of what has happened in Yugoslavia demands more than a study of either national averages or national policy and planning goals alone.

This work illustrates the need for increased study of local administrative institutions and regional growth as well as central power structure and national economic planning. Once the general functioning of the central government has been described, it is of equal, if not greater, importance to examine the impact of federal policy on local agencies and the restraints which local bodies generate over central authority. This federal-local balance is a subject of unusual importance in the United States as local governments evolve a "new partnership" arrangement with the federal government as a result of increased public expenditure in public housing, transportation, and urban renewal on the one hand, and larger-scale regional development schemes such as that for Appalachia on the other. Throughout Eastern Europe and the Soviet Union various approaches to decentralization are emerging which have as their goal the shift of greater financial responsibility and decision making to local and regional authorities. Little serious research is devoted to these significant readjustments in internal institutional arrangement.

The policies which will be examined are those which have been for the most part in the hands of local communes and cities, the fundamental agents of Yugoslavia's decentralized administrative system. Chapters Two and Three provide a general orientation to the problem, and discuss the regional variation as of 1961 of selected indicators of economic development in the light of various historical, political, and economic processes which through the centuries produced extreme differences in levels of

---

[1] Janez Stanovnik, "Planning Through the Market—the Jugoslav Experience," *Foreign Affairs* (January, 1962), p. 263.

economic and social development between the northern and southern areas of the country. In general, the 1797 boundaries between the European powers of Venice and Austria-Hungary and the Ottoman Empire coincide today with the borderline between Yugoslavia's advanced and underdeveloped provinces. The contemporary boundaries of the republics closely approximate areas previously under the control of these foreign powers. The major exception is the relatively recent inclusion of Vojvodina, an area of former Central European influence, into the Serbian Republic. Subsequent sections of the book put forth the view that local administrative procedures and the process of spatial planning itself are closely related in practice to underlying social and economic variations.

If the differences among the various cultural areas of the country are as important as at first appears, they would be expected to be reflected in underlying functional and demographic variations among cities and communes. Are what might be called "modern" industrial and commercial centers found in the advanced area of the country, while in other regions the centers of industry and commerce are in some way "nonmodern"? To answer these questions, a quantitative analysis and categorization was made of fifty-five Yugoslav cities having a population of over 20,000. The pattern of urban demographic and occupational variation revealed by this analysis appears to be related to historical and cultural processes operative throughout centuries of foreign domination and cultural penetration.

The first three chapters focus on regional or sectional variation, and on the objective differences and similarities among cities by means of a quantitative analysis of fifty-five urban centers. Chapters Four and Five examine the functioning of the system of local administration in Yugoslavia. This system was designed to make a viable political unit out of the heterogeneous ethnic, social, and economic mosaic which still exists within the territory of the Socialist Federal Republic of Yugoslavia. In Chapter Five the analysis moves to a more comprehensive level, utilizing the same factor analysis technique, but employing spatial units covering the total area of the country rather than fifty-five urban "points." This latter analysis, based upon a study of all the communes of Yugoslavia, provides greater detail and further insights into the conclusion derived from the more restricted initial sample.

The results of this study fall into two groups: statistical and methodological findings, and more general conclusions concerning the nature of postwar development in Yugoslavia.

FINDINGS OF THE STUDY

The principal statistical and methodological findings are:

1. An analysis of city-size distributions indicates that northern cities have a "rank-size" distribution while those of the South have a "primate-type" distribution. It has been suggested that a more advanced stage of development tends to produce a distribution of cities in terms of their size that is log-normal in form, that is, the progression of city sizes from smallest to largest is systematic and exponential. At the same time, in some less advanced cultures, there often occurs a distribution that is primate rather than rank-size in character. This primate distribution represents a situation where a stratum of small towns and cities is dominated by one or a few very large cities without intermediate size groups. There would seem to be some justification in terms of city-size distribution alone in choosing to regard the North and South of Yugoslavia as structurally different areas.

2. When the major administrative units, the republics, are grouped according to indices of economic development, the resulting picture is strikingly similar to the traditional regions of foreign domination and cultural penetration. Of greater significance, however, is the fact that when the classification is based on fifty-five major cities or "points" in the total national space, the same regional breakdown develops. In this case, varying statistical procedures using different modifiable units produce the same over-all pattern.

3. When the scale of analysis becomes more detailed, a different pattern emerges. When all of the communes or townships of Yugoslavia were subjected to factor analysis, structurally similar communes did not necessarily turn out to be spatially contiguous. There were pockets of underdeveloped or less advanced communes in the North, economically similar to less advanced southern communes. A limited number of southern communes compared favorably with economically advanced northern communes. Initially it was decided to keep the approximate maximum size limit of communes at around 100,000 people; the country's largest cities were,

therefore, subdivided into several communes. In theory, there was to be no difference in function between a "rural" detached commune and an "urban" commune which formed one sector of a city. Thus the factor analysis identified the sharp contrasts among communes within the same metropolis. Belgrade, Zagreb, Skopje, Sarajevo, and Ljubljana are currently multicommunal cities.

CONCLUSIONS FROM THE STUDY

In the general analysis of Yugoslav postwar development the following points stand out:

1. Selected indicators of economic development show a marked contrast between the northern and southern portions of the country coincidental to a line separating the regions of Western influences—Central European and Mediterranean—from the region of Byzantine-Turkish influence.

2. Classification of Yugoslav cities by means of factor analysis, utilizing 1961 occupational and demographic variables, produces a regionalization of the country into the traditional north-south dichotomy which corresponds to the regions of traditional foreign domination. That is, despite economic development and increased urbanization, the cities have preserved their relative positions.

3. "Housing quality," a composite variable and an assumed index of modernization and economic development, follows the general north-south dichotomy. The institutional administration of housing funds as well as the city planning mechanism itself varies from place to place in response to socioeconomic differences.

4. The postwar evolution of Yugoslavia might be characterized as a process in which the formal center of decision making for a variety of activities, at first located at a single federal level, gradually shifted to a diffusion of points which actively involved the greater mass of the population. The establishment of workers' self-government and the evolution of the communal system were the decisive instruments of the process. The "centralist-directive" phase of the early postwar period gradually gave way to increased regional or republic autonomy, which eventually incorporated 581 administratively independent communes; each, in theory, was

capable of chartering its own future progress within general limits set down by federal policy.

There was an attempt to induce the individual factories and communes to move toward greater independence, thereby involving greater numbers of the population in the decision-making process. Politically, this had the effect of restraining the so-called "nationality problem" and more or less justified the precarious existence side-by-side of developed and underdeveloped areas. Yet the total impact of communal "independence" has only recently been felt and economically it has raised very serious problems. Federal legislation in late 1964 and in 1965 attempted to curb the commune's investment capacity and eliminate the obvious weaknesses apparent during 1963 and early 1964.

In short, the Yugoslavs attempted to restrict potential conflict and insure progress by inducing mass participation of the country's citizens in both the local administrative organs of their communities and the governing institutions of the enterprise in which they worked. The Yugoslav goal was to obtain integration through controlled differences or ordered local diversity under an indirect mechanism of federal supervision. This goal is the distinguishing characteristic of the communal system and the fundamental philosophy of the April 1963 Constitution. Though politically successful, at least in terms of administrative decentralization, it appears that local administrative autonomy was secured at the expense of economic efficiency. The reforms of 1964 were expected to reestablish the balance through a rigorous separation of economic investments from other forms of investment at the local level.

Chapter 1

Development of the Yugoslav State

I. DEVELOPMENT WITHIN A MULTINATIONAL STATE

Each state has a body of traditions and objectives which rally the population's support. The viability of any state is measured by the degree of support the people give to the "state idea" or the *raison d'être* of the state. A modern state is one that has through political and educational measures successfully engaged the greater mass of the population in support of the state's *raison d'être*. The individual has shifted his values from those of purely regional or local institutions to the national level; he has become national in outlook. There must exist, therefore, within this broader framework, a mechanism for the integration of the individual to supraregional goals and values; restrictions and taboos on social mobility are to be eliminated. The national territory becomes the effectively utilized area. Some would maintain that political boundaries should correspond to economic and social areas so that "homogeneity" becomes a reality:

The problem here is essentially to identify the social boundaries of a community and to see to what extent they correspond to the effective political boundaries. In other words, how much of a difference does it make in holding a group together as a functioning political unit if its members have similar social, economic, or other characteristics?

The hypothesis is that social homogeneity will contribute strongly to the feasibility of political integration and, conversely, that communities whose members are very different from one another will have a very hard time achieving or maintaining political integration. Viewing the problem in inter-community terms, the hypothesis holds that the more that communities are similar, the more successful are attempts to build integrative relationships among them.[1]

There is little doubt that a state must enlist the support of the bulk of its population behind a certain body of values and goals. Is this to be done through enforced measures which attempt to superimpose a standard set of values, usually belonging to the dominant social and elite group, upon all other areas and peoples within the state? Perhaps the best contemporary model of this solution is the Soviet Union. Or is it possible, on the other hand, to tolerate diversity while increasing the degree of participation? Can individual economic enterprises in a socialist society be given freedom to set prices, distribute profits, and project their own expansion in harmony with the broad developmental goals set by the state?

Increased similarity as suggested by Jacob and Teune is not the integrative model selected by the Yugoslavs. The Yugoslav goal is to obtain integration through controlled differences or ordered local diversity under an indirect mechanism of federal supervision. This goal is the distinguishing characteristic of the communal system and the fundamental philosophy of the April 1963 Constitution.

The integrative model selected by the Yugoslavs was strongly influenced by the multinational structure of the state. Yugoslavia is a state with two alphabets (Latin and Cyrillic), three major religions (Orthodox, Roman Catholic, and Moslem), three major languages (Serbo-Croatian, Slovenian,

---

[1] Philip E. Jacob and Henry Teune, "The Integrative Process: Guidelines for Analysis of the Bases of Political Community," *The Integration of Political Communities*, edited by Philip E. Jacob and James Toscano (Philadelphia: J. B. Lippincott Company, 1964), p. 18.

and Macedonian), four nationalities (Serbs, Croatians, Slovenes, and Macedonians),[2] six republics (Serbia, Croatia, Slovenia, Macedonia, Montenegro, and Bosnia and Herzegovina), and seven surrounding nations (Austria, Hungary, and Rumania on the north; Bulgaria on the east; Greece and Albania on the south and southwest; and Italy on the west). Figure 1 (in the section of oversized figures) indicates the boundaries of these six republics, major regional place-names, rivers, and major cities; this map should serve as a basic guide for the reader throughout the book. Thus Yugoslavia is representative of the problems associated with the development of a multinational state. For example, one has but to think of Canada in North America; the Republic of South Africa in Africa; India in Asia; and Belgium, Switzerland, Czechoslovakia, and, of course, Yugoslavia in Europe. The U.S.S.R. is a specific example of the (attempted) transition from a colonial power to a multinational state.

These multinational states have, in varying degrees, problems which have evolved as a result of their diverse ethnic composition and internal variations in levels of development, plus, of course, the degree of nationalism to which each group ascribes.

The problems among the various sections of Yugoslavia related to development are greatly compounded due to the multinational structure of the country. Economic criteria have been less of a rationale for investment than the constitutional provision which suggests that equity must be shown to each of the six republics. The federal government is viewed as a mother which must divide her milk equally among all six children. Thus very real problems arise as to the location of various developmental projects: Why continue the expansion of a particular branch of industry in Croatia rather than diversify with a new plant in Serbia? Why continue port expansion in the northern Adriatic rather than develop one of Montenegro's coastal villages? Transportation systems are the least developed in the South; why

---

[2] It should be remembered that during the interwar period, the Macedonians and Montenegrins did not have a separate regional unit and were not considered as separate nations. Macedonia was viewed either as "South Serbia," by the Serbs, or as a potential part of Bulgaria by the Bulgarians. Contrary to the official Yugoslav position, I do not find sufficient criteria to separate "Montenegrins" from "Serbs." The reader should not forget that there are also many national minorities, such as Albanians, Hungarians, Italians, and Rumanians.

Terazije, one of the main avenues in Belgrade. *Foto-Tanjug*

A market square in Sarajevo.

not concentrate investment there rather than continue to improve the moderately developed North?

Perhaps one example will help illustrate the situation. Before the war not a single factory for the production of refrigerators existed in Yugoslavia. The first one was established at Maribor, a major industrial city in the North, in the Republic of Slovenia. The location was within the potential market area and in direct proximity to a well-developed transportation network. The quality of the labor force was high and the final product was therefore of a standardized quality. Under political pressure another factory was built at Cetinje in Montenegro and yet another at Bitola in southern Macedonia. The quality of the Bitola product has continued, at least by reputation, to be very poor, while the cost of shipping the products of both of these southern factories to market is extremely high. For example, the Cetinje factory, which operates under an Italian license, imports raw materials which reach the coast by ship and then must be transported by truck over mountainous terrain and unpaved roads. Cetinje has no rail connection. The final product must be sent to the coast by truck, then shipped to a northern port which has rail connections to Zagreb or Sarajevo.

A somewhat clearer picture of the differences among Yugoslavia's six republics (Slovenia, Croatia, Bosnia and Herzegovina, Serbia, Montenegro, and Macedonia) can perhaps be obtained by generalizing the contributions of each nation or region to the newly formed Yugoslav state in 1918 (see Figure 1). Serbia had an effective political and military organization which was nevertheless counterbalanced by a desire to create a "Greater Serbia." Though the economy and transportation system were undeveloped, there were significant untapped natural resources. Macedonia was an equally undeveloped area that stood, at that time, in strong opposition to Serbia. Montenegro was a barren mountainous wasteland with a great tradition of independence and courage against the Turks. These qualities appeared to be of little importance until World War II, which resulted in the emergence of the Montenegrins as a powerful political force in postwar Yugoslavia. Though Bosnia and Herzegovina was undeveloped, this area too had important natural resources. During the interwar period this multinational unit (composed of Serbs, Croatians, and Moslems) was a major point of conflict between the Croatians and the Serbs. Vojvodina was a complex multinational unit composed of Serbs, Croatians, Hungarians, and Germans, but had the advantage of rich agricultural land, some related

The newly constructed Slavija Hotel on Dimitrije Tucović Square in Belgrade.

industry, and a modestly developed transportation system. Croatia had a strong Western tradition and ties with the major European powers and with Western capital. Slovenia had the highest cultural level, was relatively developed, and showed resistance to centralism and the creation of "the Yugoslav nation."

It is the purpose of this study to examine the institutional adjustment which evolved in the postwar period as a result of the central government's desire to achieve a higher stage of development while simultaneously moving the country along the road to "integration" and thus of increased national viability. This balance was difficult to achieve, however, as Yugoslavia was in the unusual circumstance of having the dominant political group, the Serbs, culturally and economically less advanced than the Slovenians and the Croatians. The path the Yugoslavs chose proved to be an institutional compromise between these two compelling forces: a high rate of development and policies aimed at easing intergroup conflict.

2. ECONOMIC DEVELOPMENT, URBANIZATION, AND MODERNIZATION

Centuries of domination by various foreign powers stimulated the cultural

One of Sarajevo's passageways.

and developmental differences of Yugoslavia. As the terms "culture" and "development" underlie much of the discussion to follow, it seems useful to present a definition of these terms as used in this study.

Man attempts to order his environment to satisfy his needs more fully; population is distributed over the face of the earth in response to both the innate physical characteristics of man's habitat and the nature and level of his culture.[3] The use man makes of the physical features of his habitat is a function of his culture, that is, of the attitudes, objectives, and technical abilities of man himself.[4]

Yugoslavia contains at least two cultures. Centuries of foreign domination and cultural penetration have produced varying attitudes and group objectives among regions at different stages of technical achievement. The diverse nature of development within the country and its impact on postwar policy is our present concern.

Three distinct but interrelated facets of a society's development are suggested: the level of economic development, urbanization, and the extent of modernization. The degree of modernization implies a certain level of economic development and urbanization. What else is necessary for a state to be "modernized?" The level of education obtained by the bulk of the population is one factor, as is the degree and scale of individual integration into society. Modernization implies the willingness and ability to accept innovation when the new methods imply greater savings of human labor or greater capital accumulation for the individual or the society as a whole.

It should be clear that a developing country can elect to modernize as rapidly as possible, which suggests increased economic development as but one part of the total program. Countries that elect economic development alone set priorities so that only industrial output increases. These two alternatives should be kept in mind in the discussion that follows. The

---

[3] "Culture is that complex whole which includes knowledge, belief, art, morals, law, custom, and any other capabilities and habits acquired by man as a member of society." Edward B. Tylor, *Primitive Culture* (London: J. Murray, 6th edition, 1920), p. 5.

[4] "The individual learns to accept the attitudes and objectives, and to practice the technical skills of his culture. Culture is not inherited; it is a 'learned behavior.' It is man's culture that determines his relationship to his environment." Preston E. James, *One World Divided* (New York: Blaisdell Publishing Company, 1964), p. 9.

major conclusion which emerges from the subsequent discussion is that economic development, measured as increased output, occurred in Yugoslavia's southern area without substantial strides in modernization. A question remains: Is economic development without modernization self-sustaining?

For the purposes of this study, *economic development* can be measured not only by output but by the rate of increase in the efficiency of the economic process, efficiency being defined as the amount of economically valuable output that can be produced per unit of input of labor, capital, and natural resources. Economically underdeveloped societies are characterized by the fact that their level of efficiency does not change; typically, per capita income is low, but it may be moderately high if the resource base is exceptionally rich. In modern history the process of economic development has been accompanied by a reorganization of traditional society that includes a shift from agriculture to nonagricultural pursuits. Activities tend to become specialized in advanced societies; mutual interdependence becomes the hallmark of economic existence.

Contemporary economic growth and development and, in fact, all that is implied in this study by the term economic development, originated as a result of the technical revolution that began in England in the latter half of the eighteenth century, known as the Industrial Revolution. The size and organization of the production unit changed as man mastered new sources of energy and power. "The new capacity to produce and to transport requires a reappraisal of the significance of the physical features of the habitat." [5] Man blazed new routes for the new modes of transportation he created. Economic development includes, therefore, not only increased production, but also the integration of space through transportation systems that supply the raw materials and distribute the products of the country's industrial plant. The level of industrialization and the nature and development of circulation routes are indices of the degree of a region's level of economic development. The barriers to travel are reduced or eliminated by a new transportation network geared to supply vast markets. Reduced transfer costs extend markets and stimulate increased savings, which result in higher living standards and allow further expansion of

---

[5] *Ibid.*, p. 22.

industrial capacity. As individual income increases, consumers demand more goods and services; this demand in turn produces increased earnings and savings and the whole cycle begins again.

In the contemporary world, *urbanization* is often described as the direct result of the transformation of a traditional society to an economically advanced one. The two are clearly interrelated and follow closely upon one another. For our purposes here, however, it is desirable to attempt to define the nature of urbanization at various levels of development.[6]

Within the contemporary world at least three stages of urbanization seem to be present, each with specific characteristics which *may* be related to the level of development of a particular area. It is necessary in each case, however, to examine whether urbanization was a result of accelerated economic development or in fact preceded it. Urbanization is, in its simplest form, "the concentration of population." Predominantly rural areas often have a uniformly distributed network of points of population concentration (at times with a degree of density only slightly above the regional mean) to facilitate exchange of goods and services through

---

[6] "It is particularly important to call attention to the danger of confusing urbanism with industrialization and modern capitalism." Louis Wirth, "Urbanism as a Way of Life," *The American Journal of Sociology*, Vol. XLIV (July, 1938), p. 7.

New Belgrade, the Yugoslav capital's most modern section.

periodic markets. In this type of urbanization, the activities of each point of population concentration are in fact duplicated by all the other "points;" there is no specialization and, in the general model, each settlement's hinterland is a closed economy.

At the next stage, however, urbanization implies much more than population concentration. Economic development or industrialization requires increased scale and greater complexity of industrial operations. At this stage of development there is population concentration plus diversification of the demographic and occupational composition of the city's population. Demographically there is a gradual increase in the productive age group (20–50) of the population, and a gradual increase in the older dependent age groups. There is also a shift from agriculture to nonagricultural occupations which results in a diversity of employment categories within the city. The city provides the maximum quantity and variety of goods and services; it is in reality a social device serving an economic need.

For Yugoslavia the two above stages of urbanization are clearly sufficient at the present time. In the United States urbanization has moved further, resulting in a pattern which ultimately may be expected in Yugoslavia. In Parsons' words, "The most striking development is the rapid increase of the 'metropolitanizing' of the population, which has both shifted the rural-urban balance, which has been discussed for so long, substantially further in the urban direction, and has focused attention on major change in the character of urban communities." [7] By the time a country has reached this stage, the older age groups of the population form a significant portion of the dependent age groups and the tertiary sector of the economy is increasing faster than the secondary. The rapid replacement of primary production by secondary during the initial stages of development appears to be shifted in the advanced stage to an increase of tertiary activities at the expense of the secondary. Recreational activities may well become a substantial component of tertiary activity suggesting a further displacement in the most advanced stages.

Life style clearly distinguishes "metropolitanization" from the previous

---

[7] Talcott Parsons, "Comment on Trends Shown by Population Census," *Proceedings of the Social Statistical Section* (Washington: American Statistical Association, 1961), p. 127.

stage. At this later stage the differences in human occupancy between town and country have been substantially eliminated for a large majority of the population. Man's life style is essentially the same whether he lives in the center of the city, in the suburbs, or in the outlying rural areas. Housing is standardized, appliances ubiquitous, and internal residential space consumption similar throughout the megalopolis; consumption patterns are identical regardless of place of residence. As Friedmann has suggested, "Just as Karl Mannheim speaks of fundamental democratization as one of the tendencies of our age, so one may speak of fundamental urbanization as the end-result of modern economic growth. With this, the former distinction between town and country will be blurred and will leave a thoroughly organized, impersonal, and functionally rational society to carry on."[8]

The degree of urbanization, viewed within this conceptual framework, may well reflect the level of economic development that a particular society has achieved. It is suggested that the level of economic development or degree of industrialization directly influences the scale of urbanization. Does it, however, suggest the degree of modernization? Does industrialization plus urbanization equal modernization?

Clearly *modernization* implies much more than a specified level of urbanization or of economic development, measured perhaps by GNP per capita. It is a more general term referring to intellectual, political, and social as well as economic matters. Modernization implies the desire to improve one's material condition, to achieve higher levels of achievement,[9] to comprehend and generally endorse national goals, to value one's occupational role and judge oneself and others according to performance rather than custom or preconditioned status.

One sign of modernization is an expanding educational base. Traditional societies are characterized by the fact that a very small proportion of the population is literate. It is stipulated that in "modern" societies, literacy is almost universal. It is of course possible that a developing country could elect to expand its industrial base without investing sufficiently in social

---

[8] John Friedmann, "Cities in Social Transformation," *Regional Development and Planning—A Reader*, edited by John Friedmann and William Alonso (Cambridge: The Massachusetts Institute of Technology Press, 1964), p. 360. Reprinted from *Comparative Studies in Society and History*, Vol. 4 (July, 1961).

[9] David G. McClelland, *et al.*, *The Achievement Motive* (New York, 1953).

A view of Sarajevo.

overhead: public utilities, schools, housing, transportation, and related facilities. To "modernize" implies an investment in people which simultaneously allows society to expect more of them.

3. THE POLITICAL BACKGROUND

Considerable socioeconomic variation and marked contrasts in living standards characterize modern Yugoslavia. Though subsequent sections will illustrate these differences in terms of economic and demographic variables, the reader should also keep in mind the varying types of human occupancy or man-to-land relationships in the mountainous Karst, the level Pannonian Basin, the upland areas of Slovenia, and other physiographic areas of the country (see Figures 1 and 4). History and geography have interacted to produce heterogeneous groupings of economic, cultural, and social variables. Superimposed on this physical and cultural landscape is a political system that has been in constant flux as a result of external pressure and internal variability.

Yugoslavia has attempted to form a viable political state from a diversity of cultural, social, and political elements.[10] Centuries of foreign penetration and control under various political systems have led to great regional variations in administrative practice, economic standards, land utilization, urban patterns, and language among the three basic cultural areas—Central European, Byzantine-Turkish, and Mediterranean. One Yugoslav analyst has described the situation, suggesting that past political fortunes created administrative areas which continue to influence contemporary policies and territorial reorganization:

The various economic and political systems which through the centuries have existed in the present territory of Yugoslavia were so distinct in their nature as to represent, in reality, different civilizations. They left us the heritage of a long tradition of established spatial frames, both the large territorial units (the historical nations—today's people's republics), and the medium and small territorial units (former *oblasts*, *okrugs*, districts and rural townships), with which today, during the formation of the territorial units of our new communal system, we have much concern . . .[11]

The complex evolution of the country stimulated and maintained individual loyalty to local subgroups. In the South, kinship ties predominated. In the North, which shared in the economic and social advances of Western Europe, both the rural and the urban population tended toward greater involvement with local authorities. Ethnic fragmentation further reinforced group cohesiveness. Political response was therefore regional; in the prewar period there were many regional parties centering on ethnic and/or cultural identity. The most notable postwar example of massive support of a national goal was the backing of Tito in the 1948 conflict with the rest of the Bloc. In this case an external force, momentarily at least, consolidated the various national groups in support of a potential threat to the state.

---

[10] For a valuable discussion of the formation of Yugoslavia, see Ivo J. Lederer, *Yugoslavia at the Paris Peace Conference* (New Haven, 1963).

[11] Rude Petrović, *Prostorna determinacija teritorijalnih jedinica u komunalnom sistemu Jugoslavije* (Sarajevo, 1962), p. 20.

The Kingdom of the Serbs, Croats, and Slovenes, established in 1918, initially maintained the distinctive regional administrative groupings that had evolved during the centuries of foreign rule. The Vidovdan Constitution (1921), however, reorganized the country into a single administrative system, comprising 393 districts and 7,085 *opštine*.[12] Above these were various higher-level units, except in Dalmatia, Slovenia, and Vojvodina. In 1931, the country was organized into nine *Banovine* (see Figure 2) which again resulted in an alteration of communal and district boundaries, as a further attempt to undercut the significance of the traditional regional units.

The interwar period was marked by bitter conflict between the Serbian-dominated government, and the Croatians and the national minorities. In order to counteract the growing centrifugal tendencies of the Croatian nation, a political solution was reached in 1939 that created a separate Croatian unit, corresponding to the areas traditionally inhabited by this people (see Figure 2). The failure of the entire interwar political process was perhaps symbolized by the ease with which the Axis occupation forces divided the former states among themselves (see Figure 3).

Between the two World Wars, Yugoslavia was a state but never really a nation. Now, two decades after its establishment, the state vanished. Created by one war, it was destroyed by another. The same war was soon, however, to give birth to a new Yugoslavia, very different from its predecessor, yet in many ways much the same.[13]

This situation was the basis on which the new—now Communist—administration had to attempt to create a politically viable state after the war. The initial compromise worked out by the new government to soften the "particularist" tendencies of the various nationalities, which had been fanned to frantic proportions by the terror of war and the policies of the occupation forces, was a federal system comprising six republics (see

---

[12] The Serbian term *opština*—*općina* in Croatian—historically referred to a specific area, defined by the collectivity or commonalty of the land and the inhabitants' use thereof. In the prewar period the term lost this meaning and signified only an administrative unit, such as a borough, district, municipality, or community.

[13] George W. Hoffman and Fred W. Neal, *Yugoslavia and the New Communism* (New York: Twentieth Century Fund, 1962), p. 65.

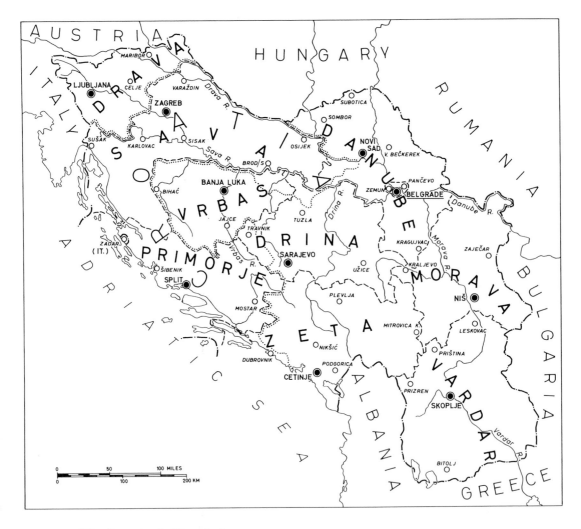

FIGURE 2. The *Banovine* in Yugoslavia, 1931.

Source: Milan Šenoa, *Geografski Atlas* (Zagreb, 1934), pp. 18–19. The 1939 "compromise" with the enlarged Croatian unit is indicated.

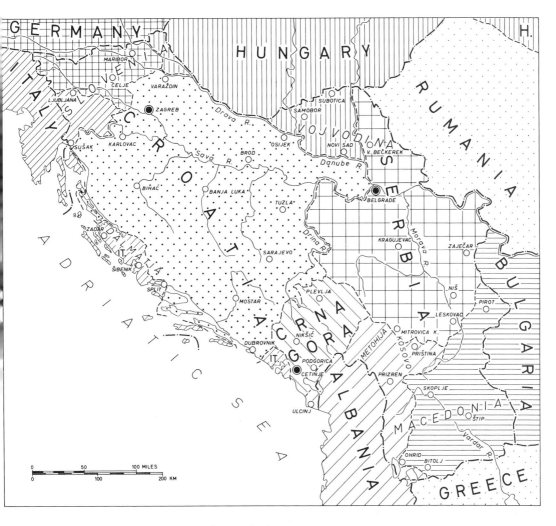

FIGURE 3. The Dismemberment of Yugoslavia, 1942.

Source: *Ljudske i materijalne žrtve Jugoslavije u ratnom naporu* 1941–1945 (Belgrade, 1945), p. 13. An independent Croatian state was created. Germany annexed two-thirds of Slovenia while Italy took the rest of Slovenia and the Adriatic coastal area. Montenegro (*Crna Gora*) was made a separate kingdom, which was in personal union with the Italian king; Italian Albania obtained Kosovo-Metohija and part of Macedonia; the remainder went to Bulgaria. Hungary received parts of Slovenia and Croatia and part of Vojvodina (Bačka and Baranja). Serbia became a separate unit administered by the Germans.

Figure 1).[14] Though the new state was federal in theory, the political system was clearly centralized and dictatorial in practice. A recent Yugoslav study has described the period from 1947 to 1951 as "centralistic-directive," [15] while another account in a publication prepared for foreign consumption clearly states that "the local organs of government, although elected directly by the citizens, existed primarily to implement the law and the decisions of the central organs." [16]

After 1950 a number of major changes, generated from above, completely realtered Yugoslavia's institutional pattern:

. . . it is desirable to recall the outstanding features of the present-day Yugoslav economy, the only experiment of its kind in the world. While the Yugoslav economy retains in common with the Eastern countries as a characteristic that the principal means of production (except agricultural smallholdings) are nationalized and that a planning system is applied, it has since 1949–50 differed in two important and novel respects. First, the Workers' Councils elected by all the workers in each enterprise in the socialized sector ("Economic Organizations" in Yugoslav terminology) have acquired extensive powers of management, both in the allocation of net disposable income between the remuneration of workers and the enterprise's investment fund and in the orientation of production and in consequence of the pattern of gross investment, whatever the source of financing. Secondly, this introduction of a factor of relative autonomy of enterprises by the decentralization of production and investment decisions, has been accompanied by the restoration on an increasing scale of a genuine market both for end products and also for the production factors of capital and labor. The sovereignty of consumers has been recognized and in more and more cases (now forming the rule) the consumer's choice, through the mechanism of supply and demand and of prices, is increasingly allowed to affect the pattern of investment decisions.[17]

---

[14] Evgeni Dimitrov, "Position of the Republics in the Federal System of Yugoslavia," *Selected Problems of Social Sciences and Humanities*, Papers from the Yugoslav-American Colloquium, Ohrid, August 27–September 2, 1962 (Skopje, 1963), pp. 113–124.

[15] Borivoj Jelić, *Sistem planiranja u jugoslovenskoj privredi* (Belgrade, 1962), part 2.

[16] Sreten Bjeličić, *Communal System in Yugoslavia* (Belgrade, 1961), p. 10.

[17] *Socialist Federal Republic of Yugoslavia* (Economy Surveys of the Organization for Economic Co-operation and Development, Paris, 1963), pp. 5–6.

The two decisive steps which eventually led to the communal system as described in the April 1963 Constitution occurred during 1952 and 1953. A constitutional provision was passed which provided for local responsibility over all activities not expressly reserved by law for higher governmental levels. This provision meant, in essence, that local administrative agencies directly responsible to the central government could be created only by law and not by executive decree. The second step was the stipulation that local administrative agencies were responsible only to their own local political bodies or councils, not to higher governmental agencies. Higher administrative units could intervene only when local units or officials committed illegal acts. It is a long process, not as yet completed, for the implications of these two laws to be implemented fully in practice. It is significant, however, that the intent was legally stated as early as 1953 and that there has been a gradual administrative evolution since then in harmony with these two regulations.

The post-1950 institutional reforms were political measures undertaken by the state to organize the diversity resulting from centuries of domination by various foreign powers. Cultural homogeneity or increased uniformity appeared politically impossible. Therefore, it was decided to stabilize and control the existing diversity by means of increased local participation of the individual in both economic and political life.

The post-1950 period witnessed the evolution of an administrative system tailored to the peculiarities of the country's socioeconomic characteristics. The establishment of workers' self-government and the increased authority of the communes were the basic building blocks of Yugoslavia's new decentralized format. Decision-making power was formally transferred from the federation to the districts, rather than the republics, and finally to the communes. Thus political response to regional variation produced an administrative reorganization, which increased the authority of local institutions under formally indirect federal supervision and control, thereby providing a microregional approach to development. The establishment of the communal system after 1950 was intended to temper economic variation as well as social and cultural differences.

Chapter II

Historical Background and Regional Variation

I. HISTORIC REGIONS OF FOREIGN DOMINATION AND INFLUENCE

Yugoslavia, created in 1918 as a new state, was composed of areas which had never enjoyed a common government and which for centuries had been under the domination of different foreign powers. The urban centers which had developed in these regions of foreign rule and cultural penetration had evolved distinctive urban patterns responding to the value system of the dominating power and to the events which occurred within the city's surrounding area. The direction and extent of alien influence over what is now Yugoslavia is more understandable when viewed in relation to the country's general physical characteristics (see Figure 4 in the section of oversized figures).

It is a basic truth about Yugoslavia that an understanding of its geographical situation and physical properties is essential for an understanding of its stormy past and present problems . . . Let us consider how far economic and cultural changes have restricted the negative influence of natural factors in Yugoslavia; how each of the major regional divisions—the mountainous heartland and the peripheral zone—and each of the regions within these divisions have acted upon the other and contributed to the formation of a unified state.

The mountainous heartland largely coincides with the Dinaric ranges; the peripheral zone consists of fertile plains, hill lands, and basins connected with interior valleys . . . The mountainous part of the country (over 1,500 feet) comprises 45 per cent of the total area, while 29 per cent is classified as lowlands (below 600 feet). The varied relief separates the people of one valley from those of another, bringing about local particularism and political fragmentation.[1]

Four foreign centers—Byzantium (Istanbul), Vienna, Budapest, and Venice—dominated various parts of the area at different times from the Middle Ages until the creation of the unified state in 1918. A symbolic description of the influence of the four centers has been provided by Robert Wolff:

Byzantium, Vienna, Budapest, Venice, shone like great searchlights sending out level beams of light and heat, which penetrated up the valleys, through the passes, and across the plains. These beams were halted only as they advanced farther from their source and encountered effective mountain barriers or met the fierce glare of a beam sent out by a nearer rival beacon. Thus, Montenegro was but faintly illuminated by the light sent out from Constantinople. In the Bosnia hills, the Turkish and the Habsburg beams petered out together.[2]

The effect of these "beams" led to regional variations in human occupancy under the different political systems which introduced varied administrative systems, economic standards, land utilization, and urban patterns.

Across the length and breadth of Yugoslavia have moved enormous migrations of peoples. Some left few traces; others left both tangible and intangible heritages. Greece, Rome, Byzantium, Venice, the Ottoman

---

[1] George W. Hoffman and Fred W. Neal, *Yugoslavia and the New Communism* (New York: Twentieth Century Fund, 1962), pp. 10–11.

[2] Robert Lee Wolff, *The Balkans in Our Times* (Cambridge: Harvard University Press, 1956), p. 20.

Old Travnik in Bosnia and Herzegovina, with buildings and monuments from Turkish times. *Agencija za Fotodokumentaciju*

Husref-Bay Medres in Sarajevo, the capital of Bosnia and Herzegovina. *Agencija za Fotodokumentaciju*

Empire, Hungary, and Austria contributed strands to the Yugoslav
tradition. The Slavic inhabitants themselves were various. If foreign
elements were the warp of the complex design, Croats, Serbs, Slovenes,

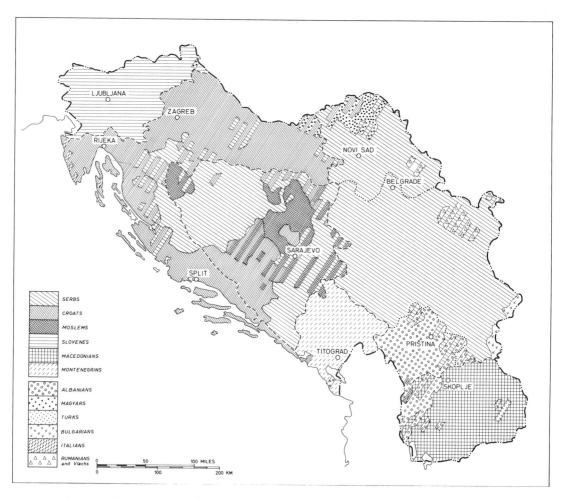

FIGURE 5. Ethnic Map of Yugoslavia.

    Source: *Konačni rezultati popisa stanoviništva od 15 Marta 1948 godine. Knjiga III, Stanov-
ništvo po Narodnosti* (Belgrade, 1954). This map was made on the basis of average values for
each *kotar;* nationalities comprising less than 30 percent of the total population were not included. The 1948 census was utilized rather than that of 1953, as in 1948 the designation "Yugoslav" was not included among the categories an individual could select. Thus it gave a much
clearer and less distorted picture of the classical ethnic and social differences existing in the
country, particularly of the area of Bosnia and Herzegovina where a large majority of people
of Moslem origin declared themselves "Yugoslav" in 1953.

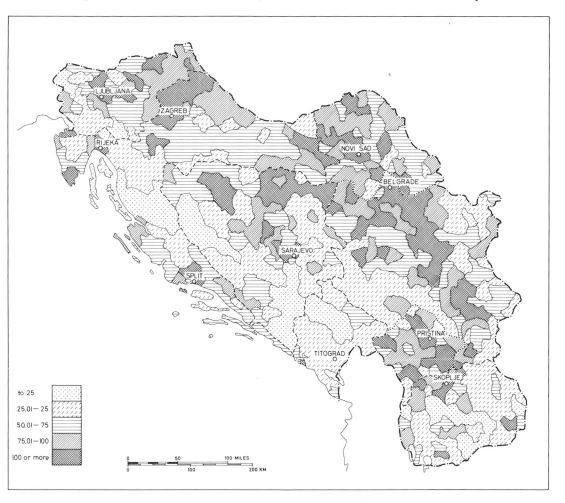

FIGURE 6. Population Density per Square Kilometer in 1961.
Source: *Statistički godišnjak SFRJ* (Belgrade, 1963), pp. 508–531. Data are by communes.

Macedonians, and Bulgarians were the woof. Physical configuration and, much more important, political conditions further complicated the pattern, resulting in a subdivision of existing groups. Figure 5 presents the diverse ethnic fractionalization of the country as of the 1948 census.

This ethnic variety has made Yugoslavia a land of many languages. The major languages today are Serbian, Croatian, Slovenian, and Macedonian. Serbian and Croatian are the most similar; the major difference between them is that Serbian uses the Cyrillic alphabet, while Croatian uses the

Latin one. "Serbo-Croatian," a Latinized amalgamation of both tongues, is used in the federal government and the Army.

Throughout these centuries of war and upheaval, and in spite of long periods of subjugation during which entirely different and alien cultures were at times superimposed upon them, the South Slavs succeeded in living, on the whole, on the originally settled lands. The geographic diversity of this land and the many cultural-political influences are expressed in differences in the way of life of the people, their customs, speech, religion, and in the demographic structure of the population. The centuries-long conflict on the territory which makes up today's Yugoslavia resulted in many difficulties for the inhabitants which continued after they were unified into one state. The process of working together is still new and often fraught with hazards.[3]

It is convenient to divide the foreign impress upon the Yugoslav landscape into three broad regions of foreign cultural penetration: Central European, Mediterranean, and Byzantine-Turkish. Cvijić and others (Maull, Krebs, Kayser) propose a fourth, purely "Yugoslav region."[4]

The "Yugoslav region" is a wide "patriarchal" zone consisting of the Central Dinaric Mountain Area of Yugoslavia. According to Cvijić, the Central European and Byzantine-Turkish cultural impact was effective only in certain areas within this "Yugoslav region." Because the foreign impact upon Yugoslavia was so important in shaping variations in social and economic development, discussion will be confined here to the three regions of foreign influence. Nevertheless, it is interesting to study the results of the give-and-take between the political and cultural forces emanating from neighboring spheres towards the Dinaric Mountains and the national movements away from the mountains towards the periphery. It was within this central mountainous zone of Yugoslavia that Central European, Mediterranean, and Byzantine-Turkish cultural penetration overlapped, with the consequence that any single impact was minimized and foreign influence generally had fewer permanent effects than in the peripheral areas.

---

[3] Hoffman and Neal, *op. cit.*, pp. 27–28.

[4] Jovan Cvijić, *Balkansko poluostrvo*, Book One, (Zagreb, 1922); Elizabeth von Lichtenberger and Hans Bobek, "Zur Kulturgeographischen Gliederung Jugosla-wiens," *Geographischer Jahresbericht aus Österreich* (Vienna, 1956), pp. 79–154; Rude Petrović, "O problemu geografske rajonizacije Jugoslavije," *Geografski pregled* (Sarajevo, 1957), pp. 104–134.

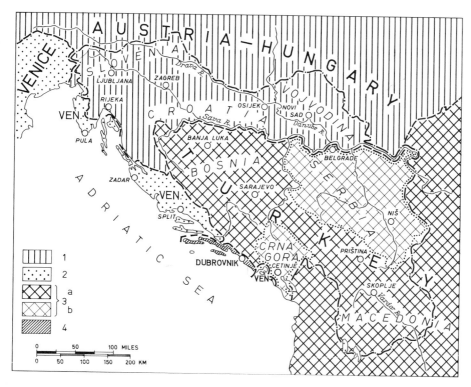

FIGURE 8. Political Regions of Foreign Domination.

Figure 8 indicates the political boundaries of the three major areas of foreign political domination: Central European, Mediterranean, and Byzantine-Turkish. These are regions over which foreign powers held absolute control for centuries. They are defined by the political area occupied by the conquerors whose cultural contributions are evident and traceable in the landscape. The Central European region of political domination is defined as those areas of Yugoslavia under Austro-Hungarian control between 1699–1718 and from 1737–1878 and lasting until 1918.[5] The western-most area of Yugoslavia was under Austrian domination as early as the Eighth Century. The last area to come under Austrian control was Bosnia and Herzegovina in 1878. The area [2] designated on the map (Figure 8) as Mediterranean is enclosed by the boundary lines maintained,

---

[5] The use of the term "Austro-Hungary" can refer technically only to the period after 1867.

and subsequently enlarged, by Venice from approximately 1420 until 1797 when Austria occupied the area. The city-state of Dubrovnik is designated separately [4], for though independent through the centuries it was "Mediterranean" in culture and orientation.[6] The Yugoslav region of Byzantine-Turkish control is encompassed by the 1699–1718 boundary line which was in force until 1878. After this date, the land was subdivided by the occupying powers as follows: (1) Bosnia and Herzegovina, the area of Austrian occupation; (2) the emerging Serbian State [eastern 3b]; and (3) Montenegro [western 3b] which never was completely under the effective political domination of the Ottoman Empire. The remaining area [3a] (excluding Bosnia), remained under the control of the Ottoman State until 1912.

---

[6] Josip Roglić, "The Geographical Setting of Medieval Dubrovnik," in Norman J. G. Pounds (ed.), *Geographical Essays on Eastern Europe*, Russian and East European Series, Vol. 24 (Bloomington: Indiana University Publications, 1961), pp. 141–159.

Baš-Čaršija Square in Old Sarajevo, with narrow streets, passages, and small shops dating back to Turkish times.

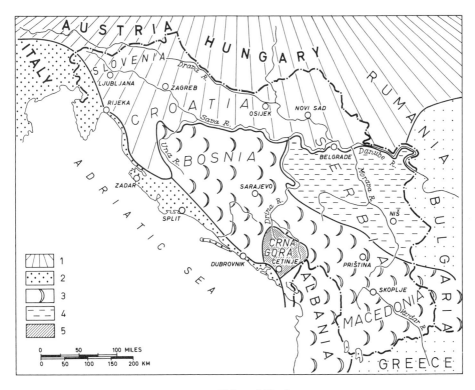

FIGURE 9. Cultural Regions.

Figure 9 generalizes the areas of foreign domination as defined above into cultural regions as follows: Central European [1], Mediterranean [2], and Byzantine-Turkish [3]. Separately designated is the area of the Serbian State which evolved after 1817 [4] where the tangible vestiges of Ottoman occupation were systematically destroyed, and the core area of Montenegro which, because of the ruggedness of the terrain and the distance from Constantinople, was never completely under the effective control of Ottoman authorities [5]. Professor Halpern provides a description of some of the social differences within the country which evolved as a result of the various foreign occupations:

Related to the differences in administrative techniques of the former empires is the basic nature of village organization itself, aspects of which have carried over into the present day. The most significant ties in rural Serbia, Macedonia, and Montenegro clearly remain bonds of kinship. Non-kin organizations such as are found in the western areas (soccer teams, volunteer fire brigades, political clubs, hunters' associations) never developed in the Orthodox areas. There were, however, agricultural cooperatives and village libraries in Serbia in the inter-war period, some of them locally organized. There were also some trade guilds and church organizations in small towns and villages, but all of them are relatively recent (mainly during the past fifty years) when compared to institutions in the western areas, and their total impact has been less.

Not only is the industrial tradition older in the western area, and the cities themselves more adaptable to the needs of an expanding technology without being completely redesigned, but also the existing types of social systems in rural areas have facilitated urbanization. Peasantization of the towns is not so clearly noticeable in Croatia and Slovenia because there has been more continuity and interdependence in rural-urban relationships.

It is not possible to formulate any rigid typologies, for the processes are complex and in many ways seemingly contradictory. Thus, while kin ties are valued and maintained in Serbia, urbanization here presents more cultural discontinuity than is apparently the case in many areas of Slovenia, Croatia, Dalmatia and even the Vojvodina. To become a townsman and particularly a professional person, it is felt necessary to explicitly reject one's peasant past. Often the parents and other close relatives aid willingly in this process, since to become an urbanite of status is viewed as a great accomplishment. Those who have attained this desired status often emotionally reject their past by emphasizing elements of urban culture most distinct from their backgrounds: disdain for physical labor or even for an avocation like gardening; meticulous and expensive dress; stress on the acquisition and care of non-functional material possessions; preference for classical rather than folk music; and a general concern with formal status and position.

A different situation has existed in the western areas where peasants had many of the prerequisites of urban status—reading and the possession of books, the desire and ability to travel for purposes other than selling agricultural produce or visiting relatives, and acknowledgment of the value of education and its compatibility with village life. Feudal and capitalist tradition is also significant here, where there has been constant contact with an upper class concerned with investment and economic development. The deeply rooted historical conceptualization of alternate models and modes of behavior strongly affected the nature of the urbanization process, the results being vastly different than emergence from a homogeneous peasant society after the removal of foreign overlords.

Slovenia, Croatia and Dalmatia were colonial areas, the first two without a developed commercial or professional class. They were, however, tied in with

Western European economic and industrial developments, and the Turkish areas, while geographically contiguous, were in some respects less affected by the industrial revolution and accompanying urban and administrative changes than were some of the overseas colonies of the European imperial powers.[7]

Economic and social conditions and the accompanying administrative systems varied greatly from region to region. Slovenia and central Croatia emerged as partially industrialized and agriculturally advanced zones within the region of Central European domination. In discussing the development of this area, and particularly the city of Zagreb, one contemporary Yugoslav writer has accurately written: "Zagreb was in reality, in this period, the last point (of capitalist exploitation) in Europe; further to the east was Balkan, in other words, Orient . . ."[8]

The major cities of the Mediterranean zone, though experiencing periodic cycles of economic stagnation, developed as strong cultural, commercial, trade, and, to a limited degree, industrial centers. After 1817, Serbia became a major exporter of agricultural products. The remaining portion of the country stagnated under the centuries of Ottoman domination.

2. REGIONAL VARIATION AND URBAN DEVELOPMENT

Yugoslavia's cities were profoundly affected by the foreign occupations. All the major cities, with the exception of Sarajevo, developed near the periphery of the present territorial boundaries close to a major foreign center. There, where the intensity of the influence was greatest and could more easily "penetrate up the valleys, through the passes, and across the plains," evolved the cities of Zagreb, Ljubljana, Belgrade, Skopje,[9] Split, and Rijeka.

The effect of Central European influence upon the development of the

---

[7] Joel M. Halpern, *Peasant Culture and Urbanization in Yugoslavia*, mimeographed (Brandeis University, 1964), pp. 36–39. Halpern is the author of *A Serbian Village* (New York: Columbia University Press, 1958).

[8] Andre Mohorovičić, "Analiza historijsko-urbanističkog razvoja grada Zagreba," *RAD*, Book 287 (Zagreb: Jugoslavenska Akademija Znanosti i Umjetnosti, 1953), p. 38.

[9] "Skopje" is the Macedonian spelling of the city's name; "Skoplje" is Serbo-Croatian.

region's cities can be illustrated by looking at the history of Zagreb.[10] Located near the Sava River on the southwest rim of the Pannonian Basin, Zagreb from the beginning was under the direct influence of its northern neighbors. Upon the site of the present city of Zagreb existed two independent centers: a feudal religious community (founded by the Hungarians) and a Slavic civil community under royal charter. For six centuries these two communities existed side-by-side, often engaged in economic warfare and armed conflict. In time, each gradually expanded, and finally the two merged physically, making some form of over-all administration necessary. This was accomplished by royal decree in 1850.

The evolution of Zagreb's urban pattern falls into two distinct periods, in both of which the policies of the Central European powers shaped the nature of the urban pattern. Prior to 1850, Austrian policy confined Zagreb's urbanized area to its original upland location above the Sava plain. After 1850, the development of the railroad to the south of the urbanized area, the process of industrialization, and conflicting Austrian and Hungarian economic policies produced rapid expansion of the city onto the lowland area. In both periods it was the policies and objectives of Budapest and Vienna which produced spatial changes in Zagreb's urban pattern (see Figure 10 in section of oversized figures).

The Yugoslav region of Mediterranean influence, for centuries under the political domination of foreign Mediterranean powers (Greek, Roman, Byzantine, and Venetian), is in the character of its climate and the nature

---

[10] For a detailed discussion of the impact of the varying political policies upon Zagreb's urban structure, see Jack C. Fisher, "Urban Analysis: A Case Study of Zagreb, Yugoslavia," *Annals of the Association of American Geographers*, LIII (September, 1963), pp. 266–284. This article provides a concrete example of the views which have been suggested here.

"Although the traditional urban pattern established during the centuries of foreign domination was interpreted in different ways by the Croatian planners of Zagreb and Split, the master plans for the socialist city of the future are, in each case, an adaptation of trends inherent in the distinctive traditional urban pattern . . . The forces, especially those related to the industrial revolution, which altered the respective urban patterns in the nineteenth century set into motion development trends which continue to influence the urban pattern and will continue into the foreseeable future." J. C. Fisher, *The Continuity of Urban Patterns under Socialism: The Yugoslav Experience* (Syracuse University: PhD Dissertation, 1961), p. 17.

Zagreb, industrial and commercial center of Croatia. *A. Roca*

The Diocletian Palace in Split,
port city in Croatia.

of its occupancy similar to other Mediterranean areas. The Adriatic coastal cultural landscape, limited in its extent by the Karstic conditions of the interior, may be identified as a very narrow zone with characteristic olive groves and vineyards, mixed cultivation, carefully built terraces, and flat-roofed stone houses. The Mediterranean coastal cities developed a distinctive pattern with a compact walled area of relatively high dwellings and extremely narrow streets for pedestrians. The city's activity was centered around the square, cathedral, and town hall, which were usually located directly on or near the shore.

Split, a typical city of the Mediterranean region, went through five distinct patterns of urban change and growth in response to a variety of political circumstances: (1) the founding of the Greek-Illyrian-Roman community of Salona which emerged as the capital of the Roman province of Dalmatia; (2) the construction by the Emperor Diocletian of a palace south of Salona which, after the Slavic migrations in the Seventh Century, became a haven for Latin refugees from the interior and the first nucleus or frame of the city; (3) the expansion of the city to the west, and the addition of a new series of walls in the Fourteenth Century to form the second frame or city pattern; (4) the construction of an entire series of fortifications in the Seventeenth Century during the Turkish-Venetian wars; and (5) the eventual destruction of the former fortifications and the gradual transformation of the entire urban complex in an attempt to link the isolated suburbs beyond the walls to the "old city."

Skopje, under Turkish occupation until 1912, is representative of the Byzantine-Turkish region. Until well into the Twentieth Century the urbanized area of the city was confined to the left bank of the Vardar River. The structure of this area was, prior to the earthquake on July 2, 1963, characteristic of the Turkish-Oriental type of city—numerous mosques and minarets, turkish baths (*hamami*), and a distinctive Turkish-type motel (the *han*) for weary travelers. Perhaps most interesting of all, however, was the commercial section of the city, the bazaar or *čaršija*, with its innumerable tiny stores and narrow, crowded streets. The alterations and fluctuations of Skopje's urban pattern reflected concretely the ebb and flow of Turkish fortunes in Europe and politics in Istanbul.

Once an urban complex was founded, the pattern of the original format or layout was maintained without significant alteration. To the original complex, however, events and foreign-directed policies brought distinctly different stimuli. The coming of the railroad and subsequent industrialization conditioned a vast expansion of Zagreb's urbanized area and the emergence of the newly urbanized lowland area as the center of commercial, industrial, and cultural activity. The Austro-Hungarian restriction of trade to the ports of Trieste and Rijeka, and the lack of a rail connection to the interior, frustrated Split's development. The resources of Split's own immediate area, however, allowed the city to increase its nineteenth-century port activity without significant alteration or expansion of the urban pattern.

The scope of this volume precludes extensive discussion of the varying social and economic characteristics of the distinct cultural regions which were grouped together to create a new state in 1918. However, some indications of the conditions prevailing in the separate provinces, and the impact of the destruction of the Austro-Hungarian Empire, can be obtained by observing the effect of the change in political boundaries on Croatia.

The new Yugoslav state formed in 1918 was from an economic point of view both quantitatively and qualitatively heterogeneous. In the former Turkish areas, including Serbia, there was little industry: these areas possessed only 15 percent of the factories in the country.[11] The creation of Yugoslavia produced for Croatia an absolute decrease in the size of its market area. Removed from its economic and political union with Austria-Hungary, Croatia was made part of a nation which had a population of only twelve million people. Croatia's market area decreased from Austria-Hungary's 677,000 to the new Yugoslavia's 248,000 square kilometers. This new market was not only more limited in area but much poorer; its productive capacity was small and its purchasing power still less. Before 1918, Croatia's predominantly agricultural products were consumed in the industrialized areas of Austria-Hungary. In 1918, Croatia found itself in an economic region having a complementary economic structure. The economic position of the province changed radically as a result of its incorporation into the new state; instead of being one of the most

---

[11] S. Kukoleča, *Industrija Jugoslavije 1918–1938* (Belgrade: Balkanska Štampa, 1941), p. 74.

underdeveloped regions of the Empire, it was one of the most highly developed areas of Yugoslavia.

In this new state, Zagreb was the largest industrial and commercial center. While Belgrade gradually concentrated political authority and thus became the center of political power during the interwar period, Zagreb had the greatest concentration of capital in Yugoslavia. In 1924 Croatian banks which depended on Zagreb as their financial center contained approximately 50 percent of all Yugoslav capital.

The 1918 boundaries removed politically a whole series of large cities which traditionally had been supplied from the Yugoslav area: Klagenfurt, Graz, Pécs, Szeged, and Timişoara. Especially serious was the loss of access to the port cities of Trieste, Rijeka, Zadar, and Thessalonike which traditionally served Yugoslav territory. The industrial and port cities of Trieste and Rijeka were separated from their economic hinterland, in a political upheaval which changed the trade structure of the ports as well as the economic conditions of their former hinterlands. Particularly hard hit was Slavonia,[12] which had supplied most of the food for Graz and Trieste. Physically diverse, culturally and ethnically fragmented, economically backward, the Kingdom of the Serbs, Croats, and Slovenes began political existence.

It is within a framework of quantitatively delimited regional differences that we can most profitably examine the nature of the system of local government that has evolved since 1950. Chapter Three describes the underlying structure of the Yugoslav economy in the 1960's and attempts to discover similarities or differences between areas previously under Austrian and Turkish occupation.

---

[12] Special attention should be paid to the area which is called "Slavonia." This name has been used for a variety of areas. During the Middle Ages, Slavonia referred to that area between the Drava, Sava, and Kupa Rivers, or Pannonian Croatia. Later "Slavonia" referred only to the area between the Drava and the Sava, and from the first half of the Eighteenth Century on, only to the eastern portion of this area. "Croatia" has usually had reference to that organized state which steadily moved northward under pressure of Venetian and Turkish advances. After the initial formation of the Croatian State on the territory of present-day Dalmatia, the name "Dalmatia" has generally excluded reference to Croatia proper while "Croatia" has come to indicate the area between the Kupa and the Drava rivers. At the present time "Slavonia" is used to refer to that area between the Sava and Drava from east of the Ilova River to the Croatian Republic boundary with Serbia.

Before proceeding, however, it seems advisable to examine the implications of the previous discussion for contemporary Yugoslavia. The impact of the historical consequences described previously are evident today in the country's landscape, including its urban network. Yet these tangible differences, spatially diverse though they may be, are only one facet of the effect of centuries of domination by various foreign powers. The remainder of this chapter examines city-size distributions in Yugoslavia, and briefly presents varying regional mores or attitudinal differences, and the economic goals generated by cultural and social differences, which—reinforced by ethnic dissimilarities—condition the contemporary political process.

3. NORTHERN AND SOUTHERN YUGOSLAVIA

Since much of the subsequent discussion will focus on Yugoslav cities it seems desirable to examine the nature of the size distribution of urban

Sarajevo townhall, constructed in 1896 in Moorish-Byzantine style.
Agencija za Fotodokumentaciju

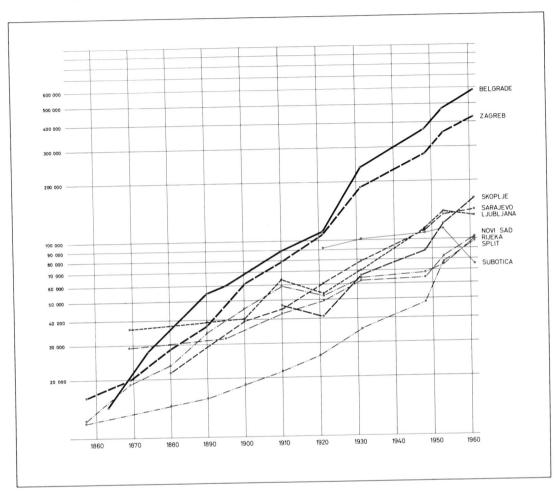

FIGURE 11. Growth of Major Yugoslav Cities.

Source: Official statistics 1921–1961; both official sources and various articles prior to 1921. The decline of populations of Ljubljana and Subotica was, in part, due to a decrease in each city's administrative area.

settlements in the country.[13] City-size distributions were examined in the country as a whole and in the North and South. The northern area corresponds generally to the previously described Central European and Mediterranean regions of foreign domination and cultural penetration or the contemporary republics of Slovenia and Croatia plus the northern part of Serbia, Vojvodina. The southern area corresponds to the Byzantine-Turkish region of domination and influences consisting of the existing republics of Serbia (except for Vojvodina), Macedonia, Montenegro, and Bosnia and Herzegovina. The distributional characteristics of fifty-five cities over 20,000 are shown in Table Two.

Table One. PRIMACY INDEXES AND PRIMACY SCALES

Country	Primacy Index	Primacy Scale
Yugoslavia	41.9	Low
North	55.0	Medium
South	56.8	Medium
Poland	39.7	Low
U.S.S.R.	54.8	Medium
Thailand	94.2	High

Source for Poland, U.S.S.R., and Thailand: Norton Ginsburg, *Atlas of Economic Development* (Chicago: University of Chicago Press, 1961), p. 36.

The first concern was to create an index of primacy for each of the three areas. This primacy index, similar to that suggested by Mark Jefferson, is a measure or ratio of the population of the largest city in a country or region

---

[13] "Students of urbanization have recognized two kinds of city size distributions: *rank-size*, according to which the distribution of cities by population size class within countries is truncated log-normal; and *primate*, whereby a stratum of small towns and cities is dominated by one or more very large cities and there are deficiencies in numbers of cities of intermediate sizes. Rank-size regularities have been associated with the existence of integrated systems of cities in economically advanced countries, whereas primate cities have been associated with overurbanization and superimposed colonial economies in underdeveloped countries or with political-administrative controls in indigenous subsistence and peasant societies." Brian J. L. Berry, "City Size Distributions and Economic Development," *Economic Development and Cultural Change*, Volume IX, Number 4 (July, 1961), p. 573.

to the combined population of the four largest cities.[14] Comparing the primacy indices computed for Yugoslavia with Berry's results suggests that the country as a whole is low on the primacy scale[15] but, considered separately, both the North and South show average degrees of primacy.

It is maintained that low primacy is correlated with log-normal city-size distribution, and conversely, that primate countries do not have rank-size distributions. Although small countries (such as Switzerland, Finland) may also have log-normal distributions, it is more likely that large countries will produce the complex conflicting forces that lead to a rank-size distribution. Thus, breaking a country up into small pieces would tend to show *less* log-normality in the pieces, unless the same *set* of forces was at work in each piece. Working from the opposite direction, sections which showed high degrees of primacy when separated might show a greater degree of log-normality when combined *if* the sections were essentially different. For the case of Yugoslavia, the North and the South exhibit sufficiently different characteristics so that when they are combined a significantly higher degree of "entropy" exists, as indicated in Figure 12.

Table Two. CHARACTERISTICS OF YUGOSLAV CITY-SIZE DISTRIBUTION

Percent of Population (cumulative)			City-Size	Percent of Cities (cumulative)		
Yugoslavia	North	South	Class Interval	Yugoslavia	North	South
17.3	15.4	18.9	20,000–30,000	45.4	43.5	46.9
26.0	20.0	31.0	30,000–40,000	61.8	52.2	69.7
32.4	25.4	38.2	40,000–50,000	70.9	60.9	78.1
42.5	38.0	46.2	50,000–80,000	81.8	73.9	87.5
49.8	49.0	50.6	80,000–100,000	87.3	82.6	90.6
55.8	62.1	50.6	100,000–150,000	90.9	91.3	90.6
70.5	71.8	69.5	150,000–300,000	96.4	95.6	96.9
83.3	100.0	69.5	300,000–500,000	98.2	100.0	96.9
100.0	—	100.0	500,000+	100.0	—	100.0

Source: *Statistički godišnjak SFRJ*, (Belgrade, 1963), p. 606.

The curve on log-normal paper for the South, shown in Figure 12,

---

[14] Mark Jefferson, "The Law of the Primate City," *Geographical Review*, XXIX (1939), pp. 226–232, and Harley Browning, "Recent Trends in Latin American Urbanization," *Annals of the American Academy of Political and Social Sciences*, CCCXVI (March, 1958), pp. 111–120.

[15] Berry, *op. cit.*, p. 579.

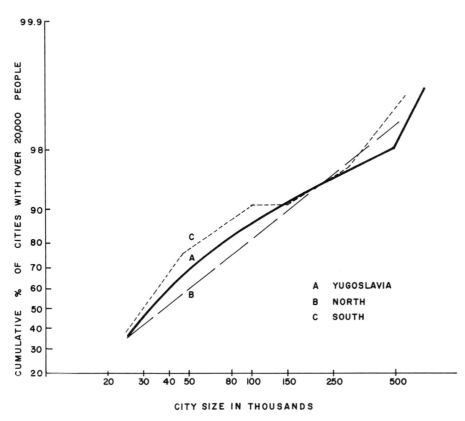

FIGURE 12. City-Size Distributions in Yugoslavia, the North, and the South. Cumulative frequencies were plotted on log-normal probability paper and are shown in Table Two.

indicates a definitely primate type of distribution when compared with Berry's graphs; the North by itself has a clearly log-normal curve, while the country as a whole would be classified as "intermediate between log-normal and primate."

Countries with rank-size distributions are either highly developed, complex societies or countries with long urban traditions. Smaller countries are expected to have steeper curves, which is consistent with the findings here. The inverse relationship between primacy and log-normality comes through fairly strongly; the South is first in the order of primacy followed by the North and Yugoslavia, while the North is first in the order of log-normality followed by Yugoslavia and the South.

In conclusion, there seems to be some justification in terms of city-size distribution alone in choosing to regard the North and South of Yugoslavia as structurally different areas. The North is more diversified and more urban, both characteristics tending to produce a rank-size city distribution, whereas the South seems to be more primate, with a higher percentage of its cities under 60,000.[16] Berry maintains that there is no general, world-

---

[16] The general lack of urban centers in the South between the 60,000 and 150,000 city-size category, indicated in both Figure 12 and Table Two, has important planning implications. It would appear that more research and attention should be given to the desirability of stimulating increased development of the smaller centers to achieve the missing size categories or to straighten out the curve. The uncontrolled and massive migration as a result of political policies in Macedonia directed towards Skopje resulted, in reality, in a "planned" restriction on the growth of middle-size urban centers.

The federal assembly house in Belgrade, constructed in 1932, with Marx and Engels Square in front.

The old section of Ljubljana below the castle, under control of a special municipal agency for preservation and reconstruction.

The western entrance into Ljubljana. The Hotel Lev, completed in 1964, is visible beside the modern two-lane approach to the city.

wide correlation between log-normality and the state of economic development, but it would appear that the South of Yugoslavia is in some sense less developed than the North according to these data alone.

Yugoslavia's unique historical evolution produced a state with no definable "core area," to use a term often employed by political geographers. In other words it has no area which, both economically *and* politically, significantly dominates the rest of the country. There are in fact two major cultural hearths or core areas each centering on a major city, as the above discussion would suggest. Belgrade and Zagreb are approximately the same size, especially if the commune of Zemun is subtracted from Belgrade's population.[17] The situation in Yugoslavia is an exception to the so-called law of the primate city, which suggests that the largest city in a country has a significant preponderance over the others (see Table One). Yugoslavia may be described as having a biprimary pattern, as the first two cities, Belgrade and Zagreb, are of almost equal size.

Until 1918 these cities were in different political, cultural, and administrative systems which had different social values. Zagreb was Western-oriented, Catholic, and semi-industrial. Belgrade was essentially Near Eastern in custom, Greek-Orthodox, and traditional in occupational structure. Around the two "core areas" evolved a network of communications which reinforced within-group contact and essentially eliminated direct or frequent interchange between the two principal South Slav groups: the Croatians centered on Zagreb and the Serbians centered on Belgrade.

Around each of the two focal points, Belgrade and Zagreb, there were a number of subcenters acting as centripetal points for other ethnic groups. Most notable of these was Ljubljana, cultural and administrative center of the Western-oriented Catholic Slovenes. Linguistically distinct from the other South Slav peoples, the Slovenes had evolved through the centuries an articulated set of national traditions and institutions.

To the south of Belgrade lay the complex area of Macedonia, focusing on Skopje. Traditional in occupational structure, Greek Orthodox and

---

[17] It should be recalled that Belgrade is a "multicommunal" city composed of nine communes. Thus the commune Zemun is in reality a city which was attached to Belgrade after the war.

Moslem in religion, oriental in custom, the area gravitated towards Belgrade, Thessalonika, or Athens, depending upon political conditions.

The varying levels of economic development and cultural background crystalized political activity in a number of urban centers. One of the contributing reasons that a distinct core area cannot be specified for Yugoslavia is that the location of greatest economic strength in Slovenia and Croatia does not correspond with the focus of state power in Belgrade and Serbia. This led to increasing internal antagonism during the interwar period, as Serbian Belgrade attempted to impose centralized political authority over the economically more advanced Croatians and Slovenes.

This cleavage between political power and economic means still lies at the root of the recurring unrest or conflict between the various nationalities. Discussion of "Danubian" or "Adriatic" orientation for Yugoslav economic development—a discussion which has reached no formal end and no final decision—refers in reality to Serbia's desire to concentrate investment along the Danube River within this republic's zone of influence and Croatian and Slovenian emphasis on the Adriatic zone. Thus the location of an iron and steel mill at Smederevo south of Belgrade on the Danube rather than in Split on the Adriatic was scorned in Zagreb and Ljubljana. The Danubian solution to development would suggest a more Eastern orientation to raw materials and markets of the Soviet Bloc while the Adriatic-Sava River emphasis would require Yugoslav access to Western markets and sources of raw materials. Furthermore, the continuing discussion among Yugoslav economists as to whether a more "centralist" or "noncentralist" planning structure is best for the country refers to differing Serbian (centralist) and Croatian (noncentralist) positions.

At present, Belgrade and Zagreb predominate, and each in turn has a set of regional or provincial centers that economically, politically, or culturally focus on them (see Figure 13). It should be emphasized that Figure 13 represents the author's estimate of regional alignment around Belgrade and Zagreb based on economic or trade orientation, local attitudes, cultural and economic conditions, and their historical antecedents—plus the typical political behavior of regional representatives on national issues. Slovenia and Ljubljana are more difficult to classify in this manner but at least three factors would tend to indicate the suggested alignment: (1) transportation connections and flow; (2) the use of the Zagreb airport by the Slovenes for international flights; and (3) strong economic, cultural and personal ties, as well as the fact that certain Croatian specialists are employed in Slovenian industry. The southeastern area of Yugoslavia is culturally and economically dependent on Belgrade, though subareas have a high degree of cultural individuality which at times is equated with economic nationalism. Macedonia, centering on Skopje, is under Belgrade's influence. Kosovo-Metohija (often referred to as Kosmet) is administratively directed from Priština, though economically dependent upon Belgrade. Montenegro may accurately be viewed as a Serbian exclave. It is the dilemma of Bosnia and Herzegovina and especially Sarajevo that the attraction is to both major cities, politically to Belgrade and economically to Zagreb.

It is significant that, both culturally and economically, Croatia and Slovenia are more advanced than Serbia or its hinterland. Since 1918,

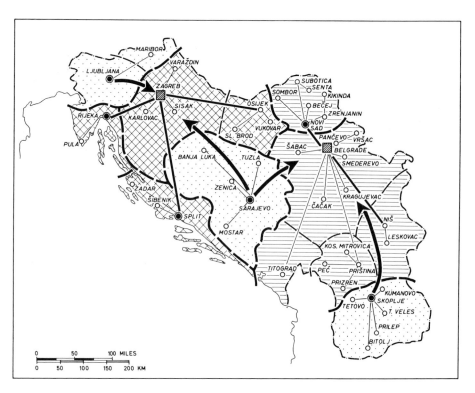

FIGURE 13. Gravitational Orientation of Major Yugoslav Cities.

however, because of the location of the federal government in Belgrade, Serbia has dominated the rest of the country.

In Chapter Three two underlying elements are discussed: the varying levels of economic development and the extent and structure of the transportation grid. In the case of Yugoslavia, a more advanced northern area is adjacent to a less developed southern zone. The existence within the same state of have and have-not areas, further distinguished by the dominance of different ethnic and religious groups, weakens at least potentially the over-all viability of the state. Though various attempts have been made to siphon off the northern economic surplus for southern development, the operation has not usually been harmonious. Even though the North is economically more attractive than the South, ethnic, linguistic, and other cultural differences restrict many southern workers from seeking jobs in the advanced North.

The major exception to the above is the relatively new phenomenon of unskilled forestry, mining, and especially construction workers, primarily from Bosnia and Herzegovina and Macedonia, seeking seasonal jobs in northern urban centers. Though there is relatively less interrepublic migration than might be considered normal, especially for the large sector between the unskilled and the highly skilled professional groups, there is apparently a very high turnover in the labor force within the same republic or city. "The Federal Statistical Office says that last year the fluctuation of the labor force was 47.7 percent (labor turnover). This is a very high percent which, of course, negatively influences the quality of production and labor relations in economic organization." [18] This same article goes on to state that some of Yugoslavia's leading factories have had well over 100 percent turnover in the labor force during the year. Desire for more favorable or attractive conditions is the main reason for this turnover. Workers and in fact all employees in Yugoslavia are free to select their place of work. Each position is competitive and the specifications for the job must be publicly announced. Yugoslav enterprises, however, often resort to methods for obtaining top managerial staff similar in character and equal in intent to those common in the United States. As salaries are essentially egalitarian,

---

[18] *Borba*, Belgrade, Tuesday, October 13, 1964.

with a small difference between the highest and lowest paid employees of the enterprise, housing is a more appealing item of barter. Increasingly the opportunity to improve oneself with more education will influence younger workers to seek employment in localities and factories that facilitate this goal.

There is also a definite hesitation on the part of high-level professional and political leaders to leave Slovenia and Croatia for Belgrade. On numerous occasions ranking Party members (that is, members of the League of the Communists of Yugoslavia) have absolutely refused to accept high position in the federal government for the following reasons: (1) great attachment to their native city, reinforced by a set of cultural attitudes that considers this attachment the normative pattern for a good Croatian or Slovenian; (2) better housing than would be available in Belgrade and the fact that an individual, who must by law give up his apartment in Ljubljana or Zagreb if he obtains one in Belgrade, would be unable to obtain another easily after his tour of duty in Belgrade is completed; (3) lack of Croatian and especially Slovenian schools in Belgrade, which usually means that one must leave his family in Ljubljana or Zagreb. Those individuals who, under strong political or occasionally professional pressure, find themselves unable to reject a Belgrade position, often leave their families at home and spend the minimum time (four or five days a week) in Belgrade. There is also the feeling in the North that one improves his general status as he moves north along the Belgrade-Zagreb axis nearer the coastal area.

Roughly, less than one percent of Slovenian party members live outside Slovenia (in other words, in Belgrade) while more than 50 percent of Montenegro's Party members reside outside the Republic, mainly in Belgrade. In Montenegro there is an entirely different trend. The Montenegrins are culturally closer to the Serbians, but have a lower standard of living and are therefore attracted by the cultural, economic, and political pull of Belgrade.

A different situation exists with respect to the Macedonians. The newly created Macedonian state has formally provided its people with the cultural and economic individuality that was so harshly repressed through the centuries. The new republic stimulated a wave of nationalism that has

The new building of the Assembly of the Socialist Republic of Slovenia, in Ljubljana.

reinforced cultural and historic differences and tended therefore to curb the outflow to the more attractive North.

The lack of adequate cultural and other amenities in the outlying areas of Macedonia produced a migration to Skopje. As shown in Figure 11, Skopje, in the postwar period, experienced the largest and most uncontrolled population increase of any major Yugoslav city; its rank shifted from the eighth largest city to the third (after Belgrade and Zagreb). In contrast to this centripetal movement of Macedonians toward their capital there was a centrifugal movement of some non-Macedonians out of the Republic. Thirty-five percent of Skopje's population in 1953 was composed of Albanians, Turks, and Gypsies. By 1962 the Turkish element had decreased significantly as a result of one of the most interesting and least known postwar migrations. Between 1951 and 1962, 37,700 "Turks" moved from Skopje to Turkey. Due to a provision of the Turkish immigration law requiring a period of residence in the city, Skopje acted as the collection center for Turks in the southern portion of Yugoslavia. Instead of destroying the slums the Turks left behind, the municipal administration allowed Albanian inhabitants from western Macedonia and Kosovo and Metohija to purchase the one-room shanties. As a result, during the late 1950's there was a considerable immigration of Albanians to the Skopje area. This process of the less-advanced Albanians moving into areas that, though depressed according to Yugoslav standards, were superior to their former conditions, took place not only in Skopje and other Macedonian cities but in South Serbia. As Serbian peasants moved from outlying rural areas to the suburban zones of major cities, their former dwellings were occupied by Albanians.

After the earthquake in August, 1963, there was a unique opportunity for the planned economic integration and development of the Skopje-Kumanovo-Tetovo-Titov Veles region which was already interconnected by good transportation lines. It appears, however, that despite this opportunity to reconsider developmental policies, Skopje will continue to dominate Macedonia at the expense of the rest of the Republic.[19] Investments in manufacturing and commerce will continue to be concentrated in the republican capital at the expense of the outlying areas of the province.

The lower developmental level of the South produced in this case a lower rate of capital accumulation, and thus tends to maintain or accelerate the differences between North and South. This fact plus the historical differences and cultural variations among the various sections of the country—where economic regions coincide with cultural-ethnic regions—has tended since 1918 to strengthen ethnic-group ties and discourage assimilation.

Yugoslavia's physical diversity, striking economic contrasts, and cultural differences have led almost "naturally" to sectionalism or regional antagonisms. The content of regional conflict during the interwar period and after 1945 was, formally at least, fundamentally different in character. Cultural and national autonomy were developed and applied during the war (which was called the National Liberation War), and as such may be said to represent basic tenets of the existing political philosophy. For the post-1945 government the overriding problems were economic in character rather than cultural and economic as they had been in the prewar period. This was a result of the economic expansion policies of the new

---

[19] See Jack C. Fisher, "The Reconstruction of Skopje," *Journal of the American Institute of Planners* (February, 1964), p. 48; and Eric Larrabee, "Letter from Skopje," *The New Yorker* (October 17, 1964), pp. 169–172.

government and the fact that cultural self-determination for the various peoples was one of the fundamental policies upon which the new state evolved. The problem, however, was and is that economic differences often evolve today into "nationality problems."

The prewar period increased the ethnic awareness of the Croatians and triggered that of the Macedonians at the same time that the government, which was Serbian-dominated, was attempting to transform itself into a privileged class to which other ethnic groups would be subordinate. The harshness of the prewar Serbian regime has left its mark on the consciousness of the other groups. It has even restricted the current federal government from taking certain courses of action they might otherwise have considered correct for fear of non-Serb minorities decrying them as "Serbian chauvinism" (for example, the initial complete hands-off policy on the part of the federal government in dealing with the reconstruction of Skopje).

The Macedonians, who officially achieved their national identity only after 1945, are the most dogmatically nationalistic in their policies and development goals. The flower of Macedonian nationality is being carefully tended. Economically dependent upon the federal government for investment capital and therefore development suggestions, the Macedonians appear most sensitive to federal pressure. It should be recalled that this feeling is reinforced by memory of the prewar period when "Serbian chauvinism" neither recognized the Macedonian people as a distinct ethnic group nor granted them any regional economic or political autonomy (even the name "Macedonia" was replaced by the term "South Serbia"). The Croatians, on the other hand, achieved national recognition at a much earlier date, had a strong, if nationally unsuccessful, party system in the prewar period, and appear therefore to be most concerned with political decisions made in Belgrade which will affect economic development in Croatia. A specific example of this is Croatian concern with federal regulation of foreign trade, as a large share of Croatian industrial capacity is destined for foreign markets.

Perhaps one of the clearest tangible examples of ethnic rivalry concerns the expansion of Yugoslav port capacity. Rijeka (Fiume), the major Yugoslav port, is relatively limited from substantial expansion by the physical characteristics of its site. The projected increase in the facilities of the port to handle the transit trade of Central Europe would appear to represent its optimum and maximum function. It is clear that further expansion of port capacity must occur at points other than Rijeka. An excellent discussion of the competition among Yugoslav coastal cities and their regional supporters is provided by Dennison Rusinow:

If Rijeka is to become increasingly important as a transit port, however, the problem of alternative ports for *Yugoslav* commerce becomes increasingly urgent. The old question, *which* alternative ports, is raised again, and the answers under consideration prove to be as much political as technical and economic.

The other ports involved in the debate are six in number: Koper, Zadar, Šibenik, Split, Ploče, and Bar. Koper (Capodistria) is the chief town of the brief 15 miles of north Istrian coastline, formerly Zone B of the Free Territory of Trieste (1946–1954), which is today the Socialist Republic of Slovenia's

Rijeka, Yugoslavia's major port city, in Croatia.

proud toehold on the sea. Bar, at the other end of the Yugoslav littoral, was wrested from Turkey in 1878 by the Principality of Montenegro in alliance with the Principality of Serbia, both landlocked until that day, and it falls now within the frontiers of the Socialist Republic of Montenegro. The other four ports are all in Dalmatia, which is part of the Socialist Republic of Croatia.[20]

The major problem of the "political ports," as they are sometimes referred to, is that each of the Adriatic ports and their political supporters desire transformation into a major focal point for an extensive hinterland with widespread international connections. The Serbs back the communal leaders of Bar for expansion as this would provide Central Serbia, the Kosmet, and Montenegro access to the outside world through a "Serbian" port.

Unfortunately these considerations are not based upon sound economic calculation but on the recurrent assumption that each republic should be able to have its own "personal port." The arguments often assume a semieconomic tone. The question that must be asked, however, is which port or group of ports can most effectively handle Yugoslav tonnage requirements and maintain the lowest transportation costs in distribution. In view of the continental interior east of Bar and Ploče, as well as Split, and distance to major production centers, it would seem plausible that transport costs would be higher relative to shipments from northern ports. Also rail traffic would be brought to a standstill for certain periods of time during the winter due to the mountainous terrain of the interior.

If existing transportation rates are to be based upon more or less economic criteria or actual costs, as expected, rather than the current noneconomic, administrative rates, it is imperative that transportation development be based on sound cost analysis rather than political and emotional whims.

The development scheme of each of these ports is based upon the desire of each locality to advance its own relative position. The Republic of Slovenia, without any significant federal contribution, is hard at work constructing a major port facility at Koper. Regardless of the actual utility of the port's development, the work proceeds due to Slovenian desire to

---

[20] Dennison I. Rusinow, *Ports and Politics in Yugoslavia* (New York: American Universities Field Staff Report, Southeast European Series, Vol. XI, No. 3, 1964), pp. 8–11.

have a port of its own. In essence, the decentralization policies of the last decade facilitated this kind of local action set within a framework of serious competition or rivalry with one's neighbors. The final decision as to which port to develop and modernize in relation to a total transport development plan has unfortunately been left to various piecemeal projects generated as a result of political pressure. There has been no form of comprehensive regional planning, nor any effective mechanism through which local plans could be processed and evaluated.

Ethnic sensitivity has sharply conditioned the evolution of Yugoslavia's administrative system. The division of the country into republics in 1945 officially affirmed and consciously stimulated the self-determination of the various ethnic groups. This, coupled with the administrative centralism of the period through 1950, combined to produce a climate of discord. The discontent which resulted from the policy of economic centralism was initially balanced by granting each people the right to maintain its own schools, newspapers, and churches. Yet the initial era of good feeling was short-lived as it became apparent that cultural independence would be worth little without political and economic self-determination. In 1948, events made it possible and expedient to reconsider the policies which had permeated the initial postwar years.

Chapter III

Socioeconomic Variation and Urban Structure

I. A SURVEY OF SELECTED INDICATORS OF ECONOMIC DEVELOPMENT

The previous discussion has stressed that geographical location and historical circumstances contributed varying economic and social elements to the
diverse regions that made up the new state of Yugoslavia in 1918. This is
usually taken for granted in most studies of Yugoslavia. What is the
relationship between these traditional regions of foreign domination and
influence and the level of economic and social development in the country
today? If the variation is as marked as is usually assumed, does this mean
that there are different sets of administrative procedures and measures on
the local scene despite standard policies emanating from the federal
government in Belgrade? The latter portion of this study will concern

itself with these questions. The questions raised here are: What are the differences between the regions or republics of the country in terms of major indicators of economic development? What are the functional or occupational differences among the urban centers of Yugoslavia? Do occupational, demographic, and other selected variables vary in such a way that a classification of urban settlements within the confines of the traditional regions of foreign domination and influence bears out the assumptions concerning the development of these regions? At a level of greater detail, how do the communes, the basic administrative units of the country, vary among themselves, and what are the underlying dimensions which contribute to that variance? With an understanding of the objective variations among cities and communes, the functioning of the administrative system that was superimposed upon a heterogeneous physical, social, and economic environment can be examined.

The boundaries of the republics created after World War II corresponded (with the general exception of Vojvodina) to the traditional provinces existing during centuries of foreign domination. The level of economic and social development in these republics today reflects the conditions and policies of the foreign powers which dominated these provinces. Variations in economic and social development created distinct differences between the areas of Mediterranean and Central European domination and those under Turkish influence. The levels of development were so varied that it has become customary to speak of Slovenia and Croatia and portions of Serbia as advanced, but to view the rest of the country as essentially underdeveloped.

To distinguish the differences among the regions and their relationship to past historical process, three major indicators of economic development are examined: (1) the size and organization of industrial plants as a measure of industrial scale and·specialization; (2) transportation systems as measures of accessibility and interchange; and (3) per capita income, a summary index, as a measure of standard of living.

Following a brief discussion of the spatial distribution of these indicators, subsequent sections of this study will examine the occupational structure of fifty-five urban centers with population over 20,000 in 1961, and will classify these centers by multivariate techniques which simultaneously

interrelate occupational structure, demographic characteristics, and selected indicators of urban and economic "quality."

Our first class of variables expresses the level and degree of *industrialization*. Statistics are presented in Table Three for northern and southern
Yugoslavia, as well as for the country as a whole. Serbia, which occupies a
transitional position spatially between the northern republics of Slovenia
and Croatia and the southern republics of Macedonia, Montenegro, and
Bosnia and Herzegovina, has been placed in a separate category due to its
heterogeneous historical and cultural background. It should be recalled
that the Serbian Republic today contains not only Serbia proper, the area
which evolved independently of Turkish domination between 1817 and
1878; but Vojvodina, which forms part of the Pannonian Basin and was
under Central European influence; and the area of Kosovo and Metohija
which remained under Turkish control until 1912 (see Figure 3).

The assumed "index of economic development" or the output
capital ratio is an approximate indicator of modernization as well as
economic development since it is a ratio between output (GNP per
worker) and input (assets per worker) of activities within the socialist
sector. This ratio is a reflection of regional variations of labor intensity, of
the "quality" of the labor force (skilled versus nonskilled, educational
level, and other determinants) as well as the scope and structure of the
regional economies. Note, as indicated in Figures 14 and 15, that total assets
per worker are much higher in the South than the North, while GNP per
worker is reversed. Serbia has approximately the same index of economic
development as Yugoslavia as a whole. This transitional position of Serbia
between an advanced North and less-developed South emerges in many
statistical data.

The difference in industrial capacity and labor productivity between the
northern and southern republics is evident from Table Three. Croatia and
Slovenia, with 42.6 percent of the industrial enterprises and 44.5 percent of
the workers, contributed 48.8 percent of the total national product of the
country, while the corresponding figures for the southern regions are 20.6
percent, 21.9 percent, and 19.8 percent. At the same time it would appear
that Serbia, in terms of the variables in Table Three, is in a less fortunate
position than even the southern republics; this is a reflection of the

importance of agriculture in Serbia and the disparity of prices (low agricultural prices). Though Serbia has 36.8 percent of the factories and 33.6 of the labor force, the republic contributes only 31.4 percent of the national product. Similar comparisons are valid for the size of industrial enterprises both in terms of their labor force and the size of their contribution to the national product.[1] The older industrial plants of

[1] See *Statistički godišnjak SFRJ* (Belgrade, 1963), Tables 207–4, p. 394, and 207–5, p. 395.

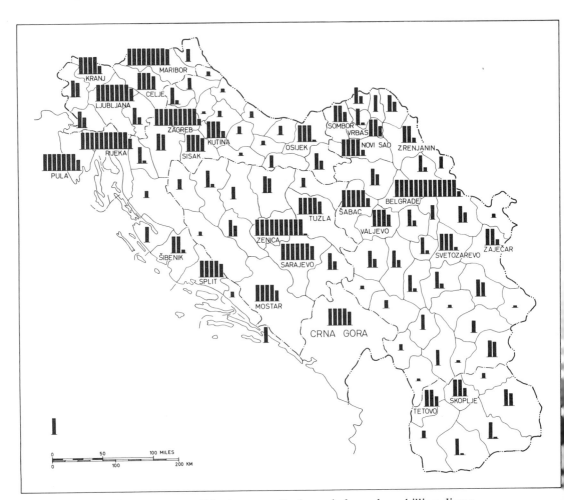

FIGURE 14. Total Fixed Assets per District, 1959. Each symbol equals 10 billion dinars.
  Source: Rudolf Bičanić, *Ekonomska Politika* (Zagreb: Birotehnički izdavački zavod, 1962), pp. 264–265.

Slovenia and Croatia are more efficiently operated with higher rates of return than the newer establishments in the South.

Figures 14 and 15 present the regional distribution of fixed assets as of June 30, 1959, in the socialist sector of the economy, excluding rail and postal facilities. Figure 14, showing total fixed assets per district, gives the

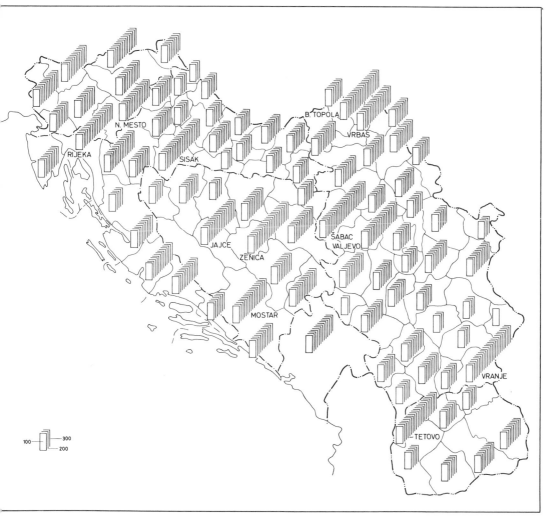

FIGURE 15. Fixed Assets per Worker, 1959. Each symbol equals one hundred thousand dinars.
  Source: Rudolf Bičanić, *Ekonomska Politika* (Zagreb: Birotehnički izdavački zavod, 1962), pp. 264–265.

Table Three. BASIC INDICATORS OF THE LEVEL OF INDUSTRIALIZATION IN 1961

	Yugoslavia	Northern Republics [1]	Southern Republics [2]	Serbia [3]
Data				
Number of industrial enterprises	2,787	1,187	576	1,024
% of total	100	42.6	20.6	36.8
Labor force	1,137,737	505,534	249,971	382,232
% of total	100	44.5	21.9	33.6
Gross national product in millions of dinars [4]	1,423,774	695,507	281,990	446,277
% of total	100	48.8	19.8	31.4
Total assets	3,782,815	1,633,927	927,913	1,220,975
% of total	100	43.1	24.5	32.4
Indicators				
Average employment per enterprise	408	425	432	372
Index based on Serbia (100%)	109.9	114	106	100
Total assets per worker in thousands of dinars	3,325	3,232	3,712	3,194
Index based on Serbia (100%)	104.1	101.3	116.4	100
Gross national product per worker in thousands of dinars	1,251	1,376	1,130	1,168
Index based on Serbia (100%)	107.3	117.5	96.8	100
Index of economic development: (GNP ÷ Total Assets)	.38	.43	.30	.37

[1] Slovenia and Croatia
[2] Bosnia and Herzegovina, Montenegro, and Macedonia
[3] Serbia proper, Vojvodina, and Kosovo and Metohija
[4] 750 dinars equalled one dollar in 1961. GNP is called "Social Product" in Yugoslavia. GNP excludes "nonproductive" activities such as health, government, and some services and therefore is approximately 10 percent less than GNP as calculated in the United States.
Source: *Statistički godišnjak SFRJ* (Belgrade, 1963), Table 207–2, p. 393, and *Ekonomika preduzeća* (March, 1964), p. 213.

picture expected from the preceding discussion, that is, a more developed North and less advanced South, with recognizable exceptions. The districts of Belgrade and Zagreb (the two largest industrial centers in the country in absolute terms), Rijeka, Zenica, Maribor, and Ljubljana predominate.

Figure 15 appears to indicate a somewhat different situation, as fixed assets per worker are larger in the South. Much greater depreciation has occurred in the older industrial plants of Croatia and Slovenia than in the new industrial complexes built after the war in the South and Southwest.

The investments in the southern areas were mainly in heavy industry, power plants, and the like; major capital consuming items. The new plants, constructed according to advanced technology, required fewer workers to operate than the older plants of the North. The major urban centers, such as Belgrade and Zagreb, have fewer fixed assets per worker than cities in which industry comprises a larger share of the economy. Activities such as commerce, construction, handicrafts, and the like, which predominate in metropolitan economies, require less investment per worker than does industry.

Transportation is often cited as a principal or a major index of economic development. Most assuredly the lack of an adequate transportation network hinders economic growth by greatly increasing transport costs, and contributes to both economic and cultural isolation.

The length of roads and railroads per 100 square kilometers in 1961 in the three more advanced areas is shown in Table Four.

Table Four. LENGTH OF ROADS AND RAILROADS PER 100 SQUARE KILOMETERS

	Yugoslavia	*Serbia*	*Croatia*	*Slovenia*
Roads with improved, hard un-paved surfaces (km)	22.8	17.4	28.4	70.0
Roads with asphalt or cement surfaces (km)	3.0	2.5	3.9	9.0
Railroads (km)	4.6	5.0	5.3	6.5

Source: "Saobraćaj i veze" *Statistički bilten* (Belgrade, 1962), No. 247, and *Statistički godišnjak, FNRJ* (Belgrade, 1962).

Figure 16 presents the rail network density and volume in millions of tons of freight hauled in 1961. A study of this map reveals the same characteristics stated statistically above. Serbia, it should be noted, is above the Yugoslav average in the length of rail lines per 100 square kilometers due to the inclusion of Vojvodina. Kosmet, on the other hand, has but 2.5 kilometers of railroad tracks per 100 square kilometers. The difference in the development of the network of roads in Serbia in comparison with Croatia and especially Slovenia is striking. Many agricultural products produced in the southern regions of the country cannot be profitably marketed due to the state of the transportation system. One analyst has

The highway connecting Zagreb and Ljubljana was built
after the war. *Agencija za Fotodokumentaciju*

A section of the modern Adriatic Highway follows the seacoast.

The new railway station at Sarajevo.

estimated that the total loss to Serbia due to the poor transportation system alone is around 16 billion dinars a year.[2]

Perhaps the variable most frequently cited as an index of development is *per capita income*. Figure 17 indicates those areas of the country that had an annual per capita income in 1961 of less than 100,000 dinars. The figures were calculated on a communal basis, dividing total personal income in the commune by the population. Bosnia and Herzegovina, Serbia proper with Kosovo and Metohija, and Macedonia stand out as areas with more than 80 percent of their territory designated as underdeveloped by this classification. Montenegro, with more than half of its territory underdeveloped, appears superficially in a more favorable condition due to the size of its administrative units (communes) which has the effect, statistically, of spreading the slightly higher incomes of the scattered settlements over the large, sparsely populated communes. Slovenia, Croatia, and Vojvodina have only a few pockets where income is less than 100,000 dinars per year. These areas will occupy our attention when a more detailed analysis of the communes is presented later.

[2] C. Popović and D. Miljković, "Problemi akumulativnosti u privredi Srbije," *Ekonomika preduzeća* (March, 1964), p. 159.

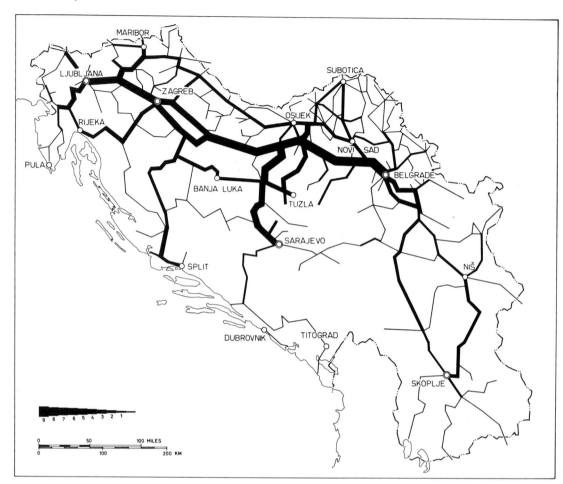

FIGURE 16. Railroad Density and Flow, 1961. Million net tons of freight hauled. Source: "Saobraćaj i veze," *Statistički bilten, No. 247* (Belgrade, 1962).

Once again a direct correspondence exists between the areas with predominantly lower incomes and the traditional region of Turkish domination. The largest group of the actively employed population in Serbia, Macedonia, and Bosnia and Herzegovina is in private agriculture (primary production), which pays much lower returns. These private holdings, largely subsistence in nature, accumulate relatively little cash return. These areas have undergone less change or remained more traditional in their occupational structure than the areas under more Western influ-

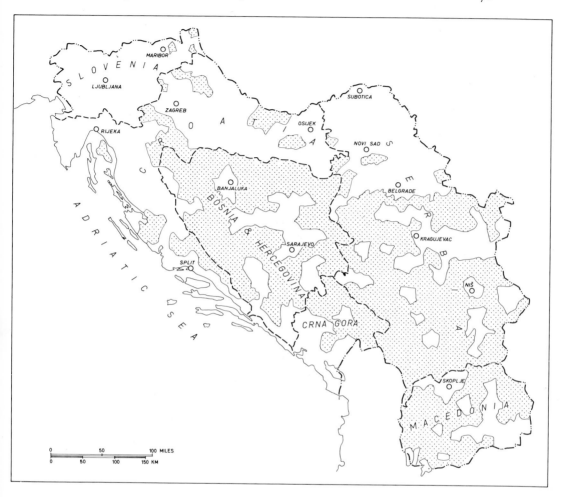

FIGURE 17. Underdeveloped Areas of Yugoslavia. Communes with less than 100,000 dinars per capita income in 1961.

Source: *Statistički godišnjak SFRJ* (Belgrade, 1963), pp. 532–555.

ence. This is strikingly revealed by the contemporary employment structure, which produces in the southern portions of the country the low incomes revealed in Figure 17. The total population of Yugoslavia in 1961 was 18,549,000, with Serbia containing 41.2 percent of the total population, Croatia 22.3 percent, and Slovenia 8.5 percent. Thus the small number of people employed in the socialist sector of the economy compared to the large number engaged in primary production in these regions accounts for the relatively low figure for incomes and also for the lower rate of saving. This statement obviously coincides with Colin Clark's generalization that economies tend to move toward more complex organization and higher income levels in a series of steps: first, intensification of primary production, agriculture, forestry, and mining, followed by an expansion of secondary and finally tertiary production.[3] The central and southern areas of Yugoslavia are traditional in occupational structure, as measured by the proportion of people in the nationalized or socialist sectors compared to the private, essentially agricultural sector.

A survey of the incomes or "budgets" of 16,567 families sampled throughout Yugoslavia indicates a considerable difference in monetary terms, not in real income, between agricultural and industrial employees. The average white- or blue-collar worker's family had 714,000 dinars income. This includes not only salaries but gifts, lottery winnings, and all possible sources of income. The rural family had 300,000 dinars less. The mixed-income families, who derived income from both agricultural and nonagricultural pursuits, had an average income from all sources halfway between the other two groups.

The average annual income per person has improved since 1960 and 1961. The estimated Yugoslav average in 1963 was 220,000 dinars (146,000 in 1960), distributed as shown in Table Five.

Table Five. Per Capita Income in 1960 and 1963 (Dinars)

Republic	1960	1963
Serbia	133,000	202,000
Bosnia and Herzegovina	111,000	149,000
Montenegro	81,000	140,000
Croatia	174,000	269,000
Macedonia	85,000	148,000
Slovenia	280,000	421,000

Source: *Statistički kalendar Jugoslavije* (Belgrade, 1965), pp. 21, 42.

If the 1960 and 1963 per capita income breakdown by republic is plotted on a simple scale, it appears that the positions of the southern, less-developed republics (Montenegro, Macedonia, and Bosnia and Herzego-

---

[3] Colin Clark, *The Conditions of Economic Progress* (London: Macmillan, 1940); Allan G. B. Fisher, "Capital and the Growth of Knowledge," *Economic Journal*, Vol. 43 (September, 1933), pp. 379–389, and "Production, Primary, Secondary and Tertiary," *Economic Record*, Vol. 15 (June, 1939), pp. 24–38.

vina) have more or less merged, while Croatia and especially Slovenia have accelerated their advances. Serbia in each case remained close to, but below, the Yugoslav average. A more extensive discussion of this occurs later.

The negative influence of the larger birth rate in the South is apparent from examining total national income growth for 1963 compared to 1960 against the growth in per capita income for the same period. The difference between the per capita income index for 1960–1963 compared with the index for total national income for all Slovenia and Croatia was only 3 and 4 points respectively below the Yugoslav difference of 5 and well below the 9-point difference of Bosnia and Herzegovina and Montenegro. Macedonia had a 7-point difference. The higher increase in population of the southern republics offset to a limited extent their gains attained in total national income increase.

The mixed-income category is another indicator of transition from a traditional to a modern social structure. In 1960, 45 percent (1,314,000) of the total labor force of the socialized sector of the economy was in the mixed-income category. This group of peasant-workers provides a large reserve of cheap labor, employed mainly in construction and mining activities. In an expanding economy, this group of laborers is often viewed favorably as they do not put pressure on scarce housing and utilities or demand agricultural products destined for urban markets. On the other hand, these peasant-workers tend to remain among the unskilled labor force and at the same time show little interest in improving production on their small land holdings.[4] They tend not to undergo the attitudinal development necessary for changing or altering traditional mores and thought patterns. In Yugoslavia, these peasant-workers remain a group apart from other workers and only seldom do they participate in the "political process," in "management" of the factory through the workers' councils.

---

[4] Recent governmental policy was directed at the mixed-income category as this group appears most reluctant to cooperate with the socialized state farms. Federal authorities now provide credit to the socialized sector to purchase private small farms. Thus there is a clear policy for the socialist sector to acquire land not properly cultivated by families having outside economic pursuits. *Economic Survey of Europe 1963, Part I, The European Economy in 1963* (Geneva: Secretariat of the Economic Commission for Europe, 1964), Chapter III, p. 34.

Table Six. RURAL POPULATION PERMANENTLY EMPLOYED OFF THEIR OWN LAND IN THE PERIOD 1953–1960

Area	Persons Employed (thousands)				Index for 1960 (1953 = 100)
	1953	1955	1957	1960	
Yugoslavia	798	880	955	1,314	165
Bosnia and Herzegovina	134	149	170	247	184
Montenegro	18	21	24	27	150
Croatia	375	370	336	351	94
Macedonia	35	56	63	94	269
Slovenia	47	61	71	139	296
Serbia	190	223	291	456	240
Serbia proper	133	153	175	366	200
Vojvodina	33	43	82	140	424
Kosmet	24	27	34	50	208

Source: P. Marković, "Društveno ekonomska kretanja na selu," *Jugoslovenski pregled*, Number 11–12 (Belgrade, 1962).

A large portion of this "peasant-worker" group commutes to the industrial complexes of the country's major cities. What is the pattern of commuting around Yugoslav urban centers? Appendix One attempts to provide some insight into this complex phenomenon. Through the use of a multiple regression model it was possible to establish the labor market area around selected Yugoslav cities: Belgrade, Zagreb, Niš, and Bor. The designated area seems to relate fairly well to each city's major economic tributary area. The analysis revealed that the quality of the means of transportation is the most important determinant in explaining the journey-to-work each day. Distance does not appear to be as significant a factor. It is hoped that the material in Appendix One will serve as source material and background for those readers interested in this most important subject.

2. VARIATIONS IN REGIONAL ECONOMIC GROWTH

A number of questions arise which are central to both the theory and practice of planning and investment in Yugoslavia today. The nature of planning itself will be discussed in a subsequent section. Despite clear statements of a planning policy to increase the economic level of the South,[5] are these republics advancing at least as rapidly as Croatia and

---

[5] One of the basic goals of long-range economic policy is:

Slovenia? Figure 17 revealed that most of the territory of southern Yugoslavia is much less developed than Croatia and Slovenia. Is it, however, less advanced relatively than it was in 1946 and 1953? If the average per capita income for Yugoslavia in 1962 is designated as 100, then Serbia's was 90.5, Croatia's 123.5, Slovenia's 193, Bosnia and Herzegovina's 69.5, Macedonia's 64, and Montenegro's 62.

In 1953, the first year the *Statistical Yearbook* had data on income by republics, it can be observed that Serbia was then in a better position than today; in 1953 it was only eight points (92) below the Yugoslav average. On the other hand, the two most developed republics, Slovenia and Croatia, were in a worse situation in 1953 than today, for Croatia's index compared to the Yugoslav average was 113, and Slovenia's index was 185. As one can see, the assumption that Serbia moved towards the Yugoslav average in production and income does not hold.[6]

What can be concluded from these figures? The index of Serbia was 92 in 1953 and 90.5 in 1962. If the index in 1962 had remained 92, one would have concluded that the rate of growth of per capita income in Serbia was as fast as in the rest of the country. The difference between 90.5 and 92 does not seem significant, as it could easily be due to slight differences in weather conditions. Crop fluctuations do have a very substantial effect on national income, particularly in the underdeveloped regions. What the author of the quotation fails to point out is that in the year 1953 crops were very good, in the year 1962 relatively bad. It could be concluded that per

---

"Rapid development of the insufficiently developed republics and regions, in harmony with general developmental policies of Yugoslavia, as one of the conditions for attaining the fundamental goals of economic policy throughout the Yugoslav territory." Jakov Sirotković, *Privredni sistem i društveno planiranje Jugoslavije* (Zagreb, 1964), p. 11.

"In order to even the material conditions of social life and work of the working peoples, for a more harmonious development of the economy as a whole and to attain the material basis of equality of the peoples of Yugoslavia, society in the general interest attaches special concern for the rapid advancement of the productive forces in the economically insufficiently developed republics and regions and in this regard, guarantees necessary means and undertakes new measures." *Constitution* of the Socialist Federal Republic of Yugoslavia (Belgrade: April, 1964); cited by J. Sirotković, *ibid.*

[6] D. Lopandić, "Pravac, tempo i izvori sredstava daljeg razvoja," *Ekonomika preduzeća* (March, 1964), p. 172.

capita income in Serbia grew as fast in percentage terms as the rest of the country—but not faster. Since Serbia started from a lower level, the republic as a whole did not catch up with national development; nevertheless the country's underdeveloped regions all (with the possible exception of the Kosmet) made relative, but slight gains if 1953/1954 and 1962/1963 averages are used. In 1963 and 1964 agricultural prices were substantially increased, which worked in favor of the underdeveloped regions.[7]

Considering the low base from which Serbia started compared to Slovenia and Croatia the question could be asked: How did Serbia achieve its actual rate of income growth? Serbia benefited from a greater percentage increase in capital goods than the more advanced republics of the country and this offset the negative effects of a traditional social and economic structure. In short, Serbia was apparently able to tread water. What worries Serbian economists currently is whether the republic will be able to experience an improvement and achieve a faster rate of growth relative to the North. Relative increases might continue though absolute growth would remain less compared to the North.

Using absolute numbers, it may be concluded that Serbia really was in a less advantageous position in 1962 than earlier:

> If one views the growth in national income per capita from 1956–1962, it can be maintained that Serbia at both the beginning and end of the period lagged 12–13% behind the Yugoslav average. Of course, the gap in the last period had a far greater material effect . . . such that the difference in income per person between Yugoslavia as a whole and Serbia in 1956 was 10,132 dinars, while in 1962 the difference in favor of Yugoslavia increased to 16,732 dinars.[8]

Due to an inferior economic structure, level of technology, and organization, the production process is inferior, transport costs are higher, and the standard of living (equated with per capita income) is lower in the southern republics than the northern. A comparison of per capita income figures by republics for 1953 and 1962 would tend to indicate that the gap

---

[7] For an excellent discussion of agricultural overpopulation and rural planning see Rudolf Bičanić, "Three Concepts of Agricultural Overpopulation," *International Explorations of Agricultural Economics* (Ames: Iowa State University Press, 1964), pp. 9–22, and Bičanić, "Tri koncepcije ruralnog planiranja," *Sociologija* (Zagreb: No. 5–6, 1964), pp. 3–24.

[8] Eva Berković, "Problemi razvoja lične potrošnje," *Ekonomika preduzeća* (March, 1964), p. 236.

between Croatia and Slovenia and the rest of the country has increased. One major topic of debate in Yugoslavia today stems from the implications that these quantitative differences have for subsequent development or future investment. Figure 17 suggests that the future rate of savings (earnings or profits) in the South will be less than in the North.

According to the most recent statistics, one dinar of investment in fixed assets (*osnovna sredstva*) leads to annual increments of retained earnings (in dinars) as follows:

in Belgrade	.44
in Ljubljana	.48
in Zagreb	.54

The annual dinar retained earnings per worker is:

in Belgrade	589,000
in Ljubljana	630,000
in Zagreb	639,000

In comparison with the Yugoslav monthly average income of 24,000 dinars per worker, Belgrade has 26,300, Zagreb 27,400, Rijeka 28,200, and Ljubljana 31,300 monthly. It is the level of retained earnings and personal income that established potential investment in both economic and non-economic activities, for from these sources investment funds of all types are derived.[9]

A clear index of the impact of the level of income on investment, which is in turn related to the level of industrialization and accompanying technology and the transportation system, is the amount spent for housing, derived in large part from a four percent tax on salaries.

Since 1957, there has existed in Yugoslavia a special institution concerned with housing policy and finance, the Fund for Housing Construction (*Fond za stambenu izgradnju*). The Fund obtains the sums at its disposal from the following sources:

(1) rents on all apartments in the socialist sector of the economy;
(2) a tax on each apartment, based upon its location or proximity to the center of the city;
(3) interest on loans previously extended;
(4) a four percent tax on the personal salaries of all people employed in the communes.

---

[9] D. Miljković, "Regionalni razvoj-Uloga Beograda," *Ekonomika preduzeća* (March, 1964), p. 183.

Figure 18 presents the average per capita value of the housing funds in 1961 for each township or commune averaged by district.[10] This map reveals the economic level or prosperity of the districts. Since these funds are largely based on the four percent tax on income they reflect the economic strength or stability of each commune or, as graphically presented here, each district. The same basic pattern of unequal development in the southern and northern areas emerges. With the exception of three districts, Bosnia and Herzegovina, Serbia (excluding Vojvodina), Macedonia, and Montenegro all fall into the lower three categories, with less than 6,000,000 dinars of housing funds per capita. Slovenia, most of the coastal area of the country, and Vojvodina stand out in contrast as highly developed areas. The districts of Skopje in Macedonia and Sarajevo and Zenica in Bosnia and Herzegovina are the exceptions. All these districts have received large amounts of federal investment (Zenica for heavy industry) or reflect the concentration of investments in the republican capital cities of Skopje and Sarajevo.

Of special significance is the fact that Belgrade has a very low per capita housing fund while at the same time having the largest volume of housing construction.[11] This is a direct index of the allocation of federal funds into Belgrade's housing program. Skopje's relatively high value reflects the concentration of investments in the republic's capital and the spillover effect on the housing fund through the tax on salaries.

Regional variation in terms of some of the indicators of economic development then clearly corresponds to the regions of foreign domination

---

[10] The averages reflect the statistics provided in "Sredstva i fondovi opština u 1961 godini," *Statistički bilten, Number 252* (Belgrade: January, 1963), pp. 8–33. My own observation would suggest somewhat higher values for Belgrade and certain other areas than these statistics indicate. Nevertheless, the general pattern would remain relatively constant.

[11] The implications of statistics similar to these may well have been in the mind of the President of the City Council of the Socialist Alliance when he was asked, ". . . when will Belgrade be in a position to guarantee an apartment to each of its inhabitants?"

Branko Pešić answered as follows, "In Belgrade there are many so-called economically-inactive people. There are over 130,000 grammar school children, close to 50,000 in high schools, and over 50,000 university students. If we add to this pre-school children and the unemployed, then we see that the burden of creating new funds falls on a relatively small percent of the population that does work" (*Borba*, Belgrade, Sunday, October 18, 1964.)

The funds for housing construction are created by a tax on salaries, thus the larger

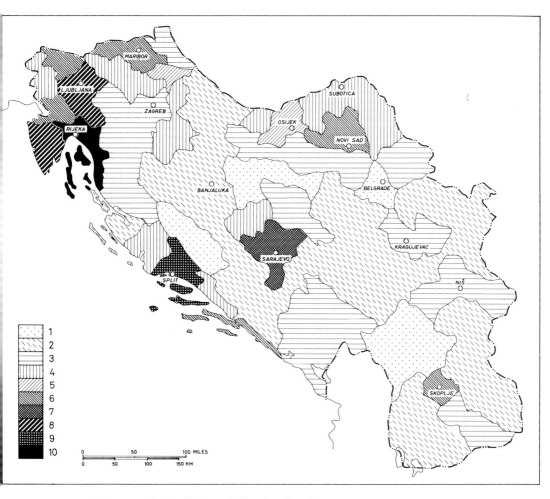

FIGURE 18. Mean per Capita Value of Housing Funds, 1961.

Source: "Sredstva i fondovi opština u 1961 godini," *Statistički bilten, Number 252* (Belgrade, January, 1963), pp. 8–33.

1. 1,999,999 dinars
2. 2,000,000 – 3,999,999 dinars
3. 4,000,000 – 5,999,999 dinars
4. 6,000,000 – 7,999,999 dinars
5. 8,000,000 – 9,999,999 dinars
6. 10,000,000 – 14,999,999 dinars
7. 15,000,000 – 19,999,999 dinars
8. 20,000,000 – 24,999,999 dinars
9. 25,000,000 – 29,999,999 dinars
10. Over 30,000,000 dinars

As these figures do not reflect the number of settlement points of population within the districts or the population density, they should be received as rough indices.

the proportion of the "economically-inactive population," the smaller will be the total housing fund in any commune or city.

and influence. The northern provinces of Slovenia and Croatia with Vojvodina correspond to the defined regions of Central European and Mediterranean domination and influence; Serbia (excluding Vojvodina), Bosnia and Herzegovina, Montenegro, and Macedonia correspond to the traditional Byzantine-Turkish region of influence. The postwar period of planning does not appear to have altered the fundamental situation but only to have kept the different areas in essentially the same relative position. In fact—and this is the basic problem plaguing the Yugoslav planners today, and in effect lies at the root of current rumors regarding the "nationality question"—it appears that the advanced republics of Croatia and Slovenia may now be progressing at a faster pace.

We have generalized here on the basis of regional or republic averages for the most part. Perhaps the main question concerns the effectiveness of the investments that were made in the last twenty years. Advanced Slovenia and Croatia had a higher labor productivity rate; thus the northern investments were more effective, or less wasteful, which resulted in a higher rate of return and capital accumulation. Does the clear demarcation apparent between economically advanced communes and have-not communes in regard to funds for housing construction remain valid for other indicators? Is there in fact some fundamental difference in function and structure among urban centers or communes that is related to underlying socioeconomic differences?

3. A QUANTITATIVE ANALYSIS OF CONTEMPORARY URBAN AND REGIONAL VARIATION

The matrix used for analyzing the structure of urban centers for contemporary Yugoslavia incorporates twenty-six variables and fifty-five cities having a population over 20,000 in 1961 (see Figure 19 in the section of oversized figures).[12] The twenty-six variables utilized in the analysis can be broken into four groups: demographic (nine), occupational (nine), "quality indicators" (three), and various combinations of the occupational variables (five). This last group combines certain occupational variables generally considered to be closely allied in order to observe concentration

---

[12] The data for this portion of the analysis were selected from a statistical source available to most readers, the *1963 Statistical Yearbook of Yugoslavia*. Data for

of grouped occupations in the cities and to enhance understanding of the degree of association among the variables. This proved to be a useful device in the initial analysis.

The underlying assumption for including demographic variables in the analysis is their presumed relationship to level of development. As a society advances the proportion of persons in the productive ages (20–50) will gradually increase while a marked shift will take place in the dependent age groups.[13]

---

seventy selected urban settlements are provided in the *Yearbook*. In principle only those places of 20,000 or more population were selected, in order to conform with generally accepted international practice for the designation of urban places. The *Yearbook* did not include among its seventy settlements two or three centers having more than 20,000 population but predominantly agricultural in occupational structure. However, two other such centers, Svetozarevo and Zaječar in Serbia, which had less than 20,000 people at the time of the 1961 census, were included in this analysis, since they have now surpassed that figure. To aid in the analysis and to eliminate the factor of population size, each of the variables was transformed into percentages; population size itself is not a variable. The major reason for not including population size was the assumption that the fifty-five selected urban settlements were "urban," at least in terms of one fundamental criterion: "Urbanization is a process of population concentration" (Hope Tisdale Eldridge, "The Process of Urbanization," *Social Forces*, XX [March, 1942], p. 311). The desire was to hold size constant and examine the other properties of these urban places. In our analysis of the communes, however, population size was a variable, as both rural and urban communes were included in the analysis.

"The data are based on definitive results of the census of population and as a rule represent the 'statistical territory' which represents the urban territory especially delimited for statistical analysis. This territory includes all independent settlements within the framework of the cities and some parts of other independent settlements which together with the city constitutes a single unified community forming a densely populated territory with common utilities funds and services consisting of a population with a common economic and cultural life." *Statistički godišnjak SFRJ* (Belgrade, 1963), p. 16.

A number of errors were found in the raw data as presented in the *Yearbook*. The numbers for total population employed in the socialist sector were in many cases incorrect and it was necessary to add up each occupational category to obtain total employment.

[13] As was pointed out by Professor Robert Morris of Brandeis University, there is evidence to suggest that more economically advanced countries may reach a point (as suggested in Chapter One) when the productive age group will decline relative to the more rapid development in the dependent range, both young and old. This change is, however, a function of a much higher stage than Yugoslavia has attained.

Age composition reflects fertility and age-selective (largely rural-urban) migration. High fertility produces a high ratio of children, or a high ratio of children to adults of an age to be their parents. Rural fertility is higher than urban. Agrarian societies which are less educated, less literate, have fewer radios or newspapers or the like, tend to have higher ratios of children to adults. Rural-urban migration selects young adults and with time, as they stay in the city and age, the urban center accumulates age groups beyond the prime age of migration; when massive migration is a recent phenomenon, few migrants will as yet have grown old and the cities will bulge with young to more or less middle-aged adults. According to Valaoras: ". . . it is easy to see that the most 'efficient' age structure of a population tends to occur towards the final rather than at the initial stages of demographic evolution . . . A sizable proportion of persons surviving beyond their 65th birthday preserves mental and physical abilities which add immeasurably to the intellectual and the material wealth of the community. Obviously a similar contribution cannot be expected from the child population. Furthermore, the cost for the upkeep and the raising of the individual child is, under most social patterns, much greater than that required for the maintenance of an old person." [14]

Fertility and migration are related to urbanization and to a wide range of economic and social characteristics. Similarly, the latter variables can be related to fertility and migration in a variety of ways.

To the demographic component, occupational variables have been added. Both urbanization and economic development in general can be "seen as a *reorganization* of activities, or a shift in social and economic *structure* that places a population in a new relationship to its total environment. It is said to involve a transition from agricultural to non-agricultural pursuits, and a concomitant increase in specialization of economic activities." [15]

The quality indicators were included in an attempt to measure urban quality. Percent of apartments completed in 1961 as a portion of the total

---

[14] Vasilios G. Valaoras, "Young and Aged Populations," *The Annals of the American Academy of Political and Social Sciences* (March, 1958), p. 82.

[15] Leo F. Schnore, "Urbanization and Economic Development: The Demographic Contribution," *The American Journal of Economics and Sociology* (January, 1964), p. 58.

housing stock is, in the case of Yugoslavia, a measure of urban maturity. The older and more "urbanized" the city, the smaller will be the observed value of this variable. The other two, percent of hard surface streets out of total street area and percent of the population having radios, are clearly quality indicators. These factors are important as they were the *a priori* concepts upon which subsequent interpretation is based.

Table Seven lists the twenty-six variables with the mean percentage ($\overline{X}$) for each variable, the standard deviation, and the range of absolute variation of each variable for the fifty-five cities. Note that the standard deviation with respect to population composition is much higher for the dependency group 0–9, and also relatively higher for the most active, reproductive age groups 25–34, 35–49, and 50–64. A closer examination of the differential urban population compositions reflects to a great extent the varying reproductive and economic structures of the cities as well as differences in migration patterns.

A ranking of the cities in terms of the percent of their actively employed population engaged in various specialties has often served as the basis of urban classification. Table Eight, utilizing a format devised by Dolfe Vogelnik,[16] lists fourteen cities having the highest percent of their actively employed population engaged in various key occupations.

Vogelnik ranks Yugoslav cities in order of the percentage of the population actively employed in several occupational categories. The top 10 percent of cities for each occupational category he calls "specialized" cities, while those in the next 15 percent are designated as "oriented." Since Vogelnik's book contains numerous maps indicating those cities which were specialized in or oriented to a particular function it was useful to employ this simple distinction as a basis for initial classification.

It is necessary to comment here on the number and significance of "urban places" in Yugoslavia. Vogelnik includes data on 315 settlements in his book. He considers as urban every settlement over 2,000, if more than 50 percent of its total population is engaged in nonagricultural activities. Dr. M. Macura, current Director of the Federal Statistical Office, uses a somewhat more complex method to distinguish urban areas. Macura's

---

[16] Dolfe Vogelnik, *Urbanizacija kao odraz privrednog razvoja FNRJ* (Belgrade: Ekonomska biblioteka, number 13, 1961).

Table Seven. Twenty-Six Variables for Fifty-Five Selected Yugoslav Urban Centers

Variables	Mean *	Standard Deviation	Range Maximum %	Range Minimum %
DEMOGRAPHIC				
1 Age 0–9	20.3	4.7	30.6	12.5
2 Age 10–14	9.2	1.0	12.0	7.5
3 Age 15–19	7.1	.8	9.3	5.5
4 Age 20–24	8.7	.9	12.0	7.0
5 Age 25–34	20.5	2.5	25.6	15.3
6 Age 35–49	17.5	2.2	21.2	12.6
7 Age 50–64	11.6	2.6	18.3	6.8
8 Over 65	5.2	1.4	9.5	2.0
9 Increase, 1953–1961	43.7	28.4	93.6	2.5
OCCUPATIONAL— ACTIVELY EMPLOYED				
10 Agriculture and forestry	6.6	7.2	38.8	.4
11 Construction	11.0	5.5	29.5	2.2
12 Transportation	8.0	4.2	19.9	1.6
13 Handicrafts	7.1	2.6	15.4	2.3
14 Utilities and housing adminis-tration	2.6	1.3	9.3	1.0
15 Cultural activities	10.0	2.6	19.4	5.3
16 Industry	37.1	11.2	57.1	7.0
17 Commerce and entertainment	10.7	3.2	23.9	6.1
18 Social and state services	6.2	1.8	13.3	3.1
QUALITY INDICATORS				
19 Apartments completed in 1961 as portion of total housing stock	5.4	2.1	10.5	1.7
20 Hard-surfaced streets out of to-tal street area	38.5	22.1	99.0	7.1
21 Population with radios	22.4	6.4	38.0	9.3
OCCUPATIONAL GROUPS— ACTIVELY EMPLOYED				
22 Construction and transportation	19.1	7.3	40.1	7.1
23 Handicraft, commerce, and en-tertainment	17.8	4.9	31.0	8.4
24 Cultural, social, and state services	16.3	3.8	29.8	10.5
25 Construction, transportation, and utilities	21.8	7.5	43.1	9.9
26 Construction, transportation, utilities, and industry	58.9	9.5	78.3	38.8

Source: *Statistički godišnjak SFRJ* (Belgrade, 1963), pp. 606–608, 610, 621, and 625. Raw data were converted to percentages.

* Raw data were transformed into percentages.

criteria also include a minimum population of 2,000, but he uses a sliding scale of tolerated percent employed in agricultural activities as follows:

Size of Settlement	Lowest Acceptable Percent of Non-agricultural Population
2,000 to 3,000	90
3,000 to 10,000	70
10,000 to 15,000	40
Over 15,000	30

Our concern here is with clearly urban places or cities; therefore, following international practice, focus is on cities of 20,000 and over. Official Yugoslav statistics maintain, however, that there are 300 "urban places," with a total of six million people or 30 percent of the total population (in 1964). In Chapter Five, regional variation and even intra-urban differentiation is examined by a study of more comprehensive statistical units, the communes.

Figures 20 and 21 in the section of oversized figures, indicate the location of those fourteen cities indicated in Table Eight as having the highest proportion of their actively employed population in each of six categories: transportation, construction, agriculture and forestry, social and state services, commerce and entertainment, and industry.[17] Agriculture and forestry, social and state services (designated as "administration" in Figure 20) and, for the most part, construction are dominant in cities south of a hypothetical line drawn between Subotica and Split. Such large employment in state services appears to be a sign of underdevelopment, in view of the southern location of these cities ranking high in administration and

---

[17] Descriptions of the historical evolution of many of the cities discussed briefly here can be found in *Geografski Horizont*, a journal published by the Geographical Society of Croatia. Each article provides a bibliography of major references on the city concerned. The following articles are useful, as they present the spatial development of particular cities: "Štip—glavno sedište istočne Makedonije," *Geografski Horizont* (Zagreb, 1964), No. 1–2, pp. 30–41; "Bitola," 1963, No. 1–2, pp. 32–45; "Niš," 1962, No. 4, pp. 17–30; "Kragujevac," 1962, No. 1–2, pp. 1–15; "Novi Sad," 1961, No. 4, pp. 1–13; "Sarajevo," 1961, No. 3, pp. 16–28; "Zadar-Split-Dubrovnik," 1961, No. 1–2, pp. 3–29; "Zenica," 1960, No. 1–2, pp. 17–32; "Ljubljana," 1959, No. 4, pp. 1–16; "Beograd," 1959, No. 3, pp. 1–20; "Skopje," 1958, No. 4, pp. 1–9; "Zagreb," 1956, No. 3–4, pp. 15–38; "Prilep," 1955, No. 3–4, pp. 23–27.

Table Eight. Cities with Highest Percentage of Actively Employed Population Engaged in Various Employment Categories in 1961

Social and State Services		Commerce and Entertainment		Industry	
SPECIALIZED CENTERS:					
Titograd	13.3%	Dubrovnik	23.9%	Kranj	57.9%
Prizren	10.7	Belgrade	15.6	Varaždin	56.2
Zaječar	10.4	Rijeka	15.2	Kos. Mitrovica	55.4
Niš	9.7	Ljubljana	15.1	Kraljevo	53.7
Tetovo	8.9	Smederevo	14.6	Pančevo	53.5
Belgrade	8.7	Titovo Užice	14.5	Zenica	53.2
ORIENTED CENTERS:					
Pančevo	8.5%	Zagreb	13.7%	Sisak	52.2%
Kraljevo	8.2	Čačak	13.5	Novi Sad	50.8
Titovo Užice	7.9	Subotica	13.5	Slav. Brod	49.4
Valjevo	7.5	Split	13.4	Leskovac	49.4
Skopje	7.4	Celje	13.3	Maribor	48.2
Peć	7.4	Šibenik	12.4	Požarevac	47.4
Titov Veles	7.1	Osijek	12.4	Kruševac	47.3
Sarajevo	7.0	Zadar	12.1	Priština	46.4

Transportation		Construction		Agriculture and Forestry	
SPECIALIZED CENTERS:					
Rijeka	26.8%	Nikšić	29.5%	Vinkovci	30.5%
Dubrovnik	19.9	Titovo Užice	28.5	Vukovar	23.2
Vinkovci	18.8	Titograd	22.3	Valjevo	16.2
Šibenik	15.9	Zaječar	21.1	Zrenjanin	16.0
Mostar	15.6	Dubrovnik	20.2	Niš	15.3
Split	14.8	Zrenjanin	19.7	Štip	13.6
ORIENTED CENTERS:					
Kragujevac	13.9%	Split	16.3%	Svetozarevo	13.1%
Zadar	13.3	Skopje	16.2	Prilep	11.9
Zenica	11.9	Bitola	15.8	Kumanovo	11.3
Titov Veles	11.6	Zadar	14.2	Titov Veles	10.7
Čačak	11.2	Titov Veles	14.1	Kruševac	9.7
Subotica	10.8	Požarevac	13.6	Peć	9.5
Sisak	10.1	Banja Luka	13.5	Subotica	8.2
Smederevo	9.2	Kumanovo	13.4	Šabac	7.6

Source: *Statistički godišnjak, SFRJ* (Belgrade, 1963), p. 608. Raw data were converted into percentages.

lacking, at least for some of the cities, specialization in something else. It is of interest to note that some of the cities which notably expanded or formed their industrial sectors in the postwar period still retain a large proportion of population actively employed in agriculture and forestry (Svetozarevo, Titov Veles, and Štip). These southern cities have merely added a new industrial component to a traditional occupational base.

The map of transportation employment (Figure 21) does in fact indicate the key transportation hubs in the country. Figure 21 clearly reveals the important port cities of Zadar (13.3 percent of this city's actively employed population is engaged in transportation, primarily in local island traffic), Šibenik (15.9 percent, aluminum and bauxite shipments), Split (14.8 percent, cement and passenger traffic), Dubrovnik (19.9 percent, tourist traffic), and Rijeka (the most important port in Yugoslavia both in terms of labor force [26.8 percent] and in terms of absolute tonnage). Vinkovci, Subotica, Kragujevac, and Titov Veles are major rail and marshalling centers, while Sisak and Smederevo are key transshipment points between rail and water carriers. There tends to be a greater concentration of industrial and commercial centers in the more advanced republics of Croatia, Slovenia, and Serbia. It should be noted that Dubrovnik is the most specialized commercial center in the country, having 23.9 percent of its actively employed population engaged in commerce.

Use of these occupational variables in order to identify the most highly specialized cities within each occupational category is important as a first step in analysis. Many authors have relied on occupational or industrial indices to group towns according to economic functions.[18] Though these simple ranking methods are useful for intraurban differentiation, they are not suitable for deriving a classification of cities in terms of their functional specialization as well as related level of development.

As a first step towards analyzing the associations among variables and isolating particularly significant or key variables, a matrix of correlation

---

[18] Chauncy D. Harris, "A Functional Classification of Cities in the United States," *Geographical Review*, XXXIII (January, 1943), pp. 86–99; H. J. Nelson, "A Service Classification of American Cities," *Economic Geography*, XXI (July, 1955), pp. 189–210; Otis D. Duncan and Albert J. Reiss, *Social Characteristics of Urban and Rural Communities, 1950* (New York: Wiley, 1956), Part III. See also Victor Jones, "Economic Classification of Cities and Metropolitan Areas," *The Municipal Year Book* (Chicago: International Managers' Association, 1953), pp. 49–57 and Tables II and IV; Victor Jones and Andrew Collver, "Economic Classification of Cities and Metropolitan Areas," *Ibid.*, pp. 67–77, 87–88, and Tables IV and VI; Victor Jones and Richard L. Forstall, "Economic and Social Classification of Metropolitan Areas," *Ibid.*, 1963, pp. 31–37 and Table I; and Victor Jones, Richard L. Forstall, and Andrew Collver, "Economic and Social Characteristics of Urban Places," *Ibid.*, 1963, pp. 85–113 and Table III, and others. As a general reference, see Otis D. Duncan, *et al.*, *Metropolis and Region* (Baltimore: Johns Hopkins Press for Resources for the Future, Inc., 1960), especially pp. 34–36.

coefficients was obtained. Table Nine presents the correlation coefficients; those with a value of .50 or higher, regardless of sign, are underlined. All variables over .26 are significant at the .05 level. The following relationships are apparent from the table:

1. A high negative correlation exists between age groups 0–9, 10–14, and age groups 35–49, 50–64, employment in commerce and entertainment, and the percent of the population with radios. In line with the previous discussion of demographic variables, this association of young dependent age group combined with a deficiency in commerce and radios suggests a condition of underdevelopment.

2. Employment in industry is negatively correlated with employment in construction, handicrafts, cultural activities, and commerce and entertainment, as well as with three of the "mixed indicators." This reflects postwar industrial expansion in the South in traditional settlements with a relatively insignificant commercial or administrative base. This association also reflects the separation in the North of industrial from commercial and especially administrative functions (for example, Ljubljana in contrast with Maribor and Kranj).

3. No variables are highly correlated with percent of population increase. This is a reflection of an interesting trend in Yugoslavia: large cities such as Skopje, Belgrade, and Zagreb, as well as much smaller centers, have been growing rapidly. The smaller settlements (under 50,000) are growing slightly faster than the larger. Thus growth is occurring at two poles of city size with but moderate expansion among the medium-size cities.

In order to test and expand the assumptions suggested by the correlation coefficients and ultimately to derive a classification of Yugoslav cities based upon the underlying communalities (the degrees of associations among variables), a factor analysis technique was utilized.

Factor analysis is a method which allows a large number of variables and a large number of observations to be handled simultaneously. Starting from a correlation matrix which determines the correlation of each variable with all others, factor analysis seeks to identify the association or underlying dimensions among variables. As it suggests which variables are most highly associated to an underlying dimension, it allows many measures to be represented by a few.

The use of factor analysis in this study has been adapted to the problems of development and designed particularly to compare the various areas of the country in relation to historical and present interdependencies. Factor analysis simply sharpens the output and makes the analysis less subjective. It was used here to provide a statistical technique which approaches the problem and suggests relationships in terms compatible with the research goals.[19]

---

[19] For a complete explanation of factor analysis, see Harry H. Harman, *Modern Factor Analysis* (Chicago: The University of Chicago Press, 1964). Berry provides an excellent brief description of the manner in which one form of factor analysis (direct factor analysis) is conducted:

"A large area is divided into n smaller areas which are the units of observation. For each of these n areas, m factors are recorded. The regionalization problem is to group the n areas into a smaller number of regions which are as uniform as possible. Actually, this is a special case of a more general classification problem: given n observations, and the values of m variables for each observation, to group the observations so that internal uniformity of the resulting groups is maximized.

"Inevitably, some of the m variables tell the same thing about the ways in which the n observations vary. This means that some variables are redundant when similarities and differences of the n areas are to be described. Therefore, when several variables display a single pattern of concomitant variation it is desirable to eliminate the redundancies, isolate this pattern and use it in the analysis instead of the several variables. Since m variables may contain several such patterns, say r, the analysis is greatly simplified by reducing the dimensions of variation of the n areas from m variables to the more fundamental r basic patterns. This is achieved in the first stage of the proposed analysis, direct factor analysis. A table or matrix which has n rows, one for each area (or in this case, city), and m columns, one for each characteristic, and which is filled out with the raw data, once these data have been transformed to common units of measurement, is analyzed. Direct factor analysis replaces the m columns by r new columns, one for each basic pattern of variation of the areas (or cities), and provides each of the n areas with a set of values which show how it rates on the new patterns. At the same time a second table is produced by the analysis, with r rows and m columns. The values in this table tell how the original m variables have been "collapsed" on the basis of concomitant variations to their r basic patterns. [In the present study we utilize more conventional principal axis factor analysis and pseudo-inverse factor scoring procedures, rather than direct factor analysis.]

"Suppose just two basic patterns emerge from the direct factor analysis. A graph

Thurstone explains the utility of the method in socioeconomic studies at the present time:

Factor analysis has its principal usefulness at the borderline of science. It is naturally superseded by rational formulations in terms of the science involved. Factor analysis is useful, especially in those domains where basic and fruitful concepts are essentially lacking and where crucial experiments have been difficult to conceive. The new methods have a humble role. They enable us to make only the rudest first map of a new domain. But if we have scientific intuition and sufficient ingenuity, the rough factorial map of a new domain will enable us to proceed beyond the exploratory factorial stage to the more direct forms of psychological experimentation in the laboratory.[20]

Direct factor analysis of the cities produced four unrotated factors which accounted for 65.05 percent of the total variance as indicated in Figure 22. The chart indicates that there was a break in the curve between successive variables or factors, including a slight break between Factor Four and Five (the cut-off point). Varimax procedures produced a rotated normal varimax factor matrix composed of four factors or components

---

can be drawn with two axes and the n observations located as points in it on the basis of their values on these two basic patterns. Two points close together in this graph are, of course, very much alike. The further apart the points, the less alike the areas they represent. Distances between points are, in such a graph, accurate indices of the degree of multi-factor similarity of observed areas.

"With more basic patterns the problem of measuring similarities is hardly more complex. If there are r patterns we assume that an r-axis graph has been drawn, and the points located in it. Distances are then measured, and the result is a matrix containing distances which tells the similarity of each pair of observations. This second stage of the analysis is called the distance-scaling of similarities." Brian J. L. Berry, "A Method for Deriving Multi-Factor Uniform Regions," *Przegląd Geo-graficzny* (Polish Geographical Review), Vol. 33 (1961), pp. 263–264.

Factor analysis has long been a basic tool in psychology and more recently in other social sciences. Berry, a few years ago, introduced it in the field of geography and since that time a number of studies have appeared: Brian J. L. Berry, "An Inductive Approach to the Regionalization of Economic Development," *Essays on Geography and Economic Development*, Norton S. Ginsburg, editor (University of Chicago Press, 1960), pp. 78–107, and J. H. Thompson, *et al.*, "Toward a Geography of Economic Health: The Case of New York State," *Annals*, Association of American Geographers, Vol. 52 (1962), pp. 1–20.

[20] L. L. Thurstone, *Multiple Factor Analysis* (University of Chicago Press, 1961), p. 56.

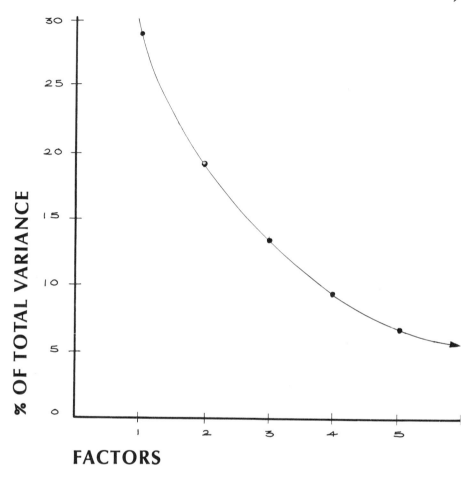

FIGURE 22. Yugoslav Cities. Variance explained by five unrotated factors.

which under rotation account for the four factor common or explained variance of 14.2 (total variance was 26), in the following manner:

	Eigen Value	Percent	Cumulative Percent
Factor 1	4.1	28.98	28.98
Factor 2	3.4	24.02	52.99
Factor 3	3.7	25.97	78.96
Factor 4	3.0	21.04	100.00
Common Variance	14.2		

Each of the 26 variables contributes towards the explained variance of each of the factors. Table Ten lists the four factors derived from the analysis and those variables out of the twenty-six having a loading of at least .50 are underlined.

A brief description of Table Ten may be useful for readers unfamiliar with factor analysis. The coefficients on each factor vary in size; some are

Table Ten. THE VARIMAX FACTOR MATRIX FOR YUGOSLAV CITIES

	Rotated Factor Loadings			
Variable	*Factor One*	*Factor Two*	*Factor Three*	*Factor Four*
1 0–9	.95	−.10	−.09	.21
2 10–14	.77	−.16	−.06	−.06
3 15–19	.15	−.12	−.16	−.44
4 20–24	.21	.10	−.06	.65
5 25–34	−.21	.07	−.04	.87
6 35–49	−.81	−.05	.14	−.22
7 50–64	−.78	.07	.06	−.56
8 Over 65	−.37	.08	.15	−.78
9 Population increase	−.05	.23	.18	.17
10 Agriculture and forestry	.10	−.02	−.25	.00
11 Construction	.12	.75	.22	.19
12 Transportation	−.26	.57	−.22	−.09
13 Handicraft	−.07	−.04	.45	−.02
14 Utilities and housing administration	.03	.08	.03	.12
15 Cultural activities	.02	.09	.74	.11
16 Industry	.03	−.53	−.65	.10
17 Commerce and entertainment	−.41	.14	.52	−.08
18 Social and state services	.21	.01	.51	.03
19 Apartments completed in 1961	.17	−.02	.00	.54
20 Hard-surfaced streets	−.04	.01	.28	.17
21 Population with radios	−.79	−.08	−.04	.12
22 Construction and transportation	−.00	1.00	.00	.00
23 Handicraft and commerce	−.31	.06	.61	−.07
24 Cultural and social and state services	.00	.06	.83	.11
25 Construction, transportation, and utilities	−.00	1.00	.00	.00
26 Construction, transportation, utilities, and industry	.00	.09	−.71	.20

larger, some smaller. The coefficient or "loading" is the correlation of a particular variable with a factor. Therefore variables with higher coefficients are making a greater contribution or are more important in explaining that factor than variables with low loadings. Some coefficients are negative, others are positive. When a factor has both high positive and negative coefficients, as in this case, it is called a bipolar factor. Bipolar factors thus contain opposites.

Factor One, by its high rating on dependency age groups 0–9, 10–14, and negative coefficients for age groups 35–49 and 50–64 and the proportion of the population having radios, is a measure of economic and social status as well as a demographic indicator. As suggested before, in less advanced areas the very young predominate as the dependent age group while in more advanced regions the reverse is true. This factor, which could be considered as a component of underdevelopment, shall be defined as an "index of relative development."

Factor Two is strongly related to construction-transportation employment, and Factor Three is strongly related to traditional employment; that is, the cultural, commercial, and administrative variables contribute significantly to the explained variance of the factor. Factors Two and Three both have high negative industrial coefficients. Factor Four consists of the young active population, age groups 20–34, positively associated with a high percentage of apartments built in 1961. These variables in Factor Four have a strong inverse relationship with older population groups (50–64 and over 65). The association of these variables describes rapidly expanding centers with a significant addition to the total housing stock during 1961. This is the effect of creating new industrial complexes which stimulated recent massive migrations so that the cities bulge with young to more or less middle-aged adults.

These four factors explain to a significant extent (specifically 65 percent) the variance among Yugoslav cities contributed by the original twenty-six variables.

The factors produced by the 55 × 26 correlation matrix suggest by their interrelationships significant elements contributing to the demographic and functional similarity or diversity among urban centers. In short, given these variables, the factors are a most appropriate index of the likenesses and differences among urban places in the territory of the entire country, that is, at the largest possible unit of generalization. The small number of high correlations in the original correlation matrix *may* suggest, however, that considerable diversity exists, implying great contrast among cities and perhaps regions.

In an attempt to ascertain regional variance in terms of the twenty-six variables, the factor analysis was repeated for each of five republics: Slovenia, Croatia, Serbia, Bosnia and Herzegovina, and Macedonia. Table Eleven indicates the correlation coefficients for selected variables for Yugoslavia (55 × 26 matrix), Slovenia (4 × 26 matrix), Croatia (14 × 26), Serbia (23 × 26), Bosnia and Herzegovina (5 × 26), and Macedonia (7 × 26). The reader must remember throughout the discussion that with the smaller number of observations only very high coefficients can be considered significant, and that sample size in this case may be a severe problem. Concern here is only with an examination of the similarities among republics in terms of the original variables and consequently in terms of the factors which suggest regional differences in occupational and demographic structure.

The first element which stands out in an examination of Table Eleven is the similarity in the correlation coefficients for Serbia and Yugoslavia as a whole. Statistically, of course, the larger number of observations for Serbia compared to the other republics might suggest that this would be the case. It is postulated, however, on the basis of the previous discussion of the industrialization "indicators," that Serbia is in fact transitional between North and South and would represent the Yugoslav "average." It should be recalled that the "index of economic development" in Table Three indicated approximately the same value for Serbia and Yugoslavia as a whole. One notable exception is the strong inverse relationship for Serbia between population increase from 1953 to 1961, and the percent of the actively employed population engaged in industry. This comparison of a "change" variable to a "level" variable is highly revealing and in itself warrants further study. This suggests that in Serbia population increases more rapidly outside of the predominately industrial centers (Belgrade and Titovo Užice). For both Slovenia and Bosnia and Herzegovina, population increase is inversely related to the number of new apartments built in 1961. For Slovenia, the order for the two variables was exactly reversed, as confirmed by the correlation coefficients. Maribor, Celje, Ljubljana, and

Table Eleven. SELECTED CORRELATION COEFFICIENTS
EXPRESSING VARIANCE WITHIN REPUBLICS

	Yugoslavia (55)	Slovenia (4)	Croatia (14)	Serbia (23)	Bosnia and Herzegovina (5)	Macedonia (7)
0–9/10–14 (1/2)	.75	.44	.70	.80	−.28	.60
0–9/radios (1/21)	−.72	.16	.04	−.80	−.12	.16
25–34/65+ (5/8)	−.58	−.02	−.64	−.54	−.77	−.07
Industry/construction (16/11)	−.50	.86	−.57	−.66	−.21	−.82
50–64/radios (7/21)	.54	−.12	−.20	.53	−.21	.33
New apartments/state service (19/18)	.00	.60	−.19	.00	−.82	.14
0–9/industry (1/16)	.14	.96	.16	.16	.95	.40
Industry/new apartments (16/19)	.12	−.07	.54	−.05	.76	−.40
Industry/utilities (16/14)	−.05	−.82	.08	.03	−.92	−.16
Industry/state services (16/18)	.12	−.83	−.61	.04	−.83	−.33
Population increase/industry (9/16)	−.19	.02	.20	−.52	−.89	.79
Population increase/new apartments (9/19)	.20	−.99	.50	.27	−.68	.41
Population increase/commerce (9/17)	.16	−.07	−.16	.22	.88	−.03
0–9/population increase (1/9)	−.09	−.17	−.19	−.16	−.90	.80
Agriculture and forestry/industry (10/16)	−.07	.35	−.31	−.37	.86	.81
Paved streets/commerce (20/17)	.28	−.44	.79	.04	−.15	.09
Radio/new apartments (21/19)	−.00	.64	.01	.03	.48	.11
Paved streets/radio (20/21)	.08	.71	.07	−.19	.35	.23
Handicraft/new apartments (13/19)	−.01	−.34	−.47	−.07	−.69	.35
Population increase/radio (9/21)	.03	−.59	−.19	.09	.57	−.27
Population increase/paved streets (9/20)	−.20	−.48	.06	.14	.52	.41

Kranj were so ordered in terms of population increase and in exactly the reverse order in terms of the percentage of new apartments built in 1961 compared to total housing stock. The same general characteristics existed for Bosnia and Herzegovina.

Many other conclusions might be drawn from the relationships implied by the correlation coefficients should the reader so desire. It is sufficient here to suggest only that there are significant differences among the republics in terms of the correlation coefficients of selected variables.

In Appendix Two, Tables II-1, II-2, II-3, II-4, and II-5 indicate the factors produced by factor analysis of the original twenty-six variables for the cities of each of the five republics. An examination of the tables reveals a distinct difference among the republics in terms of the factors, suggesting underlying social-economic and demographic variation. For example,

Slovenia, with three factors, has no clearly identifiable factor suggesting underdevelopment. The young dependent age groups are associated with industry and construction and with the total amount of paved streets.

Though beyond the scope of the discussion here, further generalizations are evident from examination of the rest of factor breakdowns for each of the republics. The relationships which appear are those which are implied in the subsequent discussion of the optimum grouping of the fifty-five cities on the basis of each city's four factor scores. This technique of factor analyzing subareas of any particular study or problem region provides useful insights into the structure of regional differences plus the fact that the distinctive combinations or associations among the variables, which underly the social-economic variation expressed in the factors, are the prime elements towards which desired development policies must be directed.

It is necessary to return now to the discussion of the four factors produced by the initial 55×26 matrix. As a first step, interpretation is confined to Factors One, "index of relative development" and Three, "the traditional employment component," or more specifically to the scores of each of the observations (fifty-five cities) on these two factors.[21]

Figure 23, in the section of oversized figures, indicates the distribution of urban settlements in terms of their rating or score on Factors One ("relative development") and Three ("traditional employment"). In reading the graph it should be recalled that the zero value lies at the intersection of the two axes with negative values falling below and to the left. Those cities with positive values for Factor One, the factor of relative development, have a large number of children, few people in the middle-aged groups, and few radios. Cities with negative values for Factor One have proportionately few children, a larger population in the active age groups, and a large number of radios. Cities with positive values for Factor Three have a large proportion of their population engaged in traditional occupations, while those cities with negative coefficients for this component have a large percentage of population employed in industry. A comparison of Figure 23 with Figures 20 and 21 and Table Eight reveals that the factor analysis technique segregates at the extreme negative and

---

[21] The correlation between Factors One and Three is −.14, which is not significantly different from zero (that is, Factors One and Three are orthogonal).

positive poles of Factor Three those cities having the absolute highest percent of their employed population engaged in traditional and industrial occupations, especially the industrial cities of Kranj, Varaždin, Pančevo, Zenica, Sisak, and Slavonski Brod and the commercial or administrative cities of Titograd, Titovo Užice, Ljubljana, Dubrovnik, Belgrade, Zaječar, and Skopje.

Examination of the quantitatively derived distribution of Yugoslav cities on these two factors allows the following interpretation to be made of the distribution of urban centers shown on Figure 23. The less developed areas of the country to the most advanced and cities with a strong traditional occupational structure to those uniquely industrial are charted proceeding from top to bottom and from right to left. Observing the distribution more closely, it is possible to separate the cities into four groups: those having a positive score of more than 2.0 on Factor One and those with less, and those having score on Factor Three on either side of a clearly identifiable zone between +.8 and −.8. The sole exception to this is Zadar, a Dalmatian city, which has unique characteristics to be described later.

Those cities with positive values on Factor Three have through the centuries been the traditional administrative, cultural, and commercial centers, regardless of the foreign power dominating the local area. The cities with less than a 2.0 positive rating on Factor One are in Slovenia, Croatia, and Vojvodina—the traditional regions of Mediterranean and Central European domination—plus Serbia proper and Sarajevo, the capital of Bosnia and Herzegovina.

The cluster of cities with a positive score above 2.0 on Factor One includes all the cities of Macedonia, Montenegro, Kosmet, and Bosnia and Herzegovina, except for Sarajevo. These cities represent or indicate areas that today are designated by the Federal Planning Commission as underdeveloped, and which correspond to the historic region of Byzantine-Turkish domination and influence described in Chapter Two.

Cities with less than a 2.0 score on Factor One (relative development) and positive values on Factor Three (traditional employment), designated by the letter "A" on Figure 23, are the commercial and administrative centers of the more northern and developed provinces of Yugoslavia. These cities include Ljubljana and Celje, two major administrative centers of Slovenia and the major centers of the Adriatic coast, each a traditional administrative and commercial settlement for an interior hinterland and the islands; Novi Sad, Zrenjanin, and Subotica, the administrative centers of Vojvodina; and Sarajevo, the capital of Bosnia and Herzegovina. The traditional regional or central places of Croatia—Zagreb and Karlovac—and those of Serbia also fall in this group.

Those cities designated by "B," with loadings or scores of more than 2.0 positive on Factor One and positive values on Factor Three, represent the older cities in the traditional zone of Byzantine-Turkish influence and domination. They specifically include Skopje and Bitola, the two traditional administrative centers of Macedonia; Banja Luka, the second major administrative center of Bosnia and Herzegovina; Prizren and Péc, two major cities of the Kosmet; and Titograd, the capital of Montenegro.

Cities with values below 2.0 on Factor One and negative values on Factor Three, designated by the letter "C," comprise the traditional industrial centers of Yugoslavia. (There are two exceptions, in that the largest industrial centers in terms of the number of employed people in industry were and are Zagreb and Belgrade.) This group of centers is predominantly industrial as measured in terms of their actively employed population engaged in industry (compare the cities designated here with those listed under the industrial category in Table Eight).

Those cities with more than a score of 2.0 on Factor One and negative values on Factor Three which suggests an industrial emphasis (designated by the letter "D") are all located in traditionally underdeveloped Bosnia and Herzegovina, Macedonia, Montenegro, and Kosmet. This reflects substantial investment in industry in these areas during the postwar period with little alteration in other socioeconomic characteristics.

A number of general implications emerge from the above picture. Modern societies are not built by industrialization alone; something more, much more, is needed. One reads of the slow rise in productivity in communist countries, countries which have emphasized the need for rapid industrialization on a scale unmatched in human history.[22] The obsession with new industrial plants obstructed these societies from modernizing as rapidly as might be assumed. The lack of investments in social overhead—utilities, housing, and transportation—decisively decreed that these areas,

---

[22] For a general survey see: Stanley J. Zyzniewski, "Industry and Labor," *Eastern Europe in the Sixties*, edited by Stephen Fischer-Galati (New York: Frederick A. Praeger, 1963), pp. 82–117.

industrialized though they might be, were to move slowly along the developmental scale. All the newly "industrialized" countries of Eastern Europe, including Yugoslavia, tend to have some of the following characteristics:

1. Industrial workers have increased while the agricultural population has decreased from approximately 75 percent to 50 percent in fifteen years. This represents on the face of it an outstanding rate of transformation. These changes were, however, essentially horizontal (that is, with greater clustering around selected points), and not vertical. There were few significant or even proportionately moderate increases in skilled employment categories, compared to the general growth of a vast unskilled, but "urban" labor pool. Tertiary activities progressed very little above prewar conditions. The exception to this has been the rapid increase in administrative personnel due to the special nature of the system which bestows increased income on higher administrative positions and increased prestige on the entire occupational category.

2. Housing, measured by any index, has stagnated and deteriorated until very recently. The discussion of housing has been reserved for Chapter Four.

3. Mobility and social interaction has been regional, not national in scope. Identification with local areas has not decreased, a national consciousness has not evolved, and in Yugoslavia, traditional individual allegiance to a single regional group may have increased. It must be stated that in some areas of the country—certainly in Vojvodina—and for certain social groups, changes involving social interaction were great in absolute terms, but slight in relative terms.

4. The combination of these factors, especially housing deterioration and increased congestion coupled with poor transportation facilities, produced striking restrictions to, or lag in, increased labor productivity. Economizing in social overhead proved to create an eventual and severe bottleneck to increased economic expansion and a strong barrier to "modernization."

In 1918 or 1945 extensive areas of the Republics of Slovenia and Croatia were "modernized," in the more comprehensive definition of the word. That is, there existed in these areas a skilled industrial labor force and a corresponding agricultural sector technically able to supply the needs of the urban population (with the major exception of wheat) and still have a surplus for export. Lack of an overpowering kinship attachment, coupled with the acceptance of innovation and rising productivity were characteristic of an increasing majority of both the urban and rural population in these northern republics. In short, the entrenched attitudes or mores of traditional peasant society had been gradually eradicated to a large extent. This was in sharp contrast to the rest of the country, where traditional occupations and life styles predominated. The postwar policies which placed new industrial enterprises in these traditional settings resulted in "economic development" as measured by conventional statistical variables described in Part 1 of this chapter; the nature of this "developmental process" had little impact on life style and attitudes or, in general, on all those composite elements—intellectual, political, and social, along with economic—which contribute to our general concept of "modernization."

4. A CLASSIFICATION OF URBAN SETTLEMENTS

The preceding discussion reflects the distribution or arrangement of the urban centers on only two factors. However, four factors or principal components were obtained which have been reasonably well explained in terms of the original variables. Each city has a score on each factor, for example:

	Factor One [1]	Factor Two [2]	Factor Three [3]	Factor Four [4]
Belgrade	−5.7	2.2	7.1	0.3

[1] Relative development
[2] Construction-transportation
[3] Traditional employment
[4] Active population

As indicated in Figure 23 the cities tended to be clustered into a number of groups which facilitated interpretation on the basis of two factors. Grouping the observations on the basis of the four factors or components is only slightly more complicated. An "optimum grouping" technique exists and can be programmed for the computer. The major aim of the technique is to minimize distances within groups and to maximize the distance between groups. The optimal grouping procedure has been used to classify the fifty-five Yugoslav cities on the basis of their scores on each of the four factors (see Table Thirteen).

The factor scores or distances among all of the observations, cities in this case, were squared and the output resulted in a distance squared matrix.[23] First, two most similar observations are drawn from the fifty-five individual group members. Then the next most similar are extracted, and so on until the entire group of observations have been grouped. For example, the two most similar observations were Karlovac and Rijeka which were .5659 apart. The total within-group distance was, of course, .5659. Štip and Priština were the next most similar, being separated by .6874 and the total within-group distance was now 1.2533 (.5659 + .6874 = 1.2533). Other groupings are shown in Table Twelve.

Table Twelve. EXAMPLE OF OPTIMAL GROUPING TECHNIQUE USED TO CLASSIFY YUGOSLAV CITIES

Opera-tion	Most Similar Cities Based on Distance Squared Matrix	Distance Apart	Total Within-Group Distance
1	Karlovac/Rijeka	.5659	.5659
2	Štip/Priština	.6874	1.2533
3	Sarajevo/Čačak	1.3626	2.6159
4	Smederevo/Valjevo	1.5897	4.2056
5	Leskovac/Šabac	1.7411	5.9467
6	Peć/Prizren	2.0539	8.0060
7	Kranj/Pančevo	2.0633	10.0639
8	Kraljevo/Leskovac	2.5226	12.5866
9	Mostar/Zadar	2.9116	15.4981
10	Niš/Smederevo/Valjevo	2.9353	18.4334

It should be noted that in the tenth operation, Niš was placed in the Smederevo/Valjevo group created by operation 4. This process was continued until four major groups or categories emerged. Table Thirteen describes the characteristics of the four major groups and Table Fourteen

---

[23] This procedure was first presented in 1960 at the Chicago Conference on Quantitative Geography. There has, unfortunately, been great delay in publication of the proceedings; see eventually Brian J. L. Berry, "Grouping and Regionalizing: An Approach to the Problem Using Multivariate Analysis," in W. L. Garrison (editor), *Quantitative Geography* (Northwestern Studies in Geography, 1965).

Table Thirteen. MAJOR CATEGORIES OF YUGOSLAV CITIES PRODUCED BY THEIR GROUPING ON THE FOUR FACTORS

Group One	Industrial cities in Macedonia, Montenegro, Bosnia and Herzegovina, and the Kosmet
Group Two	Traditional central places of Macedonia, Bosnia and Herzegovina, Montenegro, and Serbia proper
Group Three	Traditional central places in Croatia, Slovenia, and Vojvodina
Group Four	Existing industrial centers of prewar Yugoslavia

Table Fourteen. CLASSIFICATION OF YUGOSLAV CITIES BY FACTOR SCORES

| | Factors | | | |
	One *Relative* *Development*	Two *Construction-* *Transportation*	Three *Traditional* *Employment*	Four *Active* *Population*
GROUP ONE				
Ia				
Tuzla	6.1	−0.3	−2.6	4.1
Štip	7.5	−3.3	−1.7	3.3
Priština	8.1	−3.7	−1.5	2.5
Kos. Mitrovica	8.2	−5.5	−1.5	2.3
Kumanovo	5.9	−2.1	−2.7	−0.6
Prilep	4.8	−4.3	−2.4	−3.5
Tetovo	5.9	−4.6	−0.8	−1.8
Titov Veles	4.5	1.6	−4.0	−0.6
Peć	7.4	−4.2	2.2	−2.2
Prizren	7.3	−3.4	3.6	−3.3
Ib				
Zenica	5.1	−0.8	−8.5	8.0
Nikšić	4.8	8.5	−5.8	7.3
GROUP TWO				
IIa				
Banja Luka	2.2	1.8	1.5	2.3
Mostar	2.4	2.3	−1.2	2.9
Zadar	1.0	3.6	0.1	2.4
Sarajevo	0.8	1.7	3.7	3.5
Čačak	−0.7	2.2	3.9	3.8
Niš	−0.6	1.8	1.3	1.8
Smederevo	−0.6	1.2	3.2	2.0
Valjevo	−0.1	0.1	2.6	3.1
Bitola	3.4	1.1	2.7	−1.6
Skopje	3.5	1.6	5.1	0.4
IIb				
Titograd	6.2	5.1	4.0	6.6
Titovo Užice	1.3	6.0	8.2	6.8

	Factors			
	One *Relative* *Development*	*Two* *Construction-* *Transportation*	*Three* *Traditional* *Employment*	*Four* *Active* *Population*
GROUP THREE				
IIIa				
Karlovac	−4.9	−0.8	1.0	−0.6
Rijeka	−4.4	−0.4	1.8	−1.0
Pula	−1.6	−1.6	3.0	1.7
Vukovar	−2.1	−2.1	2.3	−1.8
Split	−3.4	5.6	2.9	−2.0
Zrenjanin	−3.1	3.0	3.0	−2.4
Šibenik	−2.1	4.2	.9	.4
Belgrade	−5.7	2.2	7.1	.3
Zaječar	−2.6	3.5	6.9	−0.3
IIIb				
Zagreb	−6.6	− .6	3.0	−4.1
Celje	−6.0	−4.3	2.4	−4.0
Ljubljana	−6.1	−3.1	6.1	−4.1
Subotica	−8.0	2.7	3.2	−8.0
GROUP FOUR				
IVa				
Osijek	−2.8	−2.2	−2.0	−2.3
Kranj	−2.6	−2.9	−4.4	−0.4
Pančevo	−0.7	−3.3	−4.2	0.0
S. Brod	−0.5	−2.6	−5.1	−3.4
Leskovac	1.1	−1.8	−3.7	−0.2
Šabac	.8	−1.2	−2.0	−0.4
Sisak	−0.7	−0.6	−7.0	2.1
Varaždin	−0.4	−2.1	−6.4	−0.3
Kragujevac	−4.2	1.6	−2.2	1.5
Požarevac	−1.3	1.5	−4.2	−0.3
Kraljevo	−0.8	−5.5	−1.5	2.3
Kruševac	−0.5	−5.1	−1.3	0.2
Svetozarevo	−1.3	−2.8	−1.0	0.4
IVb				
Vinkovci	−1.1	4.0	−3.6	−3.8
Maribor	−4.7	1.6	−5.2	−5.0
Sombor	−4.6	0.1	−2.8	−5.7
Individual Group Member Novi Sad	−5.9	−5.3	−1.9	−1.3
Individual Group Member Dubrovnik	−8.8	11.7	8.5	−5.9

lists the cities and their factor scores. In other words, given factor scores for the fifty-five cities, Table Fourteen provides the best ten-group classification: Group 1a had ten cities, with two cities in Group 1b, ten cities in Group 2a, two cities in Group 2b, nine cities in Group 3a, four cities in Group 3b, twelve cities in Group 4a, three cities in Group 4b, and finally two single-member groups. These subgroups would have merged with the four main groups described above at further levels of generalization.

In Figure 24 (based upon Figure 23), in the section of oversized figures, the cities are plotted according to their factor scores on Factors One and Three, and for orientation the groups or clusters presented in Table Fourteen have been indicated. Note that the grouping indicated here is on the basis of all four factors, not only Factors One and Three.

GROUP ONE: *Industrial Cities in Macedonia, Montenegro, Bosnia and Herzegovina, and Kosovo Metohija*

The cities of Group One are all in the historic zone of Byzantine-Turkish domination and influence. With two exceptions all of these centers are industrial in character. Many of these cities have the lowest percent of their active labor force engaged in commerce of all the fifty-five cities (Štip, Tetovo, Nikšić, Zenica, Titov Veles, Prilep, etc.). Peć, a mining center, is sixth in the country in the percent employed in handicraft, and Prizren has the second largest number of people actively engaged in state services. Both of these centers were placed in Group One due to high ratings on Factor One.

Zenica and Nikšić are distinguished from the main group by their high loadings on Factor Four. Thus these two centers have a relatively high percent of their population in age groups 20–34, and, in the case of Zenica, a large percent (the highest among the fifty-five cities) of new apartments constructed in 1961 (10.5 percent of the entire housing stock). This reflects a radical alteration in the investment pattern of earlier years when little if any capital was available for housing and utilities, particularly in such cities as Zenica.

The Old Bridge at Mostar was erected in 1566, during the rule of Suleyman the Magnificent, by Hajrudin, pupil and assistant of the famous architect Mimar Sinan. The high stone arch was built over the river Neretva. *Agencija za Fotodokumentaciju*

As the Old Bridge is a monument to the past, the new one is an expression of modern times. The new part of Mostar, with wide boulevards and modern buildings, is on the right bank of the Neretva.

GROUP TWO: *Traditional Central Places of Macedonia, Bosnia and Herzegovina, Montenegro, and Serbia proper*

The cities in this group have a significant portion of their actively employed population engaged in traditional occupations such as commerce, administration, and handicrafts. Both Mostar and Zadar were traditional trade centers for their immediate hinterland. Zadar, a Dalmatian city, falls in this group because of its scores on Factor One. This city has a large young dependent age group and fewer radios than the cities of Group Three, with which it shares similar scores on Factors Two, Three, and Four. It should be recalled that Zadar was isolated from Yugoslavia during the interwar period and that the area directly adjacent to it (called "Bukovica") is one of the poorest in the country.

Titograd and Titovo Užice are placed in Subgroup 2a, due to their rating on Factor Four. They both have an unusually high proportion of young active age group 20–34 and newly constructed apartments, reflecting the massive migration to these cities. Titograd had the third largest

Titograd, capital of the Republic of Montenegro. This city was built after World War II and is Yugoslavia's major "new town."

number of apartments built in 1961 as a proportion of the total housing stock (9.3 percent) and Titovo Užice was sixth (8.4 percent). Though similar in these respects, the cities have entirely different functions. Titovo Užice has 14.5 percent of its population employed in commerce and is sixth among the fifty-five cities in this function, while Titograd has the highest proportion of people employed in state service in the country (13.3 percent). Scores on Factor One reflect Titovo Užice's (1.3) location in north central Serbia and Titograd's (6.2) in underdeveloped Monte-negro.

Taken as a whole the cities of Group Two are the classical adminis-trative, commercial, and handicraft centers of the historic Byzantine-Turkish zone (with the noted exception of Zadar which was isolated between 1918 and 1941 from the other Dalmatian cities and the interior). Banja Luka was the northernmost Turkish capital. Mostar, Sarajevo, Bitola, and Skopje were all major administrative and/or commercial centers in the Byzantine-Turkish era.

GROUP THREE: *Traditional Central Places in Serbia proper, Croatia, Slo-venia, and Vojvodina*

These cities fulfill the same traditional functions as those in Group Two. The distinguishing element between the two groups is their scores on Factor One, which implies not only a different demographic composition but underlying social-economic variation. Zagreb, Celje, Ljubljana, and Subotica form a subgroup due to their low score on Factor Four. These four cities had a larger proportion of their population over 34 years of age and fewer newly constructed apartments in 1961 relative to total housing stock. This suggests a more "urban" tradition and a somewhat more mature or skilled labor force; this is certainly the case for Zagreb, Celje, and Ljubljana.

Subotica's score on Factor Four (8.0) is twice that of the other three cities, indicating an unusual emigration of the younger active age groups. During the interwar period Subotica was the third largest city in Yugoslavia (see Figure 11). The impact of the new political boundaries of 1918 placed the city on the frontier and within a new state administration hostile to Hungarians in general, which naturally influenced the treatment of this dominant ethnic group within and in the vicinity of Subotica. Unfavorable external conditions continued to restrict Subotica's development, though for different reasons, after 1948. After the break with the Bloc, fear of foreign invasion sharply curtailed investment in Subotica and in fact a distinct process of "disinvestment" occurred. Factories were dismantled and moved into the interior of the country. Few, if any, significant investments were made until after 1953, and the situation did not really improve until after 1956.[24]

------

[24] Few detailed sources exist which reveal the impact of the 1948 threat on the exposed area of Vojvodina. The following quotation, taken from an official planning document, reveals the negative effect on economic growth federal policy had on the area:

"The first period after the war was characterized for Vojvodina, in distinction to the rest of the country, by the following:

"(1) renewal, getting the economy functioning again.

"(2) investments were not made for development but only to renew prewar capacity.

"(3) in response to federal policy there was a decrease in the capacity of several sectors of industry due to the dismantling and displacement of capacity to other areas of our country.

"Independent of the general conditions and economic policy of the country as a whole, the economy of Vojvodina in various periods actually declined. In the period 1948–1952, for known reasons, economic growth was oriented to other regions and the realization of national economic goals was not based on the potentialities of the Vojvodina area. In this period the economic activity of Vojvodina measured by gross national product fell:

Table Fifteen. AVERAGE ANNUAL GROWTH RATE OF GROSS NATIONAL PRODUCT IN VOJVODINA

1948–1952	1953–1956	1957–1960	1948–1960	Sector
+.8	8.0	14.3	7.0	Industry
−4.1	4.7	9.7	2.7	Agriculture
−1.4	12.0	16.5	7.9	Forestry
−10.4	15.4	12.1	3.8	Construction
+3.9	10.3	12.0	8.3	Transportation
+1.8	12.8	10.2	7.7	Commerce and hotels
+7.8	2.4	9.3	6.6	Handicrafts
−4.5	10.7	11.9	5.0	Total economy

While in 1947 income per person was, in Vojvodina, 24.9% above the Yugoslav average, it gradually decreased so that in 1960 per capita income was equal to the Yugoslav average." *Mogućnosti razvoja privrede komune Novi Sad, 1960–1980* (Novi Sad, 1961). Unpublished mimeographed document utilized during a period of residence in Vojvodina.

Another major reason for Subotica's apparent population decline was simply a reduction in the city's administrative boundaries and to a limited degree the convenience and accessibility offered by the relatively good transportation network in Vojvodina which allowed many young men to maintain their contacts at home while working in the growing industrial complexes of Novi Sad, Belgrade, and Pančevo. It should also be recalled that Vojvodina was essentially an agricultural area which again made it a target to early postwar policies which emphasized investment in heavy industry rather than agricultural or related industries.

GROUP FOUR: *Existing Industrial Centers of Prewar Yugoslavia*

These cities of Slovenia, Croatia, Vojvodina, and Serbia proper represent the main industrial centers existing before World War II. The size or significance of the industrial sector in each city's economy is reflected to a considerable degree by the size of the negative values on Factor Three (traditional employment). See Table Sixteen.

Table Sixteen. A COMPARISON OF THE RANK ORDER OF INDUSTRIAL CITIES DERIVED FROM SCORES ON FACTOR THREE AND FROM THE PERCENTAGE EMPLOYED IN INDUSTRY

City	Percent of Active Labor Force in Industry	Rank Among the 55 Cities	Value on Factor Three	Rank on Factor Three
Kranj	57.9	1	−4.4	4
Varaždin	56.2	2	−6.4	2
Kraljevo	53.7	4	−1.5	11
Pančevo	53.5	5	−4.2	5
Sisak	52.2	7	−7.0	1
S. Brod	49.4	9	−5.1	3
Leskovac	49.4	10	−3.7	7

A comparison of the cities in Group Four with Table Eight and Figure 20 reveals that the largest industrial cities in the country measured in terms of the percent of their actively employed population engaged in industry are included in Group Four, with the exception of Kosovska Mitrovica and Zenica, which are placed among the industrial centers of Group One, and of Novi Sad which, though slightly industrialized, has characteristics which distinguish it from most other cities in Yugoslavia.

Vinkovci, Maribor, and Sombor form a subgroup due to their high negative scores on Factor Four. These centers have an older population composition.

INDIVIDUAL GROUP MEMBERS

Novi Sad and Dubrovnik stand out as centers with characteristics distinct from any of the other groups. Novi Sad's negative ratings on all the four factors imply a relatively small proportion of population in the young dependency age groups, few people employed in construction and transportation, an industrial orientation, and a rather small proportion of

Dubrovnik in Croatia, built early in the seventh century. *Vilko Zuber*

people in age groups 20–34. Novi Sad experienced for some years the full impact of Yugoslavia's isolation from the communist camp. As indicated previously, investments were curtailed or actually stopped throughout Vojvodina, and Novi Sad and Subotica, the two largest cities, felt the impact of these policies more sharply than the rest of the province. It was only after 1956 that Novi Sad began to experience rapid growth in both commerce and industry.

Dubrovnik, of course, is a different story. The city is a major resort center; this fact is reflected in the high proportion of people employed in tertiary activities (8.5 on Factor Three) and transportation and construction activities (11.7 on Factor Two). Dubrovnik has the highest scores on these two factors of the fifty-five cities and the highest negative score on Factor One. In short, Dubrovnik is not typical of either Dalmatian or Yugoslav cities in general as the amenities of its location stimulate growth in tertiary activities independent of either regional or national markets.

SUMMARY

The preceding pages have presented a general classification of Yugoslav cities derived from twenty-six original variables. Perhaps the most significant aspect of the classification is the differentiation of the cities not only in regard to occupational structure but in social-economic terms as well. The resulting classification reflects the functional significance of each city almost as well as the single variable presentation given in Figures 20 and 21. The underlying social-economic differences existing between the developed and less advanced areas of the country were related to functional variation. The resulting multivariate classification related in other words to city function, to the level of development, to the demographic and social composition of the city's population, and to their historical traditions.

On the basis of this preliminary analysis, derived from a study of fifty-five points over the total national territory of Yugoslavia, it is possible to discern quantitatively significant distinctions between the industrial and commercial centers of the advanced and those of the underdeveloped areas of the country. This classification in turn corresponds closely to the previously delimited regions of foreign domination and cultural penetration. A positive correlation has been discovered between a city's occupational and demographic structure, its traditional region of foreign domination and influence and underlying physiographic structure. The postwar process of industrialization and increased urbanization, or population concentration in cities of 20,000 and over, has not eliminated the traditional regional differences. Clearly one implication of this is that though industrialization speeded the process of urbanization in the South it did not immediately (during the last decade)—nor perhaps even necessarily—produce corresponding strides towards modernization, relative to the northern areas of the country.[25]

---

[25] This statement corresponds with the tone of the discussion by Leo F. Schnore "The Statistical Measurement of Urbanization and Economic Development," *Land Economics* (August, 1961), pp. 229–245, and Thomas O. Wilkinson, "Urban Structure and Industrialization," *American Sociological Review* (June, 1960), pp. 356–363.

Chapter IV

Housing Policy and Conditions

I. MUNICIPAL HOUSING ADMINISTRATION
AND PLANNING

Before making a detailed presentation of the communal system, it is useful to examine one particular administrative activity of cities and communes, which is also another index of development. Housing is a major factor in any developing country, and is a more meaningful index of socioeconomic variation than many "standard" indices. In this chapter, housing policy in Yugoslavia is briefly discussed, and an index of housing quality in selected communes is examined.

In Yugoslavia there are currently two major types of professional organizations concerned with city planning activities: the City Planning Department and the Fund for Housing Construction. There is also a growing trend for cities to establish an Office for Communal Construction. The Planning Department is concerned with working out the master plan for the city, supervising its implementation, and conducting research on general problems concerned with urbanization within the area of the commune. The Fund for Housing Construction is the major credit organization for housing, setting basic policy and norms. The Office for Communal Construction—not yet a universal institution throughout the country—supervises the work of various technical departments, such as those responsible for sewage and water, roads, and the like. It coordinates all construction activity in the area of the commune, including the "preparation of the ground" for construction—that is, it ensures that all required underground facilities are installed prior to construction. Each commune's administrative Department for Communal and Housing Affairs either may act as a registration or recording office (similar to the office of the city clerk in America), when the above agencies are adequately functioning, or may itself undertake most of the functions ascribed to these agencies. The latter is usually the case in smaller communes.

The general structure of the commune is similar throughout Yugoslavia, including that of the "urban communes" which are component parts of the country's largest cities. There are five of these multicommunal cities: Belgrade, Zagreb, Skopje, Sarajevo, and Ljubljana. In theory, each of the urban communes should function as independently as a rural commune. In practice, however, certain activities, especially in Belgrade, Sarajevo, and Skopje, are centrally directed under district (*srez*) administration. These

New Belgrade construction.

urban districts are, therefore, administratively more important than districts which are not composed of multiurban communes. The Zagreb District has a district assembly and executive body to which are attached agencies which serve the entire Zagreb metropolitan area, supplying water, gas, and electricity. Transportation, for example, is still decentralized and organized on a communal basis. In 1963, both Zagreb and Belgrade changed their designation from district (*kotar* [Croatian] and *srez* [Serbian]) to *grad*, meaning city. The semantic change produced no alteration in administration but may be an attempt to imply by the new term the meaning or image of a metropolitan area. It has been difficult to justify the existence of autonomous communes within these larger cities. The division has often resulted in duplication of various administrative functions at greatly increased costs coupled with the growing tendency towards localism: attempts to maximize one commune's advantage over another. This has led, at the very minimum, to a lack of cooperation among urban communes within the same metropolis. It is significant that after the adoption of the April 1963 Constitution which specifically guarantees the independent functioning of each commune regardless of location or position, there has been increasing discussion to eliminate the urban communes in favor of greater efficiency.

As is customary in Yugoslav administration, each agency, including the City Planning Department, will have a Council, composed of some ten to fifteen local citizens, usually meeting once a month. The major purpose of a Council is to restrict the administrative power of communal agencies. Thus, in theory, the Council is expected to set broad policy for administrative agencies' operation and is the funnel through which recommendations of the line agencies are passed on to the municipal assembly as regulation proposals. Theoretically, this Council is concerned with broad issues of policy, not with the day-to-day activity of the administrative agency. All too often, however, the Council deals with practical decisions of routine significance rather than over-all goals.

To document the functioning of the Council in a little more detail it might be well to discuss an example of the city planning function. In ideal practice, when the city's master plan is ready for either adoption or revision (according to the law of most republics, an approved plan must be

revised at least once every five years), the Council for City Planning—not
the City Planning Department—is required to submit the proposed new
plan to public discussion, prior to its consideration by the communal
assembly. Public discussion includes at least two operations: (1) review of
the proposed plan by a professional group of technical experts appointed
by the Council and publication of their findings; and (2) public displays of
the plan and discussions at public meetings. Through local associations, the
citizens present their criticisms and recommendations to the Council. These
views are summarized by the Council and forwarded to the Planning
Department, which must explain why the recommendations will or will
not be adopted.

There are a number of local neighborhood institutions which may, and
often do, raise issues related to planning before the Communal Assembly;
the apartment house councils, the "voters' meeting," and the local community or neighborhood units. The apartment house councils are the administrative organs of individual apartment houses.[1] The voters' meeting,
representing a number of city blocks, usually holds special meetings once
every three months to inform the public of various proposals. The local
community (*mesna zajednica*—or *stambena zajednica*, as it was called prior
to the new Constitution) is "a self-governing community of citizens of
rural and urban settlements," in which "the citizens directly participate in
self-government in activities that satisfy the basic communal, cultural,
health, social, and other needs and desires of the community."[2] Kardelj has
observed that "*mesne zajednice* [local communities], that is, *stambena*
[housing] and *seoska* [rural] communities, have primarily three functions:
first, the *mesna zajednica* is a unit of the city plan; second, it is a unit and
form of self-government in the commune; and third, it is a carrier of the
widening material-technical base for the everyday life of the family and
the individual."[3]

---

[1] For detailed information on the legal operation of the apartment house councils
and other matters relating to apartment occupancy, see *Zbirka propisa iz stambene
oblasti* (Belgrade: Službeni list, 1962), and Svetomir Petković, *Komentar Zakona o
stambenim odnosima* (Belgrade, 1962).

[2] *Mesne zajednice u komunalnom sistemu i zadaci Socijalističkog Saveza* (Subotica,
December, 1962), p. 1.

[3] Edvard Kardelj, *Samoupravljanje u Komuni*, Materijali sa godišnje skupštine
Stalne konferencije gradova Jugoslavije, Niš, 30 October-1 November, 1961

In a number of cases, the city plan and other proposals have been changed as a result of objections from one or all of the above groups. When conflicts throughout the country between local groups and planning commissions were examined, an interesting pattern applicable to most areas of planning activity in Yugoslavia emerged. When the concept or underlying principles of the proposed master plan for the city were in fact challenged by the criticisms of a local group, the plan was usually not altered. However, when the group's recommendations involved changes that would not directly alter the fundamental concept of the plan, then in many cases they were favorably received.

Recommendations by local groups—whether the communes themselves, local communities, voters' meetings, or apartment house councils—are potentially effective when the desired action conforms with general policy of higher governmental units, or when the group itself has the necessary resources to carry out the project. The implications of this principle will concern us in the next chapter, which discusses the evolution of the communal system in Yugoslavia.

At present, for example, the City Planning Department of Novi Sad conducts basic research, works out the master plan and its subsequent revision, and is responsible for over-all physical developmental goals and annual projects. The Fund for Housing Construction is responsible for setting general housing policy and selecting areas of residential expansion as ap-

(Belgrade, 1961), p. 19. For a discussion of the *mesna zajednica* in relation to city planning see Jack C. Fisher, "Planning the City of Socialist Man," *Journal of the American Institute of Planners*, XXVII (November, 1962), pp. 251–265, and "Socialist City Planning: A Reexamination," *Journal of the American Institute of Planners*, XXXI (February, 1965), pp. 31–42.

". . . the leading principles which characterize socialist planning are concerned with: standardization, the proper size of the city, the city's center, and the neighborhood unit concept. In addition, another important distinction is the division of the city into functional areas of residence, employment, and recreation. These areas are, of course, connected by transportation routes, the fifth basic factor.

"The significance of these principles, . . . was to provide a means for achieving efficiency and the ultimate maximization of impact from limited investments, while at the same time securing urban uniformity. To this I would add only that they are also a means of maintaining an established standard." Miloš Savić, "Comment," in "Socialist City Planning: A Reexamination," *Journal of the American Institute of Planners*, XXXI (February, 1965), p. 36.

proved by the Planning Department. The Office for Communal Construction is now responsible for the "preparation" of the land prior to construction and insures that all public housing is equipped with necessary utilities. In cooperation with the Fund for Housing Construction, the Office projects the annual development of various utilities as demand is anticipated.

Belgrade and Skopje have a similar system despite their multicommunal character. Though they are subdivided into communes, the municipal organs direct the planning process with little direct participation from the individual communes. In Ljubljana the formal institutional arrangement is essentially the same, but the practice is entirely different. Here the communes are independent (as of 1963), with the City Planning Department being in reality a contract organization for them. The master plan has not been approved at this date, due in large part to communal opposition plus strong criticism from individual citizens. Each commune in Ljubljana has its separate Fund for Housing Construction, which has led to intercommunal rivalry and to bottlenecks in housing. The commune of Centar has,

New apartment buildings at New Belgrade.

Figure 7

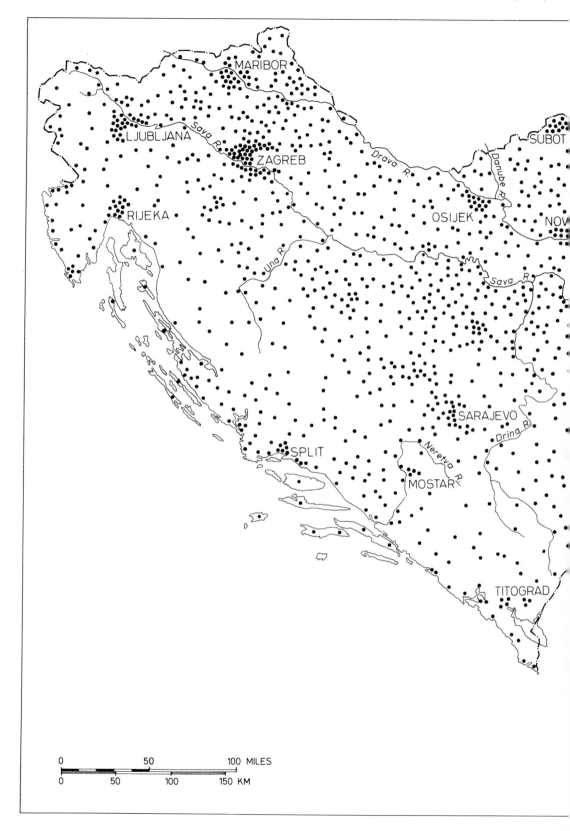

FIGURE 7. Population Dot
Source: *Statistički god.*

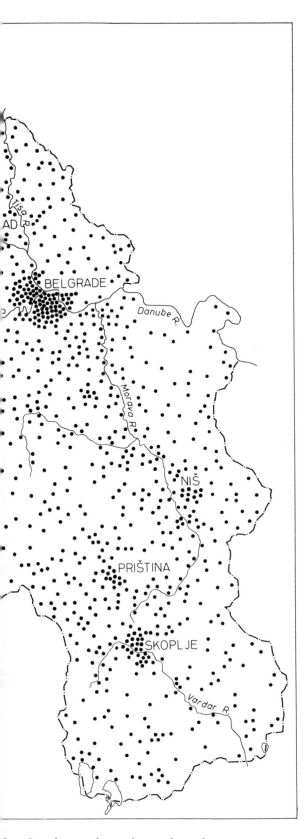

Map. One dot equals ten thousand people.
njak SFRJ (Belgrade, 1963), pp. 508–531.

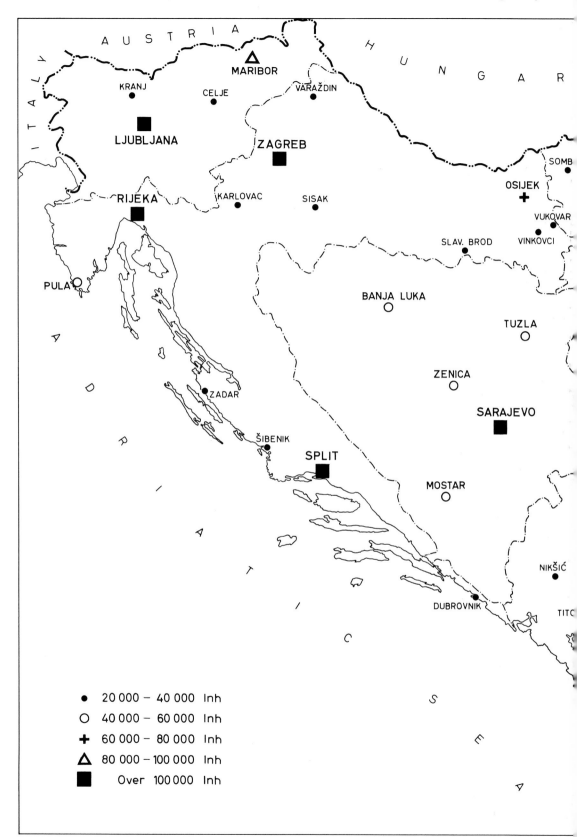

Figure 19

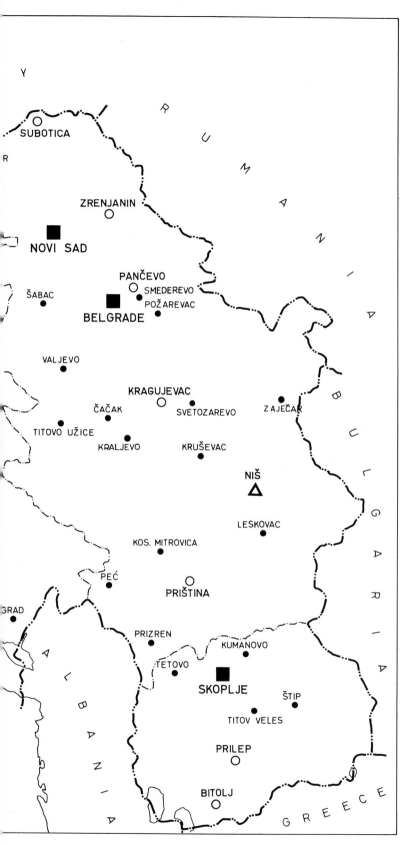

FIGURE 19. Fifty-Five Cities Selected for Analysis.

Figure 21

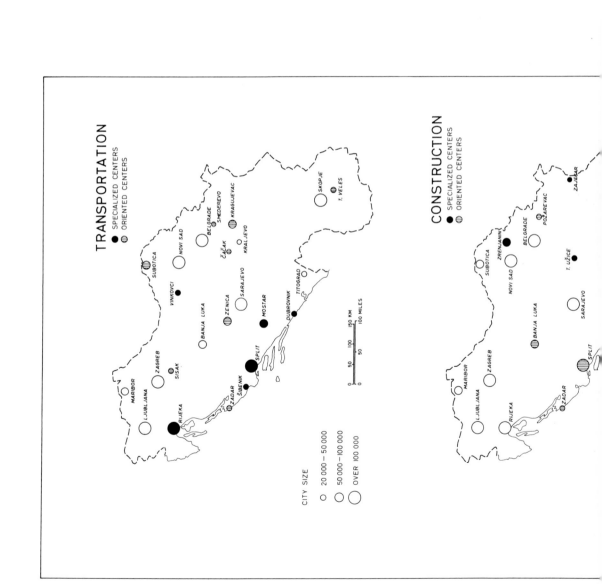

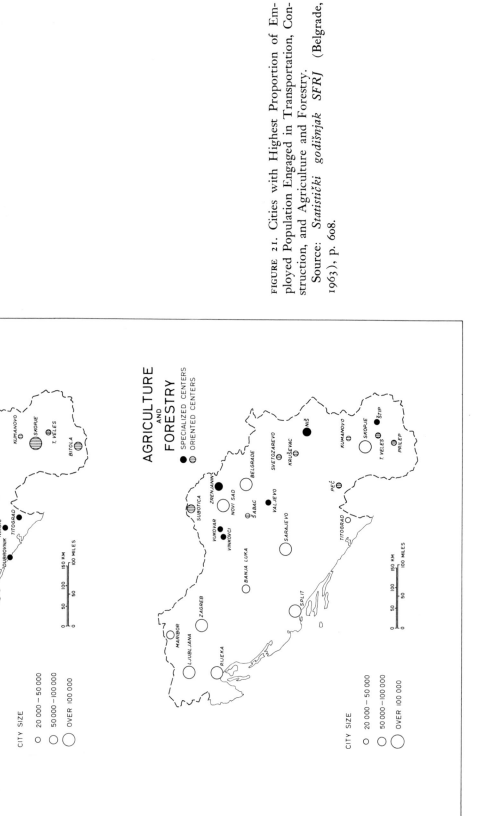

FIGURE 21. Cities with Highest Proportion of Employed Population Engaged in Transportation, Construction, and Agriculture and Forestry.

Source: *Statistički godišnjak SFRJ* (Belgrade, 1963), p. 608.

Figure 27

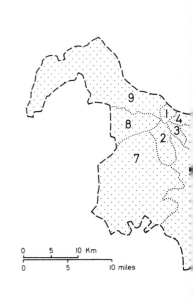

FIGURE 27. Variation of Selected Indicators of Housing Quality in Belgrade's Communes.

Source: *Popis Stanova 1961: Rezultati za Naselja* (Belgrade: Savezni Zavod za Statistiku, 1962). Original census booklets utilized in the Federal Statistical Office in Belgrade.

COMMUNES:

I	1	STARI GRAD
	2	SAVSKI VENAC
	3	VRAČAR
	4	PALILULA
II	5	VOŽDOVAC
	6	ZVEZDARA
	7	ČUKARICA
	8	NOVI BEOGRAD
	9	ZEMUN

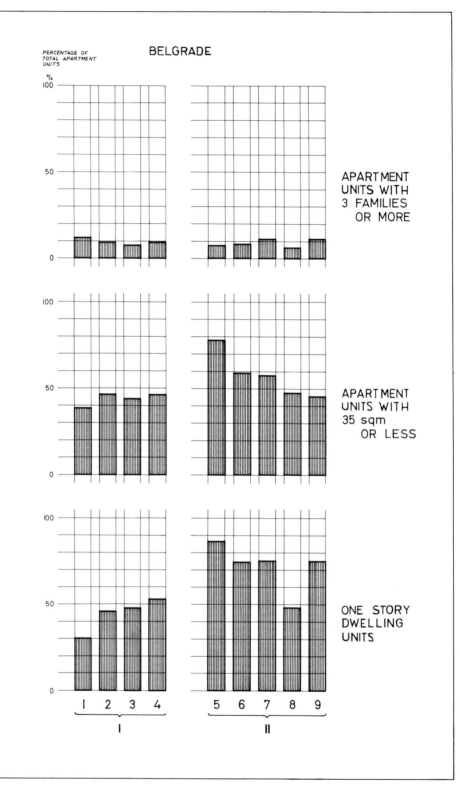

BELGRADE

Figure 29

0   5   10 Km

0   5

COMMUNES:

    1   CEN
    2   BEŽ
    3   ŠIŠI
    4   MOS
    5   VIČ-

FIGURE 29. Variation of Selected Indicators of Housing Quality in Ljubljana's Communes.

Source: *Popis Stanova 1961: Rezultati za Naselja* (Belgrade: Savezni Zavod za Statistiku, 1962). Original census booklets utilized in the Federal Statistical Office in Belgrade.

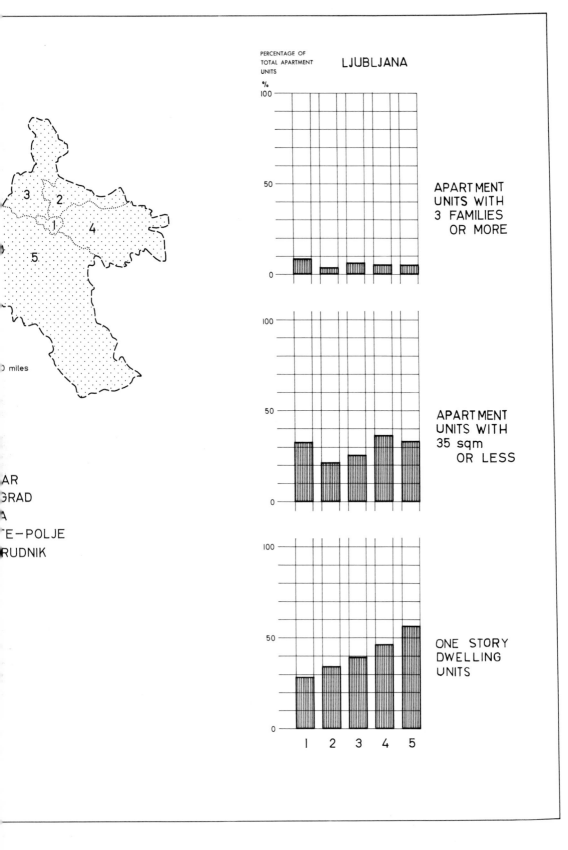

PERCENTAGE OF
TOTAL APARTMENT
UNITS

LJUBLJANA

%
100

50

0

APARTMENT
UNITS WITH
3 FAMILIES
OR MORE

100

50

0

APARTMENT
UNITS WITH
35 sqm
OR LESS

100

50

0

1 2 3 4 5

ONE STORY
DWELLING
UNITS

miles

AR
GRAD
A
E-POLJE
RUDNIK

3 2
1 4
5

Figure 31

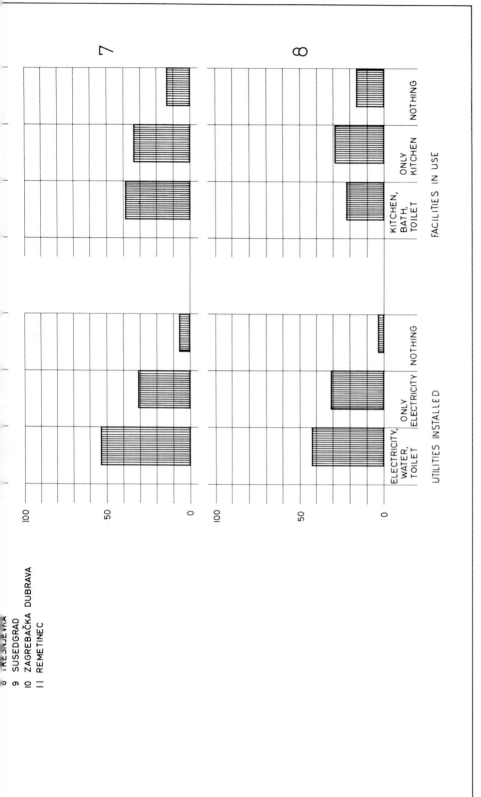

FIGURE 31. Comparison of Zagreb's Communes in Terms of Utilities Installed and Facilities Available: Maksimir, Črnomerec, Peščenica, Trešnjevka. Source: *Popis Stanova 1961: Rezultati za Naselja* (Belgrade: Savezni Zavod za Statistiku, 1962). Original census booklets utilized in the Federal Statistical Office in Belgrade.

Figure 35

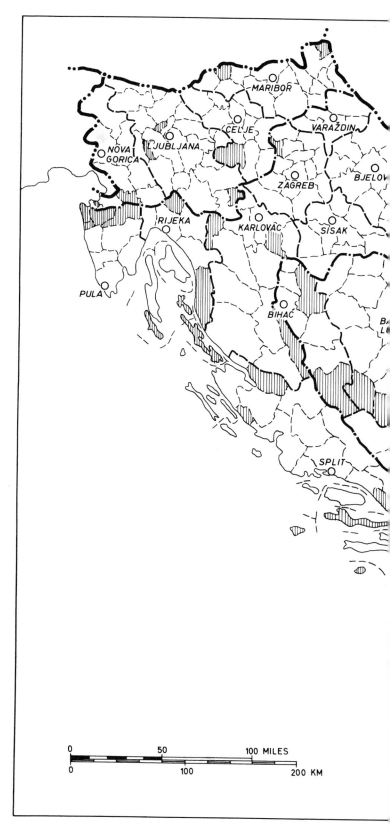

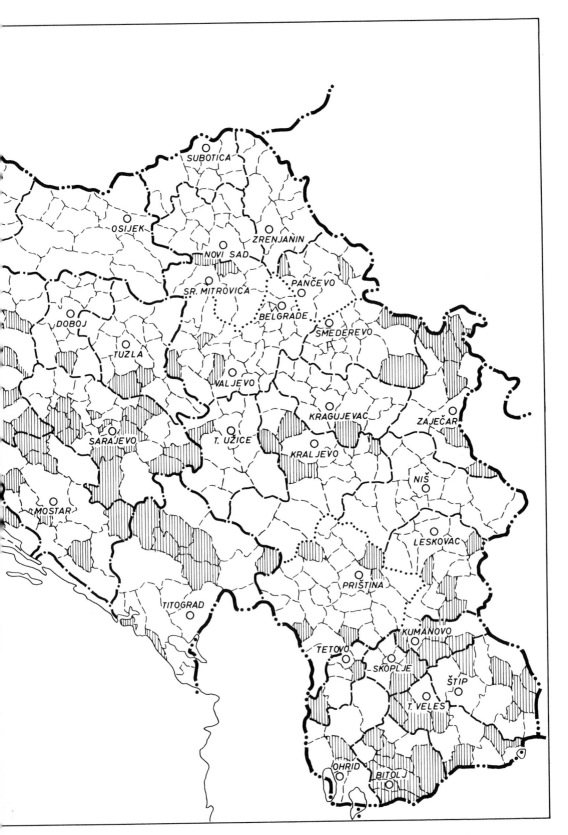

FIGURE 35. Distribution of Communes and Districts, January 1, 1963. Communes ranking in the lowest 20 percent on Factor One are shaded as indicated on Table Twenty-Five.

as might be expected, the largest housing fund but the least land. Despite innumerable attempts by the municipal government during 1962 and 1963 (which would have required a change in the regulations), that commune refused to expend any of its resources on housing construction in outlying areas, that is, in other communes. Centar maintained that renovation and reconstruction of existing housing was more expensive than construction of new stock and for them more important, and therefore it was wiser to preserve their entire housing fund for internal consumption.[4]

Discussion no longer exists in Ljubljana as to which alternative is best: a city with one or more than one commune. After many years of experience

---

[4] "The influx of new inhabitants into this commune [Centar] is minimal. At the same time the housing fund has very large resources. Since there is no vacant land for new dwellings in the commune, and these funds cannot be invested for housing beyond the commune's boundaries, there is a tendency to destroy housing and other objects too soon in order to insure 'space' for new buildings," *Borba* (Zagreb), April 19, 1964.

The Portal at Ljubljana. *Zavod za Ureditev*

they have decisively decided for five communes, which encompass 43,758.9 urbanized acres (17,709 hectares) and 179,345.2 suburban acres (72,580 hectares) with an urban population of 177,000 plus and around 43,000 suburban. There are five independent communes as well as a City Council which exists as their organ of self-management for questions of joint interest to the city. But local politicians have still not raised and answered the question of mutual interest or the manner of financing mutual needs and goals.[5]

Thus Ljubljana was the only city that really attempted to keep communal operations independent in formal harmony with the April 1963 Constitution to be described in the next chapter, which implies that all communes, whether urban or not, shall be independent organs of self-management. But Ljubljana's organization has led to the problems referred to above as well as a very low level of intracommunal cooperation and an over-all negative reaction to any measure by the City Council that might impair communal independence. One communal representative at a recent meeting of the Socialist Alliance of Centar placed the situation in perspective when he said:

> The question is whether or not the City Council should be given the right to compel or command without the preliminary approval of the communes. If the [proposed] regulation remains as is, then the City Council will become the organ of power which taxes the income of citizens.[6]

He is implying that the communes would thus be bypassed and have little representative role.

Centar's representatives also felt that since their commune was completely built up and the other four communes were not, a more realistic form of financial contribution had to be worked out to support various urban services rather than the existing one commune, one share principle.

The variation in the resource base of the cities as well as historical tradition has created varying institutional relationships among essentially uniform administrative policies. Figures 27, 28, and 29 show the large

---

[5] *Borba* (Zagreb), March 30, 1964.
[6] *Ibid.*

number of communes in Zagreb, Belgrade, and Ljubljana. Skopje has four communes. However, Novi Sad has been a single large commune since 1960.

The system of city planning, including housing administration, is operationally more advanced (as of 1963) in Novi Sad than in any of the other cities. The reasons for this are in my opinion as follows:

1. The elimination of the previous division of the urbanized area of the city into separate communes made it possible for administratively unified municipal organs to direct activities throughout the entire urban region.

2. The 1959 housing act stimulated a reappraisal of city planning procedures and led to the reorganization and strengthening of the planning function simultaneously with the creation of the Novi Sad Fund for Housing Construction. Both of these organizations were managed by capable directors having efficient staffs. Unlike most planning departments, which were composed solely of architects, the Novi Sad Planning Department gradually came to include economists, geologists, and engineers as well.[7]

3. Since they were politically secure, the Planning Department and the Fund for Housing Construction were able to set up an Office for Communal Construction. This agency was created to avoid one of the most characteristic bottlenecks in urban development, the projection and construction of utilities. Before the establishment of this agency in Novi Sad and still characteristic of much construction in the country, utilities would be constructed in one area of the city while the Fund for Housing Construction would concentrate building activities in another.

The situation in Zagreb is about halfway between that of Belgrade and Ljubljana. In Zagreb the separate communes maintain their own housing funds and receive a certain share of the total housing fund for immediate local construction needs. A number of the communes have independent

---

[7] City planning practice is beginning to experience strong criticism because the majority of the practitioners are architects. Over 65 percent of the staff of city planning offices are architects. See *Borba* (Zagreb), June 26, 1964, for an excellent discussion of the problems and deficiencies this structural composition produces in practice. A similar discussion can be found in *Borba* (Zagreb), June 7, 1964.

planning commissions which project the over-all development of their commune in harmony with the master plan for the city as a whole. These planning commissions are strong advocates of their own commune's interests as against broader city interests. The conflicts of interest which are so much a part of American planning experience are not alien to Yugoslav practice.

In the following sections of this chapter, housing policy and housing quality are examined in some detail. Before proceeding directly into this, however, it is useful to provide general data on residential space consumption and daily time budget in Yugoslavia. This kind of research is needed to further improve and understand social conditions in urban areas. These data may also be useful for cross-cultural comparisons, as such surveys are relatively rare in Eastern Europe. The survey upon which the following brief discussion is based was conducted in one commune in Ljubljana in

Aerial view of the Savsko Naselje, settlement along the Sava River, in Ljubljana.

1961 by France Ivanšek.[8] This commune, Savsko Naselje, was a residential settlement constructed soon after the war and therefore the "quality" of this postwar housing may be assumed to be average or somewhat above average for Yugoslavia. This time budget would probably be similar to that of most urban settlements in the country. The area contained 7,300 people; 195 apartments were surveyed for the study. Figures 25 and 26 present the time budget and spatial parameters of the use of dwelling space for this sample residential area.

Figure 25, in the section of oversized figures, indicates the way in which the households surveyed budgeted their time and shows which rooms within the apartment were actually in use throughout various periods of the day. Each symbol represents 10 percent of the total people surveyed. The left side of the diagram shows the percentage of women at home at various hours, and indicates whether they were asleep, in the kitchen, or in some other room of the apartment. The right side of the diagram represents the same 24-hour period and indicates when husbands were home and at what hours. Families are together mainly from 2 to 4 p.m., which is the time of the main meal of the day after work, and in the evening from 6 to 9 p.m. By 8 p.m., 30 percent of the women are in bed, while at 4 a.m., 50 percent of them are already up. This diagram reflects extremely well the rhythm of Slovenian and indirectly Yugoslav life: most workers are on the job from 7 a.m. to 2 p.m. The long periods in which the wife remains in the kitchen are a reflection of generally poorer kitchen facilities, lack of appliances, and the fact that the kitchen is usually the warmest room in the apartment during the winter, or the only one which is constantly kept warm, since the individual stoves for each room for economical reasons are but sporadically lighted. Figure 26 indicates the differences in dwelling occupancy when the wife is employed and when she is not. As most wives work in Yugoslavia, the lower portion of the diagram actually suggests the typical situation. Each square represents 10 percent of the total number of people surveyed.

---

[8] *Človek-Stanovanje-Naselje*, Seminar in razstava, Ljubljana, 12.-14.II.1962 (Ljubljana: Urbanistični Inštitut LRS, 1962).

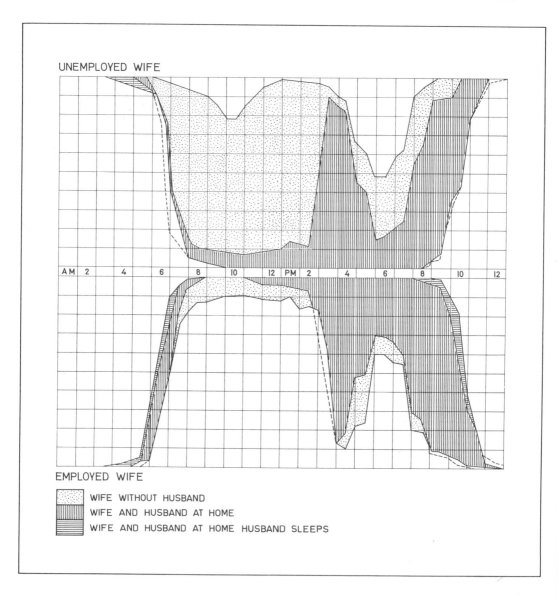

UNEMPLOYED WIFE

AM 2   4   6   8   10   12 PM 2   4   6   8   10   12

EMPLOYED WIFE

WIFE WITHOUT HUSBAND
WIFE AND HUSBAND AT HOME
WIFE AND HUSBAND AT HOME HUSBAND SLEEPS

FIGURE 26. Differences in Dwelling Occupancy Depending upon Whether Wife Is Employed.
Source: *Človek-Stanovanje-Naselje* (Ljubljana: Urbanistični Inštitut LRS, 1962), p. IX.

2. HOUSING POLICY

For the greater part of Yugoslavia's postwar existence an individual dwelling or apartment was treated as a "social good," rather than an economic good.[9] This classification implied that it was the state's responsibility to supply the individual with an apartment of the necessary size and quality. Rent was not economical; it was not intended to cover amortization, maintenance, services, and the like. In many ways the entire evolution of housing policy in the country can be summarized by examining the percent of family income expended on rent.

Table Seventeen. RENT EXPENDITURE, 1938–1960

	Percent of income spent on rent, for a worker's family of four
1938	33.6
1946	5.3
1953	4.4
1955	2.5
1958	2.4
1960	4.6

Source: *Troškovi stambene izgradnje i stanarina* (Belgrade: Zavod za unapredjenje komunalne delatnosti, 1962), pp. 58–59.

Immediately after the war, rents were lowered to half the prewar level. Due to the inflated value of the postwar dinar, this meant, as the table indicates, a substantial and continual lowering of rent expenditure. In the following postwar years, rents were maintained at approximately the same level while personal income and other household expenses increased. During most of the postwar period, rent never exceeded more than 2 to 4 percent of the average family budget.

---

[9] "An apartment in the narrow sense is an area functionally connected which is a special unit within a dwelling and has a special entrance, and serves the housing needs of one user (individual or family). . . ." *Troškovi izgradnje novih stambenih naselja* (Belgrade: Savezni zavod za urbanizam i komunalna i stambena pitanja, Dokumentacija broj 1, 1961), p. 18.

Until 1959, rents were regulated administratively in such a way that they did not represent either the real value and quality of the dwelling or the volume of residential space consumed. Nevertheless, rents were raised several times (1953 and 1955) in order to cover some of the costs of maintenance and administration. These increases, however, were far from sufficient, due to the rapid rise in the costs of services and materials.[10]

Current housing administrative practice and policy date only from 1959/1960. The main objective of federal legislation enacted during 1959 and 1960 was to create realistic economic criteria for the financing and distribution of housing construction and to increase the amount of private funds spent.[11] It was the purpose of the reforms to treat all investors—both public and private—equally in obtaining credit. The increase in rent which resulted from the reform was designed to cover the cost of various utilities, insure capital accumulation for replacement, and provide funds for the necessary maintenance and administration. The rent was expected to have some realistic relation to the value of the apartment and thus to influence the demand for existing housing stock and insure that the size and quality of new apartments matched the economic capacity of potential purchasers.

The key institutions in the housing reform of 1960 were the Funds for Housing Construction (*Fond za stambenu izgradnju*). These administrative organs, which were originally created as early as 1955, were an integral part of communal administration. The functioning of the Funds for Housing Construction within the relatively few multicommunal municipal areas (Belgrade, Zagreb, Ljubljana, Sarajevo, and Skopje) varied widely.

It is clear that these agencies represented a significant advantage over the earlier system. They are based upon the economic success of each

---

[10] "... the prices of building materials have increased thirty-two times compared with prewar, while the general level of prices has increased only fifteen times." *Financing of Housing in Europe* (Geneva: Economic Commission for Europe, 1958), p. 63.

[11] For a complete text of the law, with explanation of its basic policies see: *Reforma sistema finansiranja, izgradnje i korišćenja stanova,* (Belgrade: Kultura, 1959).

Sarajevo, with its bridges over the Miljacka River. On the outskirts is New Sarajevo. *Agencija za Fotodokumentaciju*

commune and were thus intended to stimulate economic development. A tax of four percent on the salaries and wages of all workers and employees forms a stable financial base. Further financial resources come from amortization, which amounts to half of the rents of most publicly owned residential buildings (the other half being utilized for maintenance and administration); a property tax on private holdings; annuities on loans granted; the participation or down payment of both private persons and public organizations competing for housing loans.

With the creation of the Funds there was at last a local agency concerned with long-range housing policy backed by constant sources of financial resources. This concentration of decision-making authority and resources within a single agency eliminated one of the greatest institutional barriers to an effective housing policy. Previously the responsibility had been divided among a number of communal administrative organs, resulting in the collective dissipation of responsibility. There was now an agency of local government responsible for the coordination of all housing development in the area of the commune. In contrast to the marked improvements in the quantity of housing constructed each year since 1956, one only has to observe the continuing lack of adequate commercial services in new residential areas; there is no agency directly responsible for the planning, coordination, and construction of these local services.

Through the extension of credit, the local Fund for Housing Construction and the investor emerged as financial partners distinct from the producers of apartments. This combination and the assurance of continued investment funds stimulated the building industry to increase operations, retain the necessary work force, and develop a continuing source of building materials.

The role of the Funds for Housing Construction is best summarized by an extract from an annual report of one such fund:

The dynamic development of our country demanded a change in the system of financing housing construction, the utilization of apartments, and the development of the housing economy and housing relations in coordination with the general economic and social development. Thus during 1959, the federal parliament passed a series of regulations in the housing field, among them the Law of Financing Housing Construction.

With the passage of this Law a reform was executed in financing housing construction which in essence introduced economic criteria into the system or, in other words, introduced economics *per se* into the housing economy.

The specifications of the Law of Financing Housing Construction makes the commune, as an association of producers and consumers, responsible for the total housing economy, through its organizing funds, enterprises and services, and the housing cooperatives of citizens and their funds; it is concerned with the maintenance of existing housing funds and the rational development of housing construction.

The Law gave these rights and duties to the communes, enabling them to merge local housing economy with the general economic policy of the commune so that the development of productive capacity and the growth of labor productivity automatically increases the standard of living and improves the conditions of life of the citizens, while at the same time solving the housing problem which in itself stimulates increased productivity.

With the reform of financing housing construction, the People's Council of the Commune of Novi Sad at the second meeting of the Communal Council and the second meeting of the Council of Producers held on January 21st, 1960, passed decision number 2150/60 of 25 January 1960. By this decision the Office for Constructing Housing and Public Objects in Novi Sad was eliminated and all its rights and obligations passed on to the Fund for Housing Construction. At the same time as the formation of this Fund for Housing Construction as an independent institution, whose mission it was to organize housing construction within the area of the Commune of Novi Sad, new regulations were passed governing its affairs.[12]

The core of the reforms of 1960, as well as of the major criticisms of the law since then, concerns the size and function of rents in socialist Yugoslavia. From 1954 to 1959, regulations concerning rents and housing maintenance were completely in the hands of the communes. It was assumed that rents should cover or contribute towards the costs of administration and maintenance. During this period rents were fixed according to the size and quality of the apartment. The differences in rents among cities were great.[13]

After January 1, 1960, rents were calculated according to a set of uniform criteria. A nationwide survey of all apartments existing as of 1959 was conducted and each apartment was evaluated according to an established set of criteria which estimated the apartment's quality, locational advantage, and number and efficiency of utilities supplied. Approximately forty separate items were considered, and quality rates were established within each category. These quality ratings were assigned an established

---

[12] *Izveštaj o poslovanju za 1962 godinu* (Novi Sad: Fond za stambenu izgradnju, 1962), pp. 1–2.

[13] ". . . current [1959] level of rents is very uneven among the various urban and industrial centers. For example a survey indicates that for an average apartment of the third category there is paid per square meter: in Leskovac, Čačak, Kraljevo, Kragujevac, Tetovo, Bitola, Skopje, and Koprivnica from 22 to 27 dinars, but in Sarajevo, Maribor, and Celje around 15 dinars, in Zadar, Sisak, and Slavonski Brod around 13 dinars, in Split, Trbovlje, and Zagreb around 11 dinars, in Pula and Rovinj around 10, but in Jesenice only 6 dinars." *Reforma sistema finansiranja izgradnje i korišćenja stanova* (Belgrade: Kultura, 1959), p. 12.

number of points. Once the calculation had been completed the rent for each apartment was computed as follows:

$$\text{monthly rent} = 12\sqrt{\frac{p \times 450}{100}}$$

    where p = number of points
         450 = number of dinars assigned each point
         100 = period of amortization
           12 = months of the year

The rents resulting from this system were on the average over twice as high as those applicable before the reform.

    Rents for the apartments built after January 1, 1960, were calculated in exactly the same way as above, except that the actual construction cost of the new apartment was used instead of the number of points multiplied by 450 dinars. The total points which each apartment was assigned automatically placed it in a specified housing category.[14]

    The average rent expenditure of a white-collar family was 2,480 dinars in 1961, as compared with 851 in 1959; of a worker's family, 1,838 dinars in 1961 against 612 in 1959. Rental regulations have remained unchanged since 1959, with the result that two different rent scales have developed. The cost of housing construction has increased, by conservative estimate, 50 percent since 1959; the calculated rent for a new apartment of the same size and quality rose accordingly. Variation is significant due to differences

---

[14] "IV. For the needs of planning and statistical analysis all apartments are categorized according to the square-meter value of their housing area or according to the established number of points within the following limits:

Category	Dinars	Points
I	Over 56,500	Over 125
II	47,501 to 56,500	106 to 125
III	38,501 to 47,500	86 to 105
IV	29,501 to 38,500	66 to 85
V	20,501 to 29,500	46 to 65
VI	11,501 to 20,500	26 to 45
Not categorized	to 11,500	to 25"

"Draft Regulation for estimating the portion of rent for amortization and the framework for categorization of apartments" (*ibid.*, p. 122). The original apartment classification system appeared in *Službeni list FNRJ*, Number 15, 1959.

in the cost of clearance, utilities, and construction. It is not rare for rents in new buildings in some cases to be twice those set by the 1959 reform.

Special mention should be noted in the structure of apartments, the increase in apartments built in the last three years, which means that more than ten percent of all purchasers of apartments pay significantly more rent than those who received their apartments before the housing reform. This has created pressure by those people to establish rents administratively again or to return to the level of rents established by the 1959 reform. Rent for an average apartment built now is around 5,000 dinars monthly, which is 100 to 160 percent more than the average rent. Since each year approximately 50,000 apartments are produced for rental, every year the number of purchasers with rents exceeding 10 percent of their family budget increases. If the current system continues to the end of 1970 more than one-half of all apartment dwellers in Yugoslavia will pay at least two times more rent than utilizers of apartments whose rents were established by the reform.[15]

At the end of 1962 there were 4,100,000 apartments with approximately 1,886,894,140 square feet (175,300,000 square meters) of residential space in Yugoslavia. In urban centers having 6,032,564 residents or 33 percent of the population in 1961, there were 1,430,000 apartments or 34.9 percent of all apartments in the country.[16]

In the last seven years 178,205 apartments, 13.4 percent of the entire number of apartments in the country, were constructed. Prior to 1956 the complete neglect of housing (which, as noted in the preceding sections, was due to the lack of public concern, lack of a coordinating agency with over-all responsibility, and rents too low even to cover maintenance costs) greatly affected the deterioration of the existing stock. The lack of appropriate institutions and funds curtailed new construction. The influx of rural inhabitants into the urban centers far exceeded apartment construction. "The building of apartments was limited, . . . because the

---

[15] *Usavršavanje sistema u oblasti stambene izgradnje i korišćenja stanova,* XIV Skupština Stalne konferencije gradova Jugoslavije (Zagreb, 1963), pp. 24–26.

[16] The census of housing in 1961 considered 862 large cities, industrial and tourist centers, and settlements around the larger cities as "urban settlements." Here and throughout the discussion, except where indicated, no account has been taken of damages to housing as a result of the earthquakes in Slavonia and Skopje, or the October, 1964, flooding in Zagreb.

greatest part of our wealth was directed towards building the economic foundations of society."[17]

Table Eighteen. FUNDS EXPENDED ON HOUSING CONSTRUCTION, 1956–1962
(IN BILLIONS OF DINARS)

Year	Total Funds	Social Sector		Private Sector	
		Amount	Percent	Amount	Percent
1956	67.4	43.6	64.7	23.8	35.3
1957	98.7	68.0	68.9	30.7	31.1
1958	118.2	83.2	70.4	35.0	29.6
1959	135.3	95.8	70.8	39.5	29.2
1960	192.5	134.2	69.7	58.3	30.3
1961	262.6	172.7	65.8	89.9	34.2
1962	295.0	206.0	69.8	89.0	30.2
1956–1962	1169.7	803.5	68.7	366.2	31.3

Source: Sreten Bjeličić, *ibid.*, p. 661.

In the period from 1956 to 1961 the volume of investment in housing increased five times, with public funds accounting, after the first year, for about 70 percent of the total investment in housing. Increase in the number of apartments constructed for the same period is shown in Table Nineteen.

Table Nineteen. NUMBER OF APARTMENTS CONSTRUCTED IN YUGOSLAVIA AND IN CITIES OVER 20,000, 1956–1962

	Yugoslavia	60 Cities with over 20,000 Population	46 Cities 20,000– 50,000 Population	Seven Cities 50,000– 100,000	Seven Cities over 100,000
1956	37,005	11,843	4,425	1,340	6,078
1957	44,727	15,172	5,611	1,769	7,792
1958	61,681	21,853	8,234	2,390	11,229
1959	60,614	24,189	8,179	2,821	13,189
1960	75,733	29,902	9,948	3,405	16,509
1961	100,176	39,712	15,083	5,157	19,473
1962	104,115	43,635	14,229	6,509	22,897

Source: *Usavršavanje sistema u oblasti stambene izgradnje i korišćenja stanova, osnovni referat,* XIV Skupština Stalne konferencije gradova Jugoslavije (Zagreb, October 24–26, 1963), p. 1.

---

[17] Sreten Bjeličić, "Stambena politika i naš društveno-ekonomski sistem," *Naša stvarnost* (June, 1963), p. 659.

These tables show that the number of apartments constructed in 1962 was almost three times the number constructed in 1956. Though the amount of funds invested in 1962 was five times that of 1956, the increase in the number of apartments was significantly lower.[18]

According to a census of apartments taken in 1961 in 862 urban and suburban settlements, the average space per person was 113 square feet (10.5 square meters). The regional variations, however, were striking. Macedonia had the lowest, with 86.1 square feet (8.0 square meters) per person, and Slovenia the largest, with 144.2 square feet (13.4 square meters). According to a census of agricultural households conducted in 1960, the average dwelling space in villages averaged 91.5 square feet (8.5 square meters) per person. Bosnia and Herzegovina had the lowest with 60.3 square feet (5.6 square meters), and Vojvodina the largest with 131.3 square feet (12.2 square meters).[19]

In 1962 the number of families was around 700,000 greater than the number of existing apartments. Of this total the greatest number of families without apartments of their own were in cities. According to the 1960 agricultural census estimate, there were over 100,000 more residential dwellings than existing agricultural families.[20] The degree of crowding in

---

[18] The cost of apartments varied greatly throughout the country. One average square meter of housing space in 1961 cost 55,900 dinars. An average apartment of 5,285 square feet (49.1 square meters) cost 2,746,000 dinars in Serbia: regional variations for 10.8 square feet (one square meter) of space were from 52,200 in Vojvodina to 63,300 in Kosovo-Metohija, while prices varied in Belgrade from 63,000 to 72,000 dinars. These prices were high compared to the average income of a worker's or white-collar family. The cost of an apartment was around twelve times the average yearly income of a worker or nine times the income of white-collar workers employed in industry. Many Yugoslav critics maintain that these high costs are due in part to constructing apartments of better quality and equipment than the material conditions of the country should allow. Of 12,248 apartments built in Serbian cities in 1962, around 60 percent were of the first and second categories and 27 percent in the third category. (See Footnote 14 for an explanation of housing categories). Only 13 percent fell into the fourth category. *Troškovi stambene izgradnje i stanarina* (Belgrade: Zavod za unapredjene komunalne delatnosti, 1962), p. 8.

[19] Sreten Bjeličić, *op. cit.*, p. 663.

[20] *Ibid.*, p. 665.

the major urban centers is evident from these figures for the percent of apartments containing more than one family: [21]

Belgrade	26.7%
Zagreb	24.3%
Ljubljana	23.1%
Sarajevo	23.9%
Skopje	23.6%

To provide somewhat greater insight into urban housing conditions three variables suggesting residential condition are graphically presented for Zagreb, Belgrade, and Ljubljana. These cities consist of a number of communes, as indicated in Figures 27, 28, and 29, in the section of oversized figures. Each diagram indicates the location of each commune within the city and identifies it by a number. Belgrade and Zagreb's communes have been divided at a generally accepted boundary between "urban" communes and those more rural in character. Note the general increase in one-story dwellings outward from the center.

In keeping with the use of Zagreb as a case study, Figures 30 and 31, in the section of oversized figures, and 32 indicate the percent of apartments which have various utilities installed (electricity, water, sewage lines) and those which actually have these utilities connected (stove or sink in the kitchen, toilet, or bath). Perhaps the most interesting thing is the difference between the number of apartments with utility lines available and those with corresponding kitchens and bathrooms. As would be expected, there is a gradual improvement in the situation as one approaches the center (Communes number 1 and 2 for Zagreb). For anyone familiar with Zagreb these diagrams correspond to the qualitative impression received by driving through the city. Commune 3 (Medveščak) is the zone of first-class residences in the upland area above the Sava plain.

Probably the most outstanding feature of these data is the difference in spatial distribution of units with and without utilities and fixtures or facilities. The more centrally located communities have the highest percentage of apartments with all utilities and facilities. The percentage declines very sharply with distance from the center, as exemplified by Susedgrad, Zagrebačka Dubrava, and Remetinec. These three communes

---

[21] *Ibid.*, p. 665.

are the only ones having: (1) more units with only electricity than with
electricity, water, and toilet, and (2) more units with only kitchen than
with kitchen, bath, and toilet.

The existence or availability of all utilities is much more prevalent than

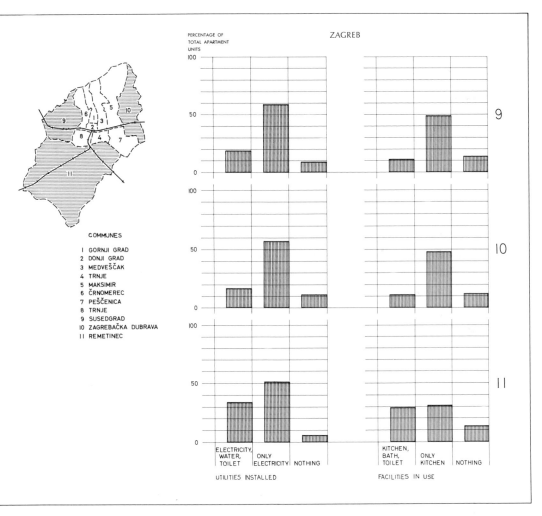

FIGURE 32. Comparison of Zagreb's Communes in Terms of Utilities Installed and Facilities
Available: Susedgrad, Zagrebačka Dubrava, Remetinec.
    Source: *Popis Stanova 1961: Rezultati za Naselja* (Belgrade: Savezni Zavod za Statistiku,
1962). Original census booklets utilized in the Federal Statistical Office in Belgrade.

the existence of all the facilities, especially in the four central communes.
Gornji Grad, Donji Grad, Medveščak, Trnje, and Črnomerec have very
few units without both water and toilet while the percent without bath or
toilet is much higher. This is probably reflective of the availability of
public utilities in the central city as compared to the more rural communes
where cost of service extension is considerably higher. It is also reflective of
the lesser importance of a bath or toilet as compared to the basic utilities of
electricity and water.

Another spatial variation can be noted in the distribution of these
variables. The three relatively central communes below the east-west
railroad line have considerably fewer units with all utilities and facilities
than do the central communes north of the tracks. Thus almost one-half
the units in Trnje, Pešćenica, and Trešnjevka have only electricity and
kitchens. This ratio is much higher than in the northern communes
(excluding the rural communes of Susedgrad and Zagrebačka Dubrava).

The following section considers these variables along with others to
create an index of housing quality; a composite measure which will
facilitate intracommunal and intraurban comparison.

3. HOUSING QUALITY

One index or indicator of development and perhaps of modernization is
"housing quality." Indeed, housing quality is a more meaningful index of
the socioeconomic character of an area than many other standard indices.
The concern here was to determine a single composite statistic of housing
quality that would suggest regional variation among selected cities (Belgrade, Ljubljana, Novi Sad, Skopje, and Zagreb) and their communes.
The usual method in processing data similar to census material is to
calculate percentages for the most important variables for the investigated
units and compare these figures. Though more than one variable is
important in determining housing quality they do not all have equal
weight. It seemed desirable, therefore, to develop a single statistical score
which would record all the variables according to their importance and
which could be used to compare quality among administrative units.

Sample cities were selected as representative of the varying regions of foreign domination previously described. The following table indicates the city, its population (according to unpublished 1961 census data [22]), and the number of communes of which it is composed:

City	Population	Communes
Belgrade	622,482	9
Ljubljana	147,991	5
Novi Sad	106,689	1
Skopje	170,373	4
Zagreb	447,133	11

The variables used to measure housing quality were similar to those of the United States Housing Census. Although limited, they are all directly indicative of housing quality. More importantly, however, they are also good indicators of broader socioeconomic characteristics. When combined, these variables make it possible to compare housing quality statistically on a broad, regional scale. The variables were age of unit, size of unit, persons per apartment, families per apartment, facilities in units (kitchen, bath, or toilet), utilities in units (electricity, gas, or central heating, and water). Any dwelling unit in the United States without at least one of these facilities or utilities could most certainly be classified as substandard.[23]

The above variables reflect not only the physical condition of the dwelling units but also the socioeconomic environment in which they are located. Persons and families per apartment are indicative of social conditions, while available facilities and utilities indicate economic conditions. Size and age reflect physical condition. There is, of course, definite

---

[22] These data were compiled from original unpublished housing census material before its synthesis and publication in standard form. The housing census was taken between April 1 and 7, 1961. There was one census booklet prepared for each commune: "Every document was made in four copies, of which one copy is retained by the commune's people's council, the county office for statistics and the office for statistics of the republic for all settlements included in the census of apartments in its area. The Federal Statistical Office retained one copy." I utilized the census material in the Federal Statistical Office in Belgrade.

[23] It must be remembered, however, that a comparison between the United States and Yugoslavia is not what we are concerned with: our aim is to measure housing quality within Yugoslavia itself for inter- and intraurban comparative purposes.

overlap among these variables; an old house, for example, is more likely to be low on facilities.

To complete the analysis, a rather simple methodology was employed. It basically consisted of the following steps: (1) Find the cumulative relative frequency distribution for each of the twelve variables among the thirty communes; (2) find the cumulative relative frequency distribution of total dwelling units among the thirty communes and five cities; (3) calculate location quotients for each variable for each commune by dividing the share that each commune had of the total amount of the variable by its share of total dwelling units; (4) give a score to each quotient according to its size; (5) weight each variable according to its importance in determining housing quality; (6) multiply the scores of the individual quotient times the weighted value of the variable to get an over-all quality score of housing in each individual commune; (7) rank these final quality scores by size to compare housing quality among the thirty communes.[24]

---

[24] The technique used to arrive at housing quality scores was quite simple. The first step was to find each commune's share of the total amount of each variable. This was done by adding up the absolute values that each commune had of each variable to find the "Total." This "Total" was then divided into the absolute number that each commune contained to find its relative share. For example, if the "Total" number of dwelling units built before 1900 in the thirty communes was 1,000 and if Novi Sad contained 100, its share would be 10 percent. This was done for each variable and also for total dwelling units. By dividing the commune's share of total dwelling units into its share of each of the variables, a quotient was obtained for each commune for each of the twelve variables. To continue with the example, if Novi Sad's shares of total units built prior to 1900 was 15 percent, its quotient for such units would be 1.50.

The formula for such a quotient is

$$Q_N = \frac{U_n}{U_t} \div \frac{T_n}{T_t}$$

where U_n = dwelling units in Novi Sad built before 1900
  U_t = dwelling units in all thirty communes built before 1900
  T_n = total dwelling units in Novi Sad
  T_t = total dwelling units in all thirty communes

The results of this type of calculation can range from zero to infinity. A quotient of 1.0 would indicate that the commune of Novi Sad had an average share of dwelling units built before 1900 in comparison with the other twenty-nine communes. If the quotient were larger than 1.0, the commune would have a larger portion of units built prior to 1900 than would be expected under a normal distribution. Conversely, as the quotient approaches zero, the commune's share of units built prior to 1900 becomes smaller in relation to its total units.

Some of the more interesting results in terms of the individual variables which reveal much about the internal structure of the cities include:

1. *Five to Ten Persons per Apartment Unit.* This variable was probably the most evenly distributed among the thirty communes. Only the communes in Skopje have higher quotients than would normally be

---

The next step involved giving scores to the resultant quotients. The main reason for this procedure was to compensate for the wide range of quotient values. By limiting the score to a certain amount the values at the extremes could be dismissed, and thus would not overweight the final quality score. For example, if a commune received an unusually high quotient for one variable but rather normal ones for the other eleven, the one high score would be overweighted in the total. The following scores were given to quotient intervals:

Quotient	Score
Below .50	1
.50– .84	2
.85–1.14	3
1.15–1.49	4
1.50 and over	5

The third step involved weighting the variables according to their importance in measuring housing quality. This was necessary because it would be incorrect to consider all the variables equally important; that is, the size of a unit is certainly less indicative of over-all quality than is the absence of a kitchen, bath, and toilet; of course such weighting is always subjective. The following values were assigned to each variable:

Variable	Weighted Value
5 to 10 persons per apartment	1
10 or more persons per apartment	2
3 to 5 families per apartment	1
5 or more families per apartment	2
Units built between 1900 and 1930	1
Units built prior to 1900	2
Units between 172.2 and 376.7 square feet	1
Units under 172.2 square feet	2
Units having only kitchen	2
Units without kitchen, bath, or toilet	3
Units having only electricity	1
Units with utilities available but not in use	1

By multiplying the weighted value of the variable by the assigned value of the quotient, a score was obtained for each variable for each commune. After adding these individual scores, a total figure was obtained for each commune. This figure represented the final housing quality score for each commune; the lower the score, the better the over-all quality of housing.

expected. All the other communes are very close to the average of 1.0. Thirty percent of the total dwelling units in the thirty communes have five to ten persons living in them.

2. *Ten or More Persons per Apartment Unit.* The distribution of this variable is much more dispersed, perhaps because of the very low frequency of its occurrence. Less than 3 percent of the total dwelling units are overcrowded to this extent. However, the communes in Skopje all have very high quotients; this severe overcrowding is two to five times more frequent than in other communes. Ljubljana has a very low frequency for this variable, with three of its communes (Centar, Bežigrad, and Šiška) having very few units of this type. Zagreb communes show more variation, with three (Trnje, Maksimir, and Črnomerec) being very low and two (Donji Grad and Zagrebačka Dubrava) being considerably high.

3. *Three to Five Families per Apartment Unit.* As with the first variable discussed above, this is rather equally distributed. The over-all frequency is much lower, however, with only 7 percent of the total dwelling units being this overcrowded. Although they have many persons per apartment, all Skopje communes have fewer units with three to five families per apartment than would be normally expected. This is due to the existence of large individual families with many children. Only Stari Grad in Belgrade and Donji Grad in Zagreb have very high quotients, and even these are not excessive. Vič-Rudnik, Moste Polje, Bežigrad in Ljubljana, and Trnje in Zagreb have less than their share of these units; the latter two also have low scores in persons per apartment.

4. *Five or More Families per Apartment Unit.* Only about one percent of all units in the thirty communes show this characteristic. As in the last variable, Skopje has a low frequency even though it was high in overcrowding as measured in persons per apartment. Donji Grad, Zagrebačka Dubrava, Medveščak, Pešćenica and Remetinec in Zagreb and Stari Grad, Zemun, and Palilula in Belgrade have the highest figures for this variable while Susedgrad in Zagreb, Bežigrad and Šiška in Ljubljana, and Idadija in Skopje are the lowest.

In summarizing the variables for overcrowding, several things stand out. The most unusual is the wide variation in the Skopje communes between overcrowding as measured in persons per apartment and as measured in families per apartment. Zagreb's Donji Grad and Zagrebačka Dubrava show excessive overcrowding in every category while all the communes in Ljubljana (especially Bežigrad and Šiška) apparently are not troubled by this problem.

5. *Units Built between 1900 and 1930.* This is another variable which is fairly evenly distributed. Communes in Zagreb show the greatest variation with Medveščak, Zagrebačka Dubrava, and Remetinec having relatively few units built during this period. Only Zvezdara in Belgrade has a very high quotient.

6. *Units Built before 1900.* This variable probably shows the widest dispersion among the communes. Surprisingly, only 14 percent of the total units were constructed before 1900. Gornji Grad, Donji Grad, Novi Sad, Centar, Vič-Rudnik, Zemun, and Kula appear to have the oldest housing units among the thirty communes, while Zagreb's Medveščak, Trnje, Pešćenica, Trešnjevka, and Skopje's Idadija have most of the new housing. Most of the housing in Belgrade's Zvezdara must have been constructed between 1900 and 1930 because it had a high quotient for variable 5 and a low one for variable 6.

It is interesting to note that there appears to be no direct correlation between age of units and overcrowding. Both Skopje's Idadija and Zagrebačka Dubrava had many overcrowded units in comparison with the other communes but they also have relatively more units constructed after 1930.

7. *Units between 172.2 and 376.7 Square Feet.* Over thirty-three percent of the total units are between 172.2 sq. feet (16.0 square meters) and 376.7 sq. feet (35.0 square meters) in area. No definite pattern seems to appear as to the distribution of these units by communes, although it should be noted that Zagreb's Donji Grad has relatively few, so that their overcrowding problems are naturally a little less severe than might appear. As a whole, these small units are fairly well distributed, with the communes in Ljubljana having the fewest and those in Belgrade having the most.

8. *Units under 172.2 Square Feet.* There are considerably fewer of these very small units although 12 percent of all units are in this classification. Belgrade again has the most while Ljubljana has the least. Otherwise the distribution is fairly close to the distribution of total units.

9. *Units Having Only Kitchens.* Over 32 percent of the total dwelling

units have only a kitchen and are without a bath or toilet. Novi Sad has the highest quotient for this variable, with Zemun and Voždovac also ranking quite high. The communes in Zagreb and Ljubljana have the lowest quotients, especially those of the latter city.

10. *Units without Kitchen, Bath, or Toilet.* This variable was given the highest score in determining low housing quality, for obvious reasons. Although the frequency is almost one-half that of the previous variable, this type of dwelling unit comprises over 17 percent of the total. The distribution again resembles the pattern where the communes in Skopje and Belgrade have the highest quotients and those in Ljubljana and Zagreb have the lowest. Two Skopje communes, Kale and Kula, have over twice their expected share of these units, while others such as Medveščak, Trnje, Vič-Rudnik, Bežigrad, Šiška, and Novi Sad have about one-half of their share.

11. *Units Having Only Electricity.* There is great variation in the distribution of this variable. All the communes in Ljubljana have extremely low quotients (only about one-quarter of their expected amount). In other cities the location of these units is very unevenly distributed. Some communes in Zagreb, such as Gornji Grad, Donji Grad, Medveščak and Črnomerec, have very low quotients, while others in the same city have very high ones (Susedgrad, Zagrebačka Dubrava, and Remetinec). This is also true in Belgrade, where Stari Grad and Vračar can be compared to Novi Beograd and Voždovac. All communes in Skopje (except Idadija) and Novi Sad have higher than average quotients for this variable.

12. *Units Having Utility Installations Available But Not in Use or Connected.* As noted, this variable probably reflects a lack of even the smallest monetary surplus among occupants. Thirty-four percent of all investigated dwelling units are in this situation, which seems remarkably high. Surprisingly, those in Skopje have the lowest quotients which, in my opinion, reflects the lack of adequate census coverage of the city's gypsy area. Otherwise, the distribution follows no definite pattern in relation to results of the previous variables.

By combining all the weighted scores for the above variables, a final ranking of communes by housing quality can be achieved. Such a ranking appears in Table Twenty.

Table Twenty. Urban Communes Ranked by Housing Quality

Commune	Score	Commune	Score
1. Medveščak (Z)	32	16. Remetinec (Z)	56
2. Bežigrad (L)	32	17. Gornji Grad (Z)	57
3. Šiška (L)	36	18. Pešćenica (Z)	57
4. Maksimir (Z)	43	19. Kisela Voda (S)	59
5. Črnomerec (Z)	45	20. Novi Sad	59
6. Vič-Rudnik (L)	46	21. Palilula (B)	60
7. Moste Polje (L)	47	22. Savski Venac (B)	61
8. Centar (L)	49	23. Zagrebačka Dubrava (Z)	62
9. Trešnjevka (Z)	50	24. Donji Grad (Z)	62
10. Susedgrad (Z)	50	25. Zvezdara (B)	63
11. Trnje (Z)	50	26. Voždovac (B)	66
12. Novi Beograd (B)	52	27. Čukarica (B)	68
13. Idadija (S)	52	28. Zemun (B)	74
14. Vračar (B)	53	29. Kale (S)	74
15. Stari Grad (B)	55	30. Kula (S)	74

Note: Z = Zagreb, L = Ljubljana, B = Belgrade, S = Skopje.

Several important things stand out in analyzing the above table. Probably the most dominant is the definite division between communes in Zagreb and Ljubljana as compared to those in Belgrade, Skopje, and Novi Sad. The eleven highest ranking communes are all in the first two cities. In fact, the scores of the five Ljubljana communes are among the first eight. A few of Zagreb's communes are found in lower positions in the ranking, especially Zagrebačka Dubrava and Donji Grad. It is important to remember that these communes had high quotients for all the variables measuring overcrowding but were below average for variables measuring actual physical condition or nonavailability of facilities and utilities. If it were not for the overcrowding scores, these two communes would also be in the top one-half. Three other communes in Zagreb (Remetinec, Gornji Grad, and Pešćenica) also have slightly lower positions but again, their position is related to the overcrowding variables. The five poorest communes (Voždovac, Čukarica, Zemun, Kale, and Kula) are definitely separated from the other twenty-five and have relatively high quotients for almost all variables.

In conclusion, it appears that the relationship among cities in the postwar period has changed little insofar as housing is concerned. Each city has essentially maintained its relative position, and better housing conditions continue to be characteristic of Ljubljana and Zagreb.

The heavy emphasis on capital investment after the war left little available resources for "nonproductive" items such as housing. Housing deterioration and overcrowding were natural consequences of this policy. Though specific federal measures since 1959 definitely improved the over-all situation, vastly increasing the number of dwelling units constructed each year, the deficit is still extremely large and financing is increasingly geared to the mobilization of individual reserves which, of course, are extremely limited. It is also true that more attractive items such as cars and vacations usually have greater priority in the individual budget than apartments, which originally were considered as a "social good" to be supplied by the socialist state. The belief that the state owes each family an adequate dwelling unit with minimum standards appears to be one of the pillars of the socialist creed that was universally accepted.

Chapter V

The Communal System

I. THE ADMINISTRATIVE EVOLUTION OF THE COMMUNAL SYSTEM [1]

The development of the communal system in Yugoslavia was made *possible* by post-1948 policies, but it was made *necessary* by the heterogeneous groupings of nationalities, the varying levels of economic and social development, and the long shadow of the past. In accepting the Soviet-inspired federal solution in 1946, Yugoslav authorities were prepared to grant "cultural determination," but sought to ensure uniform economic and political direction by means of a central apparatus backed up with sufficient force. The solution did not survive for several reasons: (1) The nature of the Yugoslav "revolution" was significantly different from those

---

[1] Portions of this section are based on my article, "The Yugoslav Commune," *World Politics* (April, 1964), pp. 418–441.

in Soviet-dominated Eastern Europe; the local partisan groups that emerged throughout the country provided a leadership in which mutual trust was never betrayed. (2) The existing physical and socioeconomic differences from place to place soon produced powerful internal pressure for greater regional latitude. This factor was deeply felt by the authorities in 1948 due to cultural allegiance of Yugoslav ethnic minorities to neighboring states: the Albanians, Hungarians, and to a much lesser degree the Rumanians. (3) A changed external situation placed the Yugoslavs on the side of the anti-Stalinists and thus of implied liberalization. Liberalization was of course an element of the policy evolved to enlist massive support against the threat of invasion and the assumption (in 1948) that another partisan war, which would depend upon popular support and sacrifice, was in the offing. In contrast to the Soviet "federal" system, where centrifugal pressures have found no outlet, the Yugoslavs have been attempting to build an economic and political system that provides regional autonomy within the framework of federal supervision. This essentially has been the nature of the Yugoslav pragmatic experiment since 1950, and especially since 1955. Once the end was decided upon, however, there appeared to be no ideal means of achieving it. So-called "centralist" and "noncentralist" factions developed. There is a tendency for every action of the central government in a federal system to be viewed with suspicion in the provinces as another "centralist solution," which in the case of Yugoslavia implies a "Serbian solution." The significant point is that though other underdeveloped countries have similar centralist and noncentralist conflicts, the situation is greatly compounded in Yugoslavia by ethnic differences and historically based variation.

The communal system was offered as a solution to the conflict of regional interests, or the "nationality question." In this regard, however, it must be emphasized that the prewar nationality question was quite different from the regional conflicts that disturb the country today. At present, there is "cultural determination" by the various peoples of the country; there is no attempt to "Serbianize the population." Regional conflicts today center on economic and social inequality and, since they are colored by varying historical traditions, often emerge as "nationality questions." The communal system has attempted, through diffusion of the points of decision-making, to solve the political aspects of the traditional conflict.[2]

After 1950, the concept of the commune or *komuna* was introduced. This term "implies a defined socioeconomic community and not merely a political machine and an autonomous political organization." [3] Thus the word *komuna* suggests something entirely different from the purely administrative prewar *opština*. In all legal and official documents, the term *opština* is still used; the term *komuna* occurs in political and economic literature and refers to a unit that is economically and socially as well as administratively homogeneous. The direct source of the word *komuna* can be traced to the Paris Communes of 1871, and indirectly to the fascination of Yugoslav leaders with forms of local government observed in Western Europe (especially Sweden, Switzerland, and England) in the 1950's.

The Constitution adopted in April, 1963, employs the word *opština* in the sense implied earlier by both *opština* and *komuna;* this indicates that in theory the administrative-territorial changes that had taken place after 1950 were expected to transform purely administrative units into "defined socioeconomic" communities. The *opština* has under the 1963 Constitution become a central feature of the effort to find a solution through administrative decentralization to the problems of national diversity and economic and social heterogeneity peculiar to Yugoslavia.

"Communal system" and "communal self-government," as distinct from "commune," are frequently-used expressions in Yugoslavia. They are applied to both the *opština* and the district or county (*srez*), and are also used to describe smaller political and social units, such as the *stambena* or *mesna zajednica*, a neighborhood association. In accordance with current Yugoslav usage, *opština* is translated here as "commune" and *srez* as "district."

The forerunner of the communal system was the transfer of management of industrial enterprises to workers' councils by a federal law enacted

[2] The principle "to each according to his work" is used to politically justify the extreme variations in economic standards.

[3] Jovan Djordjević and Najdan Pešić, "The Communal Self-Government System in Yugoslavia," *International Social Science Journal*, XIII, No. 3 (1961), p. 390; see also Sreten Bjeličić, *Communal System in Yugoslavia* (Belgrade, 1961), p. 10.

in June, 1950.[4] Under the present pattern of "workers' self-government" the workers of any factory or enterprise constitute a working collective. The collective elects by secret ballot the workers' council of the enterprise, with, for example, one representative for each thirty-five workers. A standard regulation stipulates the size of the workers' council for various size enterprises. The workers' council elects a management board for the enterprise and recommends the director of the enterprise. Each larger enterprise is usually divided into functional units known as "economic units." The workers' council is the key organ of the enterprise and the following matters are under its jurisdiction:

1. Determination of the enterprise's economic plan, which sets the kind and assortment of products, the quantity, and the price.

2. Distribution of the enterprise's income after certain taxes have been paid. Two basic taxes after interest on capital loans and amortization payments are a turn-over tax on the selling price of products or services and a tax on remaining gross income.

3. Labor relations—arbitration and supervision over the hiring and firing of workers, disciplinary measures, and the like.

4. Recommendation of changes in the organization of the factory and the production process.

The process of decentralization implied by the 1950 law placed the local governmental organs in new and more responsible positions through the "gradual substitution of bodies of social-government for the state apparatus and its competence."[5] In other words, the local territorial units, the communes and districts, were to be restructured in order that they might better supervise the "self-management" of industrial enterprises.

Prior to the adoption of the new Constitution of April 1963, two federal laws governed the communal system in Yugoslavia: a 1952 Law on the People's Committees (the main organs of administration in both the *srez* and the *opština*),[6] and a 1955 Law on the Organization of Communes and

---

[4] The most recent discussion of workers' councils is available in Adolf Sturmthal, *Workers Councils: A Study of Workplace Organization on Both Sides of the Iron Curtain* (Harvard University Press, 1964), pp. 86–118.

[5] Stane Kavčič, *Self-Government in Yugoslavia* (Belgrade, 1961), p. 9.

[6] *Službeni list Federativne Narodne Republike Jugoslavije* (Belgrade), No. 22 of 1952.

Districts.[7] A basic aim of the 1955 law was to replace the purely administrative bodies by a "commune" that would increasingly become a "special political form" created to administer the business of society.[8] The new law stressed, first, that all *opštine* were to be equal in status, thus in theory eliminating any administrative difference between the rural and urban *opštine*, and second, that the district or *srez* was no longer to be a higher administrative unit but simply an "association" of theoretically independent communes.[9] It should be remembered that, when reference was made to the "communal system" prior to 1955, ". . . in reality the *srez* was thought of. The building of self-government in the *srez* was understood as the first step in building the self-government of the *opština*." [10]

An International Labour Office publication, summarizing developments in Yugoslavia up to 1957 in terms of their effect on the development of workers' councils, makes the following statement relevant to the commune:

From the standpoint of workers' management, the main measures were the establishment of 'producers' councils [one of two chambers of the communal assembly, to be discussed below] to give the Yugoslav system an element of representation based not on political viewpoints but on the shared interests of the various collectives, [and] the granting of a large measure of administrative autonomy to the communes, enabling them to settle the great bulk of public

---

[7] *Ibid.*, No. 26 of 1955.

[8] *VII Kongres SKJ* (Belgrade, 1958), p. 146. Cited in *Materijali o statutima opština* (Belgrade, 1962), p. 89.

[9] The decline in the importance of the *srez* was strikingly underlined by their elimination in the Republic of Montenegro and the Autonomous Province of Kosovo-Methohija: *Službeni list N.R. Crne Gore*, No. 27 of 1957; *Službeni list N.R. Srbije*, No. 50 of 1959. Contrary to the current Belgrade position, a representative from Montenegro at a national congress quite frankly stated: "In Montenegro, districts have not existed for almost four years. Districts in Montenegro, during this very short time, have been completely forgotten . . . After the elimination of the districts, there began a significant growth in the incentive of the commune to solve economic, communal, cultural, health, and other problems." *Samoupravljanje u komuni*, Materijali sa godišnje skupštine Stalne konferencije gradova Jugoslavije, Niš, 30 October-1 November, 1961 (Belgrade, 1961), p. 152.

[10] Rude Petrović, *Prostorna determinacija teritorijalnih jedinica u komunalnom sistemu Jugoslavije* (Sarajevo, 1962), p. 28.

and economic matters at a level as near as possible to the individual undertaking, with regular direct participation by the latter's representatives . . . Naturally, the introduction of these reforms came up against the variety of obstacles, such as the lack of resources, the shortage of qualified supervisors, survivals of the bureaucratic and authoritarian habits of the earlier period, lack of balance as between different parts of the economic system, etc. Nevertheless, the measures taken during this period were important in that the broad guiding principles for the future development of the whole system of workers' management based on the commune and the independent enterprises finally emerged.[11]

The enactment of the 1955 law marked the inauguration of the full-scale development of the communal system. Prior to 1955, five distinct types of local administrative units were in existence: provinces (*oblasti* or *okruzi*); cities ranking as provinces; districts; cities ranking as districts; and cities within districts. The purpose of the new law was to reduce the number and variety of local units and at the same time ensure "sufficient [economic] strength to maintain all those social institutions which provide an elementary social standard for the citizens at the current level of our development."[12] The structure produced by the 1955 law reduced 4,519 separate units to a more manageable 1,479 *opštine* and 107 districts.[13]

The Constitution of April 1963 of the Socialist Federal Republic of Yugoslavia introduced significant organizational and functional changes in the commune.[14] It is not easy to describe these changes, for at least three reasons: (1) differences between theory and practice; (2) the variations in function among communes at different stages of economic and social development in a variety of physical settings; and (3) the complicated question of control on the part of both local and higher administrative

---

[11] International Labour Office, *Workers' Management in Yugoslavia* (Geneva, 1962), p. 8.

[12] Vladimir Kokole, *Komuna kao urbanistička pojava*, Annual Congress at Lake Bled, 1963: Savez Urbanističkih društava Jugoslavije (Belgrade, 1963), p. 8.

[13] *Teritorijalna podela Jugoslavije na opštine i srezove sa označenjem sedišta redovnih i privrednih sudova* (Belgrade, 1963), pp. 16, 18.

[14] "In regard to the socialist federal community and the placing of the word 'socialist' before the word 'federal' in the Constitution, it was desired in this way to attract the common interest of all working people and all the nations of Yugoslavia to the further development of socialist relations within the various nations and in the entire Federation." Veljko Vlahović, "Položaj i uloga gradjana," *O Ustavnom sistemu Socijalističke Federativne Republike Jugoslavije* (Belgrade, 1963), p. 91.

bodies, including the implementation of federal and republican policies at the local level. These factors will become more critical after a discussion of the socioeconomic variation among communes in Part Two and will occupy our attention in Chapter Six.

Article 73 of the 1963 Constitution states that "self-government by the citizens in the commune is the political foundation of the uniform social-political system." [15] Article 96 presents the general functions of the commune:

1. To provide the material and other conditions necessary for the operation and development of the productive forces;

2. To guide and coordinate economic development and the development of the social services;

3. To determine and distribute the means for common communal requirements;

4. To create the conditions required to satisfy the material, social, cultural, and other common needs of the citizens; and

5. To coordinate individual and common interests with the general interests.[16]

It is hoped that these functions can be carried out by balancing the various centrifugal forces which of necessity must exist within the commune. The most important check is expected to be the individual himself—the prime producer and the ultimate consumer.[17] The same man who participates in the workers' council of his enterprise which is struggling for increased pay will, it is believed, as a citizen of the commune and member of the assembly of the commune, suggest legislation and other measures to restrict unwarranted increase of salaries above levels of productivity.

This thread of "social self-management" runs throughout the entire fabric of current Yugoslav theory and practice. It is intended that there should be direct management of the factories and social institutions by the people engaged in them, with corresponding decentralized managerial functions assigned to the local administrative units. Great stress is placed on

---

[15] "The Constitution of the Socialist Federal Republic of Yugoslavia," *Socialist Thought and Practice* (Belgrade, June, 1963), p. 47.

[16] *Ibid.*, p. 58.

[17] *VII Kongres SKJ, op. cit.*, p. 1011, cited in *Materijali o statutima opština*, p. 138.

individuals participating in the "self-management" apparatus of their factory or institution and at the same time in the agencies of local government. The potential conflict between individual self-interest and the public or social good is self-evident.

According to the Constitution, within the commune individual workers and their organizations resolve fundamental questions of social, cultural, and political life by the process of self-government in production and consumption, according to the principle that *each will receive his share according to his work*. It is emphasized, however, that this "form of economic inequality" is only temporary—the result of a harsh history—and is necessary now as "the sole powerful base for conquering the tendency toward, and appearance of, monopolistic and bureaucratic deformation of socialist development." [18]

In carrying out their tasks the communes independently pass their own laws, create their annual plan (*društveni plan*) and budget, and set specific sums aside for various special funds. In conformity with the law, the *opština* independently establishes and distributes its own income. Communes with insufficient means for their tasks and the maintenance of minimum required social services are guaranteed additional funds from republican and federal sources.[19] In practice, however, this rule is somewhat difficult to interpret: what is the minimum standard for a commune in developed Slovenia, or for one in underdeveloped Macedonia? Such questions have never been satisfactorily answered.

The communal administrators are required to enforce compliance with federal and republican laws except where this function is expressly reserved to the higher administrative bodies. Every *opština* independently passes its own statutes, based on the federal and republican constitutions, which specify the rights and duties of the commune, and establishes the manner in which they will be realized. Communes may mutually cooperate, utilize their funds for joint projects, and create institutions to administer common needs.

The 1963 Constitution clearly tips the formal administrative scale in

---

[18] "Nova uloga države u razvoju socijalističkih odnosa i uspostavljanje osnove za razvoj samoupravljanja," *Politika* (Belgrade), October 26, 1961.

[19] Kardelj, "Komuna i prednacrt našeg novog Ustava," *Opština u novom ustavnom sistemu*, Materijali sa Godišnje skupštine Stalne Konferencije gradova Jugoslavije, Titograd, 1-3XI 1962 (Belgrade, 1961), p. 16.

favor of the commune. In its words, the commune shall "execute other powers of the social community, with the exception of the powers determined by the Constitution as being the rights and duties of republics or of the Federation." [20] Higher administrative organs do not formally have direct operational or administrative superiority over the communes.

In order to carry out the various functions and duties assigned to it, the *opština* has a number of administrative and consultative bodies. The name of the highest functional body has been changed under the new Constitution. The standard name *narodni odbor*, or "people's committee," was eliminated and in its place *opštinska skupština*, or "communal assembly," was substituted. Prior to the 1963 Constitution, the people's committee was the "basic and most important institution of local government." [21] The change was considered necessary because of the increased social role and responsibility projected for the commune and the feeling that the classical Communist term for the highest organ of local government, "the people's committee," no longer reflected the "new reality": ". . . the very name *odbor* [committee] is too narrow for such wide self-governing rights and responsibilities. It suggests more the meaning of power, administrative and operational direction, etc., while the name *skupština* [assembly] would more fully describe the new relations and role of the organ as the coordinating body and unit of self-government." [22]

The communal assembly is the highest representative body and organ of government in the commune. It is composed of a communal chamber or council, and a chamber of working associations or communities. The communal chamber is elected by all adult citizens, while the chamber of working associations is elected by all workers, not only those in industry and commerce but also those in education, cultural activities, social welfare, health services, and the like. This was another basic innovation of the new Constitution. Previously there had been a chamber or council of producers, elected only by workers in industry and commerce. It was

---

[20] "The Constitution of the Socialist Federal Republic," *op. cit.*, p. 59.

[21] *Report on Local Government in Yugoslavia*, issued by the Ministry of Community Development and Cooperation, Government of India (Jaipur, 1960), p. 19. This is an excellent account of the formal character of local government prior to the new Constitution.

[22] Dragutin Kosovac, "Uvodno izlaganje," *Samoupravljanje u Komuni* (Belgrade, 1961), pp. 62–63.

hoped that through this change the interests and specialties of all types of enterprises would be represented in the assembly and reflected in its legislative acts. The tenure of office for an assembly member is four years; half of the house changes every two years.

The communal assembly elects a president, who holds office for a maximum of four years, from among the members of the assembly. Subordinate to the president and in charge of the commune's administration is a secretary, who is appointed by the president for four years and may be reappointed.[23]

2. THE LEVEL OF DEVELOPMENT AMONG COMMUNES

The postwar evolution of Yugoslavia might be characterized as a process in which the formal center of decision making for a variety of activities, at first located at a single federal level, gradually shifted to a large number of points (the communes) which actively involved the greater mass of the population. The establishment of workers' self-government and the evolution of the communal system were the decisive instruments of this process. From a political point of view, the change can only be viewed as a beneficial and truly unique innovation in local government. The "centralist-directive" phase of the early postwar period gradually gave way to increased regional or republican autonomy, which eventually included 581 administratively independent communes; each, in theory, capable of chartering its own future progress within certain general guidelines.

As of January 1, 1963, Yugoslavia was made up of 581 *opštine* and 40 districts, as shown in Table Twenty-one. These 581 communes were the territorial and institutional basis upon which the new administrative system embodied in the April 1963 Constitution was to evolve.

Chapter Three has illustrated the use of factor analysis to arrive at a classification of fifty-five Yugoslav cities based not only on functional specialization but also upon underlying social-economic differences. The data matrix (55 × 26) was relatively small and easily manipulated. With

---

[23] For specific discussion of the functioning of one particular commune, including its organization chart, see Jack C. Fisher, "The Yugoslav Commune," *World Politics* (April, 1964), pp. 418–441.

the communes, however, we are faced with a more difficult problem. Here the number of observations and variables would far outweigh our ability to order our findings meaningfully in terms of even a few variables. But through the use of factor analysis we can produce a ranking of the communes in terms of the degrees of association or communalities among a large number of variables; thus our observations can be meaningfully arranged into a comprehensible whole.

Table Twenty-One. COMMUNES AND DISTRICTS BY REPUBLIC

	Opštine	*Districts*
Bosnia and Herzegovina	106	7
Montenegro	20	—
Croatia	111	9
Macedonia	61	6
Slovenia	66	4
Serbia	217	14

Source: *Jugoslovenski pregled*, No. 6 (Belgrade, 1963), p. 247.

Factor analysis will, as indicated in the analysis of Yugoslav cities, show which demographic and occupational variables are interrelated. Here again, the grouping of variables may suggest the varying dimensions of development. The contribution which each variable makes to any given factor can suggest which variables tend to cluster together, while the rejected variables may well be related in varying combinations to other factors.

Utilizing 1961 census data published in 1962 by the Federal Statistical Office, a data matrix comprising 611 communes and sixty-three variables was structured. Though there were 611 communes at the time of the 1961 census, they were reduced to 581 by January 1, 1963. The sixty-three variables included thirty population variables, distinguishing between total population and male population (fifteen variables), three income variables, sixteen education variables (which also distinguish between male and total population categories), and finally fourteen occupational variables. Identification of these variables is given in the first column of Table Twenty-three.

Figure 33 indicates that 87.35 percent of the total variance was accounted for by four factors which were then rotated by the varimax procedures. The chart reveals that there was a break or steep slope between successive factors, including a slight break between Factors Four and Five (the cut-off point). The varimax factor variance for the four rotated factors produced by the varimax procedures summed to 100; that is 100 percent of 87.35 percent is explained.

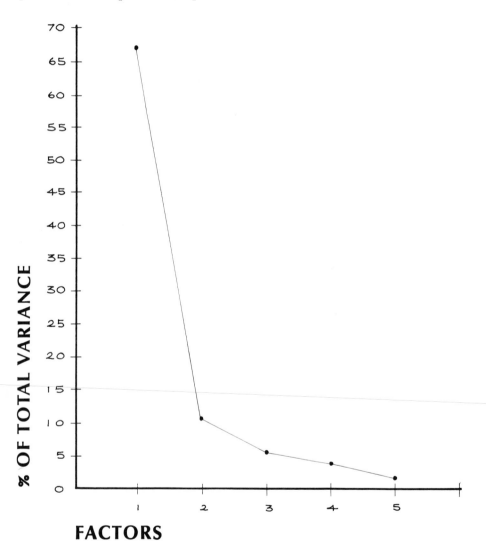

FIGURE 33. Yugoslav Communes. Variance explained by five unrotated factors.

Table Twenty-Two. Yugoslav Communes: Common Variance Explained by Rotated Factors

Factor	Eigen Value	Percent	Cumulative Percent
One	22.78	43.85	43.85
Two	9.63	18.55	62.40
Three	3.61	6.97	69.37
Four	15.91	30.63	100.00
Common variance 51.93			

Each of the 63 variables contributes towards the explained variance of each of the factors. Table Twenty-three lists the four factors derived from the analysis and those variables out of the 63 having a coefficient of at least .50 are underlined.

Table Twenty-Three. The Varimax Factor Matrix for Yugoslav Communes

Variable	Rotated Factor Loadings			
	Factor One (Urbanization)	Factor Two (Relative Development)	Factor Three (Professional)	Factor Four (Agricultural)
POPULATION				
1 Total	.50	−.47	.09	−.64
2 Age 0–4	.27	−.86	.08	−.37
3 Age 5–9	.28	−.61	.04	−.31
4 Age 10–14	.45	−.62	.10	−.57
5 Age 15–19	.50	−.61	.11	−.56
6 Age 20–24	.56	−.59	.10	−.52
7 Age 25–29	.63	−.48	.08	−.55
8 Age 30–34	.65	−.43	.07	−.58
9 Age 35–39	.69	−.26	.08	−.63
10 Age 40–44	.65	−.30	.09	−.63
11 Age 45–49	.67	−.22	.08	−.68
12 Age 50–54	.60	−.18	.07	−.76
13 Age 55–59	.47	−.16	.05	−.71
14 Age 60–64	.55	−.14	.05	−.78
15 Age 65 and over	.52	−.08	.04	−.79
MALE POPULATION				
16 Total	.56	−.54	.08	−.61
17 Age 0–4	.27	−.86	.08	−.36
18 Age 5–9	.38	−.76	.08	−.49
19 Age 10–14	.45	−.67	.09	−.55
20 Age 15–19	.50	−.61	.10	−.55

		Rotated Factor Loadings			
Variable		Factor One (Urbaniza- tion)	Factor Two (Relative Development)	Factor Three (Professional)	Factor Four (Agricul- tural)
MALE POPULATION					
21	Age 20–24	.49	−.58	.08	−.49
22	Age 25–29	.64	−.49	.10	−.52
23	Age 30–34	.66	−.43	.07	−.56
24	Age 35–39	.69	−.30	.07	−.60
25	Age 40–44	.63	−.30	.06	−.59
26	Age 45–49	.67	−.26	.07	−.64
27	Age 50–54	.60	−.25	.06	−.72
28	Age 55–59	.53	−.20	.04	−.76
29	Age 60–64	.52	−.19	.04	−.78
30	Age 65 and over	.42	−.14	.02	−.63
EDUCATION OF POPULATION					
31	Illiterate or with three years of grammar school	.01	−.80	.09	−.45
32	Four years of grammar school	.50	−.24	.04	−.79
33	Grammar school	.82	−.07	.06	−.40
34	School for qualified or highly qualified work- ers	.86	−.10	.06	−.36
35	Higher technical skill	.94	−.13	.10	−.22
36	High school (gimnazija)	.91	−.02	.11	−.12
37	Higher school	.85	−.22	.09	−.15
38	University, college, or art academy	.87	.02	.12	−.04
INCOME-NUMBER OF FAMILIES					
39	Agriculture	−.23	−.17	.04	−.86
40	Mixed income	.06	−.13	−.01	−.19
41	Nonagricultural sources	.85	−.14	.07	−.24
MALE POPULATION-EDUCATION					
42	Illiterate or first three years of grammar school	−.02	−.83	.08	−.41
43	Four years of grammar school	.37	−.40	.04	−.79

		Rotated Factor Loadings		
Variable	Factor One (Urbanization)	Factor Two (Relative Development)	Factor Three (Professional)	Factor Four (Agricultural)
44 Grammar school	.76	−.19	.06	−.46
45 School for qualified or highly qualified workers	.83	−.13	.05	−.40
46 Higher technical school	.93	−.18	.10	−.24
47 High school	.91	−.02	.12	−.15
48 Higher school	.85	−.20	.10	−.17
49 University, college, or art academy	.88	.03	.12	−.06
OCCUPATION-POPULATION				
50 Mining	.00	−.31	−.02	.02
51 Industry	.67	−.30	.03	−.36
52 Agriculture	−.28	−.40	.05	−.74
53 Forestry	−.06	−.24	.01	.05
54 Construction	.55	−.51	.08	−.17
55 Transportation	.66	−.31	.08	−.28
56 Commerce and entertainment	.82	−.18	.09	−.23
57 Handicraft	.74	−.18	.06	−.45
58 Personal service	.78	−.23	.06	−.35
59 Utilities	.09	−.09	.62	−.06
60 State administration	.21	−.07	.57	−.06
61 Cultural and scientific activities	.31	−.06	.95	−.07
62 Health and welfare	.03	−.02	.93	−.02
63 Banking and insurance	−.03	−.00	.86	.01

Source for raw data: *Stanovištvo i domaćinstva-osnovne strukture prema popisu 1961*, Statistički bilten 250 (Belgrade: Savezni zavod za statistiku, November, 1962), pp. 22–168.

Factor One—with its high scores on population size, all population age groups (including male population) over 14 years of age, all educational variables except for the illiterate category, income from nonagricultural sources, and the occupational categories of industry, construction, transportation, commerce and entertainment, handicraft, and personal service—appears to be an index of diversification and population concentration and is thus termed the factor of urbanization. Urbanization denotes, therefore, not merely population concentration but demographic, educational, and occupational diversification. The importance of the educational element may well be reflective of Yugoslavia's current stage of development or degree of modernization.

Factor Two had high scores on the young dependent age groups 0–14 and the teenage and young adult groups 15–24, including the male population categories, total male population, population with only three years of school or illiterate, and population employed in construction. This suggests that this factor, like Factor One in our urban analysis, is the young dependency age factor or an index of relative development. It is important to note that Factor Two, the development factor, is distinguished from the agricultural factor (Factor Four), suggesting that these two concepts are not necessarily spatially covariate. It is postulated that the more developed society becomes, the lower the degree of association between these two factors.

Factor Three, with high coefficients on the last five variables only, is clearly a specialized professional or tertiary component. Factor Four—the agricultural factor—has high scores on total population, all age groups over 9 years old, four years of grammar school, agricultural employment, and income from agriculture.

These four factors are clearly indicators of development, which quantitatively suggest the variance that would be found among any set of observations randomly drawn from any Yugoslav population (republics, districts, cities, or communes). These four factors, and the contribution (or weight) each makes to the explained common variance, suggest the underlying social-economic variation among Yugoslav communes, territorial-administrative units which cover the entire Yugoslav area.

		Percent
Factor One	Urbanization factor	43.85
Factor Two	Index of relative development	18.55
Factor Three	Specialized professional component	6.97
Factor Four	Agricultural factor	30.63
Total		100.00

The mixture or weight of these factors in any society suggests the level of that society in a developmental sense. Thus though Factors Two and

Four are distinct and separate, at this level of Yugoslavia's development there is a marked degree of overlap between them, as indicated in Table Twenty-Four.

Table Twenty-Four. VARIMAX FACTOR COEFFICIENTS OF SIMILARITY

Factors [1]	1	2	3	4
One	1.0			
Two	−.60	1.0		
Three	.34	−.28	1.0	
Four	−.75	.77	−.27	1.0

[1] Factors Two (index of relative development) and Four (agricultural factor) are inversely related to Factor One, the urbanization factor. The four factors do not make approximately equal contributions to the total, as was the case with the cities. Also the factors for the communes are not bi-polar, as true with the cities. This may well be the result of using percentage data for the cities rather than raw scores. (As may be recalled the major reason for adopting this procedure for the urban analysis was to avoid measuring what had already been assumed, that is, that cities of 20,000 were "urban"—it was the attributes of "urbanness" which were of interest.)

In the analysis of the communes, population size, in this case both total population (variable one) and total male population (variable sixteen) were important variables reflected by their high coefficients on Factors One, Two, and Four. This may explain the high coefficients of similarity between Factors One and Two, One and Four, and Two and Four.

Factor Three is the least significant (contributing but 6.97 percent of the total common variance) of the four factors, suggesting the low level and relatively recent expansion of tertiary activities. Since this factor makes only a small contribution to the total explained variance, for reasons of space and economy, further discussion of it has been omitted.

Due to the large number of observations, it was plausible simply to order the observations on the basis of their scores on Factor One and to indicate their score and rank for Factors Two and Four. Appendix Three lists all of the communes, ranking them on the basis of their scores on Factor One and indicating their scores and rank for Factors Two and Four. It should be noted that communes with high positive ratings on Factor One have, logically, the highest negative ratings on Factors Two and Four.

Among the 611 communes, there is a great range of scores on each of the factors: from +184 to −28 on Factor One, from +22 to −89 on Factor

Two, and from $+30$ to -141 on Factor Four. The greatest variation occurs among the most advanced communes, that is those with a high positive ranking on Factor One and therefore correspondingly high negative scores on Factors Two and Four. Factor Two, which stresses high coefficients for the young dependent age group, has the smallest variance as there are children in every commune. Factor One, the urbanization factor, has the greatest variance, which is understandable for a country at Yugoslavia's stage of development.

A casual examination reveals that the factor analysis did, in fact, identify those communes that were: (1) urban ($+$) to nonurban or rural ($-$); (2) composed of a small young dependent age group ($-$) or with larger young dependent age groups ($+$); and (3) less agricultural ($-$) to predominantly agricultural ($+$).

The list of the 611 communes and their scores on the three factors given in Appendix Three provides a rough index of Yugoslav communes in terms of urbanization (Factor One), relative development (Factor Two), and agriculture (Factor Four). As the detail available is beyond the interest of most readers only very selected examples will be discussed here. The general structure of any particular area, county, or republic can be obtained by utilizing the optimum grouping technique outline in Chapter Three. Limitation of computer capacity made it impossible to employ this technique for grouping all of the communes.

Approximately three-fourths of the communes that had positive values on Factor One, urbanization, were in Slovenia, Croatia, or northern Serbia. The remaining communes were in southern Serbia and the southern republics. As expected, all of the fifty-five cities discussed in Chapter Three had positive scores on Factor One. Most of the communes with negative scores on Factors Two and Four were in Serbia, Croatia, and Slovenia.

An example of the factor analysis output is Dalmatia, which currently corresponds to the District (*Kotar*) of Split. Figure 34 suggests the impact the various reorganizations of the local units of government had on this area. Three territorial reorganizations reduced what were seventeen districts in 1954 to five in 1955, centering on the traditional central places of the region. Finally in 1962, the five districts were reduced to one, incorporating the bulk of Dalmatia and centering on the provincial city of Split.

Table Twenty-Five orders the Dalmatian communes according to their rank on Factor One, urbanization. Their rank among the 611 communes has also been given to suggest their relative position. Scores for the Dalmatian communes on Factors Two and Four roughly approximate the same order as Factor One. The dominance of Split is evident, followed by the coastal cities of Zadar, Šibenik, and Dubrovnik. The scores of the second order communes of Sinj, Knin, Imotski, and Drniš suggest better transportation connections to the coastal area, generally focusing on Split.

Table Twenty-Five. FACTOR SCORES FOR DALMATIAN COMMUNES

Commune	*Factor One*	*Scores among 611 Communes*	*Factor Two*	*Scores among 611 Communes*	*Factor Four*	*Scores among 611 Communes*
Split	145.79	5	−77.67	3	−111.80	3
Zadar	63.98	27	−46.53	11	−60.90	18
Šibenik	52.29	33	−36.80	27	−49.96	25
Dubrovnik	35.67	·57	−14.89	94	−30.29	60
Sinj	15.10	104	−20.07	69	−22.79	83
Knin	13.81	108	−15.00	92	−17.80	101
Imotski	8.59	133	−13.53	101	−16.60	108
Drniš	1.89	174	−8.02	140	−5.87	171
Metković	−1.98	215	+2.90	263	+3.68	258
Benkovac	−3.05	223	−5.55	159	−3.20	198
Omiš	−4.50	236	+3.28	272	+4.95	271
Korčula	−8.53	284	+9.53	416	+9.70	343
Trogir	−11.03	334	+7.88	366	+11.98	389
Brač	−13.99	399	+12.58	495	+15.28	452
Makarska	−17.05	469	+14.75	551	+18.98	521
Hvar	−17.61	490	+15.16	562	+17.94	505
Biograd	−18.29	502	+12.74	500	+17.80	502
Obrovac	−20.71	538	+12.16	485	+19.56	526
Vrgorac	−21.59	560	+15.17	563	+20.57	545
Vis	−21.87	569	+18.11	599	+23.73	589
Lastovo	−28.46	611	+22.24	611	+30.67	611

The picture provided here is an excellent representation of the situation in the early 1960's prior to the completion of the new Adriatic highway as far as Split. The extreme isolation of the islands is suggested both by their relative position among the Dalmatian communes and their very low rank among all communes. It must be emphasized that the factor analysis has provided a description of the spatial integration and economic advancement of the area prior to the full impact of the "tourism revolution." The projected completion of the Adriatic highway, the proximity of the area to major European population centers, and its unusual natural advantages have destined this zone for rapid transformation of both its economy and life style. Thousands of tourists and their automobiles converge in ever-increasing numbers each year to the southernmost limits of the completed highway. From there they either take a boat south to Dubrovnik and Greece or spend their weeks of leisure north of the final extension of the highway. Relatively few tourists brave the perils of the dangerous, narrow road south. The accident rate for those who do is high. But all of this is rapidly changing. It will be most interesting to compare the pattern shown in Figure 34 with the situation in 1970.

Somewhat similar developments are taking place in another coastal region, the Istria Peninsula, at the northeast corner of the Adriatic. This area declined during the interwar period for, though Italian, it lay on the peripheral border area of two hostile states and was far from the core area of Italian economic and political life. Emigration from the peninsula was considerable. The city of Pula at the very tip of the peninsula was clearly the dominant urban center. The rest of the peninsula continued to decline until the most recent period. The factor output analysis (Table Twenty-six) provides a description of the Istria Peninsula clearly compatible with other statistical and qualitative indicators.

The coastal communes of the Istria Peninsula are located in an area of

Table Twenty-Six. FACTOR SCORES OF THE ISTRIA PENINSULA'S COMMUNES

Commune	Urbani-zation (Factor One)	Rank among the 611 Communes	Relative Develop-ment (Fac-tor Two)	Rank among the 611 Communes	Agri-culture (Factor Four)	Rank among the 611 Communes
Pula	49.11	41	−21.78	59	−31.06	58
Labin	6.97	139	−4.14	177	−8.27	154
Pazin	−9.41	301	+6.23	325	+7.22	305
Poreč	−13.60	389	+9.51	415	+11.22	381
Rovinj	−14.21	405	+11.58	473	+15.45	458
Buzet	−20.99	544	+15.95	574	+20.57	546
Buje	−21.12	549	+16.06	576	+20.98	551
Umag	−21.86	568	+17.47	592	+23.91	591
Novigrad	−27.46	610	+21.16	610	+29.32	610

Yugoslavia which will or should receive the full benefits of Western Europe's continued economic advance. If Yugoslav institutions and political philosophy allow it, the Adriatic coastal area could become a recreational and resort center of a "post-industrial," fun-seeking Western Europe. In this case the problems and potentialities of this area, like most of Dalmatia, will be distinct from those of the rest of the country.

Figure 35, in the section of oversized figures, indicates the 581 *opštine* and 40 districts as of January 1, 1963. The shaded areas reflect the lowest 20 percent of the communes according to their rank on Factor One; their scores on Factors Two and Four would provide an almost identical pattern. Though some similarity to Figure 17 (communes with less than 100,000 dinars per capita income in 1961) is evident, the major area of contrast is Serbia. The failure of Figure 35 to indicate a more underdeveloped bias for Serbia as suggested in Figure 17 is due to the territorial reorganization that took place between the time of the 1961 census and January 1, 1963. If the 1961 communal organization had been provided, Figure 35 would have shown a much higher proportion of less urbanized or less advanced communes in Serbia. Figure 35 shows the communes which scored in the lowest 20 percent on Factor One according to 1961 data and were still in existence in 1963.

In summary, political circumstance in Yugoslavia has led to the evolution of a local governmental system designed to minimize internal conflict, preserve or strengthen the state's viability, and provide a mechanism that, in theory, would facilitate the self-management of each commune along a certain path of development. The first part of this chapter has traced the formal evolution of the communal system from 1950 to a point where the political goals of the reform were administratively feasible. The second section of the chapter has discussed the socioeconomic structure of the communes. The implications of this analysis suggest certain questions about the viability of the communal system, as explicitly and formally set forth in the 1963 Constitution. Is the variation among communes not too great for balanced development to be attained? Will not economic growth continue to be concentrated in a number of economic "poles"? Even more basic, in light of such variation, how can the communal system, as formally specified in the Constitution, operate? How much variance is there between theory and practice?

3. PLANNING STRUCTURE AND ADMINISTRATIVE CHANGES

Yugoslav economist Janez Stanovnik has ideally characterized the Yugoslav economic planning process:

Today Jugoslavia has what might be called 'planned guidance' of the economy. In form the plan is comparable to an economic budget, based on an analysis of national income, as used by some countries in the West. It relies on an analysis of trends revealed in the preceding period as well as on the targets set by the National Assembly, and from these it forecasts the movements in basic economic indices over the period in view. A principal task is to bring these indices, expressed in value and not in physical terms, into mutual dependence and balance.

Accordingly, the plan provides the framework within which economic activities should develop in the future. It does this in two ways:

First, the plan makes allowance for supply and demand to modify the expected development; at the same time, it guarantees that where needed there will be compensation in other sectors, so that an advance in one sector will not be checked by a slowing-down in another. Thus the actual supply and demand do not impair the plan as they do in the case of central planning, but on the contrary help achieve the planned targets. The corrections introduced by supply and demand into the planned forecasts stem inevitably from the shortcomings of economic analysis and the manifestations of free human action.

Second, the plan provides for a number of fiscal and monetary measures designed to create a favorable climate and built-in economic stimuli for achieving desired trends.[24]

Because of the communal system and its ramifications, the system of planning in Yugoslavia is basically not comparable to that of other socialist countries. One striking contrast is the lack of a regional planning apparatus between the central planning authority and the local *opštine* (communes) or, in larger conglomerations, the city planning commissions. Activities which might be designated as "regional planning" are for the most part

---

[24] Janez Stanovnik, "Planning Through the Market—The Jugoslav Experience," *Foreign Affairs* (January, 1962), p. 255.

Velenje in Slovenia, a new town.

A new town, Velenje, in Slovenia.

conducted by the central authorities and directed to designated underdeveloped areas. The sole exceptions to this are the comprehensive territorial
studies which have been made of the former *kotars* (districts) of Krapina
and Split in the Republic of Croatia. In the Republic of Slovenia, which
lacks any semblance of a regional planning body, the need for such an
agency has been expressed in a publication of the Slovenian City Planning
Institute which discusses the theoretical nature of regional planning,
implying both its utility and its current necessity.[25] Nevertheless, it seems
apparent that true regional planning, in the sense of the comprehensive
analysis and projection of basic activities and their spatial interrelationships
within a given area, does not exist in Yugoslavia.

The Yugoslav administrative system evolved under the influence of
socialist philosophy within the complexity of a multinational state having
extreme physical, economic, and social variation, and a geographic location
that allowed for greater flexibility in international affairs than was possible
for the other East European countries. Three factors contributed to the
evolution of Yugoslavia's particular planning system:

1. Strong regional demands for independent action reinforced by a
federal system which always implied, in theory, a measure of self-determination for each republic.

2. The extreme underdevelopment of a large part of the country forced
the federal government to make most investment decisions for these areas.
This was not only necessary to achieve minimum economic goals, but since
these areas lacked an adequate resource base, the federal government had
to "channel" funds to the underdeveloped areas from more advanced
republics.

3. The poor professional quality of most "planners" immediately after
the war necessitated that students be trained at the two poles of the
process: national economic planning and city planning. Regional planning
to this date does not exist as a professional discipline, nor are there any
university training programs in regional planning.

In recent years, Yugoslavia has attempted to induce individual factories
and communes to move toward greater independence in development

[25] *Osnove regionalnega in urbanističnega planiranja*, Urbanistični Inštitut L. R.
Slovenije (Ljubljana, 1962).

decisions and to involve greater numbers of the population in the decision-making process. Politically, this has had the effect of restraining the so-called "nationality problem" and more or less justifying the precarious existence side-by-side of developed and underdeveloped areas. The total impact of communal "independence" was only recently felt, and economically very serious problems were raised. Federal legislation in late 1964 and 1965 attempted to curb the commune's investment capacity and eliminate the weaknesses in the system that became apparent during 1963 and early 1964.

Since both the individual industrial enterprise, governed by its workers' council, and the territorial unit of local government, the commune, are in theory independent of direct administrative control, the question could logically be raised as to how the entire system operates.

At the time of the adoption of the new constitution in April, 1963, the following situation was clearly implied:

1. The constitutional structure provided a legal framework for direct citizen participation in the work of the commune. In theory, the citizen participates in the political process as both producer and consumer.

2. There is a desire to ensure a minimum standard of social services throughout the country, even though quantitatively and comparatively this has never been clearly defined. This means, in effect, that those communes with an insufficient resource base will be provided with outside funds to finance minimum standards of schooling, health facilities, and the like.

3. Nevertheless, though there was a definite policy of financial assistance to underdeveloped communes, the level of services—above some theoretical minimum—was to be dependent upon the economic capacity of the individual commune, thus providing an inducement for greater productivity and local investment.

There remains, however, one additional assumption which has been referred to only briefly here and is discussed even more vaguely in Yugoslavia: that the general direction of economic and social development must be in harmony with the over-all policies of the "wider social community." If the system of controls emanating from above is not taken into account, then the communal system cannot be understood. Kardelj has asserted that:

There is no self-government and freedom without responsible organized *social control* to determine that each actually lives within the framework of his rights and not at the expense of others, and second, there is no self-government without centralization and good organization of those functions that by nature must be centralized. We have always maintained, and today it is no less important to state, that for us neither centralization nor decentralization in and of itself is an absolutely good or an absolutely bad thing. . . . It is impossible to combat bureaucratic centralism successfully if we do not fight against particularist bureaucracy. What is more, there is no doubt that the society that allows the debauchery of particularist bureaucracy in its enterprises and communes will end with the victory of bureaucratic centralism in the republic and federation. The simple truth must never be forgotten that society is a living organism, and that in its organization each organ should have its own established function.[26]

"It is true," Kardelj has written elsewhere,

that supervision or control is a necessary thing. Without social control and inspection it is not possible to ensure a single system or the healthy development of our community. . . . It is in this manner that the basic activity of the League of the Communists of Yugoslavia, the Socialist Alliance of Working People, the Trade Union Alliance of Yugoslavia, etc., should develop. If we but think this way, there will be no difficulty in finding an adequate solution for the mechanism of social supervision.[27]

Two types of control, therefore, were seen as necessary: (1) control by the commune over local institutions and economic organizations, (2) supervision by the republican and federal government to ensure compliance with central policies.

How can the higher administrative organs ensure that their policies and regulations are carried out by the "independent communes"? What methods can they employ, when the entire spirit of the Constitution stresses the independence of the commune and the dependence of higher

---

[26] Edvard Kardelj, "Iz Ekspozea na sednici Savezne Narodne Skupštine od 28. Maja 1962 godine," *Materijali o statutima opština* (Belgrade, 1962), p. 105.

[27] Edvard Kardelj, "Komuna i prednacrt našeg novog Ustava," *Opština u novom ustavnom sistemu*, Materijali sa godisnje skupštine Stalne konferencije gradova Jugoslavije, Titograd, 1–3, XI, 1962 (Belgrade, 1961), p. 20.

organs on it? From observation, it is apparent that there are three ways in which control or pressure is being applied: (1) directly on the commune, by the Socialist Alliance of Working People; (2) on all investors, by the investment and credit policy outlined in the annual federal plan and directed by the Federal Planning Commission and the banking establishment; and (3) on industrial and other organizations, by the Trade Union and the Economic Chamber.

The policies followed and positions taken by the Socialist Alliance and the Trade Union, and the entire investment pattern, centrally determined in Belgrade, are the major source of indirect control and supervision. It should be noted that we are referring to social and political policy involving investment and developmental positions, not supervision that ensures compliance with overt public laws or affects the determination of economic or criminal offenses. These institutions act, or are expected to act, as counterforces to the localist or particularist positions and interests of the voters' meeting, the local community, the enterprise, and the commune.

The principal purpose of Yugoslav economic planning is long-range growth; short-range development is considered as a by-product. There are five types of policy instruments at the disposal of central planners: (1) fiscal instruments, (2) credit instruments, (3) price instruments, (4) wage instruments, and (5) foreign trade instruments. The major regulatory agencies for these controls are the banks, especially the National Investment Bank which, since it influences the allocation of approximately half of total investment funds, has great influence.

The institutional role of the Party, except in times of declared crisis or danger, might be described as "actively passive." The local Party cells seldom take a direct stand on specific proposals, but individual members are expected to argue the "merits" of the question under discussion. The cell may thus be described as a latent, but not inactive, force ready to be called upon should the need arise. Its role may be explained in part by the following factors: (1) the genuine measures against Party monopoly that were taken during the 1950's; (2) the lack of Party discipline on the local levels, coupled with the common tendency for local loyalties to prevail— reinforced, of course, by a system that focuses allegiance on the Party organizations of the individual republics,[28] the Party's tendency to retain its tactical advantage by never actually taking an overt position on a concrete proposal and thus always being in a position to arbitrate, without previous formal commitment; and (4) the fact that the complete monopoly of power exercised by the Party during the early postwar period is no longer necessary. This monopoly can formally be shared with other organizations —of its own making—without in any way undercutting the Party's over-all security.

The new system originally encouraged the basic organ to local government, the commune, to work out its own development plans in conformity with policies laid down by the federal government. The pressures for the most part were not direct, not administrative in the classical Communist sense; they were indirect, often exerted by local citizens following the guidelines of the above-mentioned social-political organizations.

---

[28] For an example of the most recent political crisis in which opposing positions were expressed by the different republican Parties, see Jack C. Fisher, "The Reconstruction of Skopje," *Journal of the American Institute of Planners*, XXX (February, 1964), pp. 46–48.

"The Macedonians have insisted, despite the structural nature of the ground, that Skopje be rebuilt on the same site. This decision, made well before any reliable research had been completed, was apparently the result of a sentimental wish to maintain the historic site of the Republic's capital. It is assumed that the buildings will be more substantial (steel frames and reinforced concrete) than in the past. There are two separate schools of thought in regard to Skopje's reconstruction. The Macedonians insist that the new city must be a direct continuation of the old. They demand a layout at least equal in size to the former area, or even more extensive, for a population between 220,000 and 300,000. The second position—the Yugoslav, meaning that of the federal government and some of the other republics—argues for a definite limitation to the city's size and function. One concrete proposal is that the city's size be no greater than 150,000 and that the "oriental" characteristics of the city be eliminated—that the gypsies, Albanians, and Turks be transferred to other areas of the Macedonian Republic. These elements of the population add still further economic and social strain to the city. The majority were not actively employed, but subsisted completely or in part through the financial allowance made by the state for each child in a family.

"The Macedonian position can best be understood as the typical desire of an underdeveloped nation to have maximum development on one site, initially without regard to the outlying provinces.

"The second approach argues for a more mature and relatively complex solution. It maintains that Skopje must be viewed within the entire regional complex of the Republic, and specifically that the nearby cities of Tetovo (27 miles from Skopje), Kumanovo (22 miles), and Titov Veles (33 miles) must receive greater emphasis than in the past. All these cities are easily accessible to Skopje." *Ibid.*, p. 48.

It appears that after the enactment of the new Constitution of April 1963 many Yugoslav authorities became aware of the economic problems such a system, carried to its logical conclusion, could create. It is clear that 135.9 square miles and 15,000 people, the average size of the commune in 1961, is in most cases far too small a unit for effective planning.[29] The establishment of a new flour mill or paper factory in one commune will have an effect on materials, personnel, and transport well beyond the commune's boundaries. In 1963 the trend appeared to be towards the stimulation of intercommunal cooperation in joint projects of mutual interest. This cooperation appeared to be both uncoordinated and ineffective; there was a need for some higher recognizable source of authority and arbitration.[30]

In early 1964 one of the Chambers of the Federal Parliament reviewed the existing economic system and made certain recommendations, which became the basis for subsequent legislation:

. . . Despite the great successes which have been attained to date, the development of social-economic relations has lagged behind the needs of our current level of social and economic development. The deficiency exists particularly in the areas of economic growth and foreign trade, where a significant portion of these activities are still dependent upon the decisions of administrative and political organs. The mutually conflicting relations between prices and the strong emphasis on administrative measures, produced disparities among various economic sectors, delayed implementation of the principal of distribution according to work, and held the producer to a lower rate of

---

[29] Approximately one-half of the communes have an area between 77.2 to 231.7 square miles and only 118 or around 20 percent have between 115.8 and 154.4 square miles. There are also certain communes with areas as small as three and seven square kilometers. On the other hand, some (in the mountain areas of Bosnia and Herzegovina and Montenegro) have areas far above the average (for example, the commune of Nikšić has 797.3 square miles).

[30] The Federal Secretary for Legislation has stated that "attempts towards the further advancement of intra-communal cooperation must be based on securing truly independent working organizations and the emancipation of economics from politics. To achieve cooperation it is necessary to adjust both laws and other regulations, which to date, have often hindered the integration movement.

"Insofar as there is a rapid elimination of the so-called territorialization of capital," he said, "so that we facilitate its freer circulation, it can be expected that economic laws will positively influence intracommunal cooperation . . . Only when we attain the situation in which social capital from developed communes is unrestrictedly circulated even to underdeveloped communes without fear that there it will be lost, can one be sure that intracommunal cooperation has achieved its goals!" *Borba* (Zagreb), May 29, 1964.

growth. This resulted in a high degree of intervention by the Federation in the form of restrictions, premiums, etc., which, in reality, was simply a tax-hold on the funds of economic organizations. All this delayed the further development of social self-management, of increased production and labor productivity. These deficiencies were manifested in unstable sources of revenue and inadequate administrative methods for financing social services, especially in the insufficiently developed areas. All this among other things conditioned the relatively slow development of self-management in social services.[31]

The Parliamentary Report of April, 1964, recommended that measures be taken to change the total distribution of public funds in favor of working organizations and to increase the share of personal income in the national product.

Since the "independence" of each commune in pursuing its own development policies depends, obviously, on the income at its disposal, the communes attempted to increase their monetary resource base at any cost.[32] Many communes have actively fought against "economic integration," that is, the consolidation of a number of separate factories into one firm. The reason has been concern for income from taxation; initially the commune, in which the administrative headquarters of the firm was located, had taxation rights on all branches of the firm. This policy was later altered so that place of an individual's residence became the taxation criteria rather than place of work. Numerous other measures, however, were utilized in attempts to secure or preserve communal ascendancy. Communes have systematically attempted to increase their income through a variety of taxation measures aimed at the factory's profits. Often there were so many

---

[31] "Rezolucija o osnovnim smernicama za dalji razvoj našeg privrednog sistema," Prilog uz *Dnevnik* (Belgrade, 1964).

[32] The President of the Permanent Conference of Cities stated that: "For the communes, according to the present system of creating funds, it was most important to have as many commercial and industrial organizations as possible, operating without a loss, but also without any regard to their general profitability, economy, productivity, and the level of personal income attained. For if the commune had working organizations there would be sources for its investment fund, and if there were no factories, there would be none . . . Such policies resulted in an extensive development of the economy. The communes invested in many new factories while old enterprises continued to use worn out equipment.

"I consider that working organizations, rather than some kind of communal investment group or other agencies outside of the economic organizations and the economy, should be investors not only for expansion and modernization of existing facilities but also in new capacity." *Borba* (Zagreb), May 8, 1964.

communal taxes and various obligatory funds cutting into an enterprise's profit "that when each had come for his there was nothing left for the factory but the pocket." [33] Federal legislation in late 1964 allowed the firm greater freedom in the distribution of its income, eliminated a variety of different taxes (by reducing the commune's income); this in essence shifted major investment authority from the commune to the individual factory. The commune's investment jurisdiction was limited to so-called noneconomic investments, that is, to schools, housing, utilities, and the like. Even if many of the problems which developed during 1963 and 1964 are eliminated, there will still be no authority to coordinate investment alternatives and conduct adequate territorial or regional planning.

Over the last few years the belief has evolved that each commune had to fight actively to insure its share of the total pie. This situation was well described by Vladimir Bakarić:

I have at home a great amount of material which in general states that Belgrade has this and Zagreb doesn't, that certain republics are held back by the low prices of agricultural products, which enables other republics to obtain a high degree of accumulation or profit. Another republic suffers from the low prices of raw materials and semi-furnished goods, Croatia is "injured" by the Federation in that a great part of its earnings or profits are invested in other areas, another area is injured in a similar manner, etc. All begin to bring the Federation to account for damages incurred during the past year, so that one might ask the following question: Who does receive something in Yugoslavia, if we are all "plundered?" [34]

In the summer of 1964 the Federal Parliament discontinued certain legislation providing selective supplementary funds to communes from local sources. This action hit at the very center of the commune's ability to chart its own over-all development course. A number of factors had led to this drastic measure. First, the communes had been increasing the funds at their disposal by legislative fiat at the expense of the local factories. This in effect increased the investment capacity of the communes while decreasing

---

[33] *Borba* (Zagreb), July 4, 1964. For another example of this see: *Borba* (Belgrade), September 24, 1964, for an article entitled, "Illegal Collection by Communes." "The County Assembly of Ljubljana insists that communes return to utility and other service organizations contributions and taxes to which the communes had no right."

[34] *Borba* (Belgrade), September 22, 1964.

that of industrial economic organizations. Another factor was the procedure known in Yugoslavia as "the territorialization of funds." Each
commune held onto its own financial resources jealously and engaged in
sharp competition with neighboring communes in a manner reminiscent of
the competition among municipalities within the same metropolitan area.
One commune, for example, passed a regulation forbidding the sale of any
cigarettes other than those locally produced. Communal investment policy
seemed to be concerned with increasing the number of operating factories
within their territory rather than improving the efficiency of existing
ones.

Vojo Rakić, Director of the Federal Planning Commission, in an
interview with the editor of the journal, *Komuna*, has provided a most
interesting and enlightened discussion of past problems and of the future
trends which may be expected as a result of recent federal legislative
action:

. . . it appears to some that all the communes will not be in the same situation
and that those communes which are less developed, whose economic capacity is
less, will find it more difficult under the new system than communes with
developed economies. Without regard to development, it appears to me that
everywhere both the function and funds of communes will be strengthened.
True, some communes which depended on major outside sources of funds from
higher social-political communities, will find themselves in a somewhat different position. But there will not be a decrease in outside funds, insofar as there is
a real sound economic need. On the contrary, outside funds may increase. In
essence there will be a "de-territorialization of funds" which will effect not
only the social-political communities as special organs which distribute such
funds, but the economy as a whole. Specifically, the investment funds under the
new conditions are not "outside" funds, but ought to move more in the
direction of those activities and areas where they will have the greatest effect.

The heart of the question is not whether outside funds will exist or not, but
that distribution will occur by another mechanism, will go through different
channels than it has to date: not on the basis of the decisions of political organs,
but on the basis of economic mechanisms and criteria, first of all within the
framework of the credit system. Certainly some communes which rely on
initial investment and resources from public credit, with a small contribution
from their own funds, will find that they must provide a larger share of money
or face a more difficult situation, in the sense that they will not be sufficiently
competitive and capable to attract outside resources. But the system will not

exclude ordered investment when it is in the public interest that some areas should be developed or some rational project realized, for which public funds can best be utilized. The existence of funds for the development of under-developed areas, so to speak, is still one such institution in our system which is able to insure the flow of resources to such areas.[35]

According to the criteria described by Rakić, the North should receive the largest proportion of capital investment as that area is the most efficient in terms of return on investments. Certainly selected key projects should be supported in the underdeveloped areas. Most decisive of all, however, is the realization that the compartmentalization of funds by commune cannot continue, that not all communes can experience an equal degree of development, and that increased specialization and differentiation must occur.

---

[35] "Ekonomske funcije komune u novim uslovima," *Komuna* (July, 1964), p. 6.

Panorama of Konjic, a town at the border of Bosnia and Herzegovina.

4. THE ECONOMIC CORE

The "Economic Core" of Yugoslavia would appear to include Slovenia, northern Croatia, Vojvodina, and northern Serbia centering around Belgrade. The northern portion of Bosnia and Herzegovina is located in direct proximity to these areas and has terrain conditions that would facilitate incorporation into the Core. The Core thus defined includes the major industrial centers and highly productive agricultural areas of the country. It is suggested that future investment in economic development, both agricultural and industrial, should be made where earnings and therefore returns are highest, that is, in the Economic Core.[36]

---

[36] Only the broadest investment priorities are suggested in this discussion. In reality each activity or set of activities must be analyzed individually. It is important that regional studies be undertaken which include analysis of the competitive advantages among regions for each industrial sector or activity mix.

For example, it would appear that there are three major potential zones of tourism in Yugoslavia, each with different recreational possibilities, and therefore each requiring a different investment and development plan. It should be emphasized that this discussion refers to but one sector of the individual region's economy and not the total economy which, for example, in the case of Slovenia is highly diversified and tourism's contribution is relatively minor.

The Republic of Slovenia should be developed as a winter and summer mountainous resort area emphasizing skiing, hiking, and hunting. Second, a broad zone across Montenegro, southern Serbia, and Macedonia should be planned and preserved as a "wilderness" area for the West European tourist market. These areas should be similar to American "wilderness areas" or national parks, developed with camp sites and access roads that will preserve the "wild" and untouched quality of the area. As Western Europe, including Italy, becomes more and more of a standardized commercial tourist region, the existence of a large area similar to New York State's Catskills or Adirondacks in close proximity to major European population centers where it is still possible to "rough it" will be a profitable asset.

The coastal area, or "Zone of Rapid Transformation" as it could be termed, should receive, at the moment, the most careful attention and the highest investment priorities. This zone must equal Western Europe, especially Italy, in the quality and variety of its facilities if Yugoslavia is to compete in the years to come for Western European and American luxury-minded tourists. Much more than a highway and hotel is necessary to create a first-class tourist attraction. If the investment priorities suggested in the above discussion are exploited, Yugoslavia has the capacity today to capitalize on the "amenities" or rich potentials of its physical landscape and geographic location.

The Core Area is the most likely zone for accelerated economic growth. Investment should be made where it will have the greatest impact and provide the highest return. Clearly the Core Area is the most likely zone. Here labor productivity is high, and can be expected to increase faster than that of the rest of the country; and the production output will be standardized, of better quality, and thus better able to compete for West European and world markets. The "earnings" of the Core should not be utilized to create competing and less effective industrial plants in the South. Given the capital outlay that has been made there in the postwar period, investment should be concentrated in social overhead that will advance the most important of all resources—people—and act as a gradual inducement to northern capital through the creation of improved utilities, housing, and transportation networks. In this way the economic and educational status of the population will gradually be improved, and in conjunction with limited but economically effective investments, the over-all economy of the South will rise in harmony with a general uplifting of the population.

It must be very clearly stated that development viewed within this framework does not in any way preclude economic growth in the South. It does, however, eliminate forced or artificial investment. A Fund for Underdeveloped Regions does exist, and (as suggested by Rakić) can provide money for selected projects in the South. The criteria for selection, however, should increasingly be geared to a realistic appraisal of projects in terms of capital outlay and expected return.

The South in and of itself, however, should become an attractive area for northern investment. This development can be stimulated by utilizing local resources (as well as outside funds) for social overhead investments (roads, school, utilities, etc.) which will make the area more attractive to northern investment. There are four major reasons for northern capital to find the South desirable for investment:

1. The increasingly higher wage structure of the North might well induce northern firms to look carefully at the possibility of plant expansion in the South.[37]

---

[37] The Yugoslav average monthly [March] salary in March 1964 was 31,200 dinars, 4,600 dinars above the 1963 average. The highest average salary continued to be in Slovenia which had 40,300 dinars, and the lowest in Macedonia, with 27,000 dinars.

2. Northern firms, operating within a limited market economy, are now attempting to increase their market area. This can often be accomplished by establishing new branches in the South.

3. It must never be forgotten that the South contains a wide variety of natural resources, especially forestry and mineral reserves, which will attract direct investment.

4. The moral significance or political value of contributing to the economic progress of the country's less fortunate areas is clearly another inducement factor.

By providing the framework or conditions that will stimulate northern investment in the South, one of the most essential requirements of over-all national growth is secured; a gradual integration of the entire economy.

It appears that the "Sava Axis" the backbone of the Economic Core, between Belgrade, Zagreb, and Ljubljana (graphically portrayed in Figure 16) is the vital heart of the country. Expansion of transportation networks outward from the Sava Axis would serve to hasten the spatial integration of the entire country. Emphasis on social overhead investment in the South would stimulate a flow of capital to move south from the Economic Core to a population educationally and attitudinally motivated to make the maximum use of it. The major flow of goods from the northern industrial centers would continue to move north. Expensive projects such as the Bar-Belgrade railroad and the expansion of the port of Bar may serve political expediency, but clearly not economic advancement—either of the under-developed areas or of the country as a whole.

In short, the political integration of Yugoslavia must be synonymous with the country's economic integration. The Yugoslav goal has been to obtain integration by means of a system of controlled differences or ordered local diversity under an indirect mechanism of federal supervision. The initial or preparatory phase of the process was from 1950 to 1955. After 1955 the emphasis shifted to the local political-territorial units, the communes. The communes took their newly defined roles too literally and development plans were little more in reality than fiscal instruments of communal administration. A realistic assessment of local resources balanced

---

Croatia, with 32,500, was above the Yugoslav average, followed by Bosnia and Herzegovina with 29,400, Serbia with 28,800, and Montenegro with 28,200. *Borba* (Belgrade), June 20, 1964.

against potential demand, either local or regional, was lacking. Investment funds became compartmentalized or "territorialized" in the hands of administrative and political bodies. Communal taxes increased communal resources at the expense of local economic enterprises. The drawbacks of this situation became manifest during 1963 and 1964.

In late 1964 and early 1965 "dominance" or control of capital investment decisions shifted from the commune to industrial and commercial enterprises. It should be emphasized that this shift made the local enterprises independent of local political organs, but subject to the control of the federal agencies and programs previously described. Essentially the federal government's control of credit was the decisive instrument. Elimination of this one portion of the commune's taxation base placed Yugoslav communes in much the same position as American municipalities. At present, "autonomous" commercial and industrial enterprises make their own investment decisions, while local (communal) administration is expected to improve the over-all climate and attractiveness of the area for business expansion. Communal investment is limited to noneconomic or social overhead items such as roads, schools, and utilities.

The postwar period has witnessed an attempt by the Yugoslavs to achieve political viability as well as economic development. The recognized failures of the Soviet system and the assumed philosophical inconsistencies of capitalism, coupled with the country's internal regional variation, compelled the Yugoslavs to seek a new development path. The country's unique historical evolution and the play of international events produced a political response to regional variation in harmony with the country's economic, cultural, and social characteristics.

An attempt was made to restrict conflict and insure progress by inducing mass participation of the country's citizens in both their local administrative organs and the governing institutions of the enterprise in which they worked. Though politically successful, at least in terms of administrative decentralization, it appears that local administrative autonomy was secured at the expense of economic efficiency. The reforms of 1964 were expected to reestablish the balance through a rigorous separation of economic investments from other forms of investment. Only the future can tell if the scales have been set accurately or whether the underlying centrifugal forces are too strong to be controlled by these measures.

Conclusion

The preceding pages have attempted to set the basic framework necessary to an understanding of Yugoslavia's development pattern and accompanying administrative system. This background comprises the building blocks essential to an understanding of the country. Unfortunately, this study must end with many of the most interesting questions remaining unanswered or at best vaguely sketched out. Hopefully, a foundation has been laid for more detailed studies into the relationship between administrative policy and economic goals.

Marked regional variation and a strong political desire for "socialist" institutions stimulated the evolution of a unique administrative mosaic which though institutionally uniform throughout the country is substantively diverse from place to place in response to varying historical traditions, social values, and levels of development. The country was in 1945, and is in 1965, run by one party, the Communist Party. There has been in the intervening years, however, a distinct shift toward increased mass participation in the decision-making structure of both local sociopolitical units and economic enterprises. This attempt to create a compromise between Western democratic institutional traditions and proletarian dictatorship lies at the root of Yugoslavia's postwar institutional development. Visible party intervention in local affairs has receded more and more into the background; party members have assumed or are expected to assume a new role of guidance, stimulation, and suggestion rather than direction or administrative intervention. The concept of "self-management" of one's enterprises evolved in part to stimulate increased motivation toward one's work through a collective structure to which each could identify in contrast to reliance on individual motivation induced under conditions characteristic of capitalism.

The general development of the communal system along with the role of the local association (*mesne zajednice*) leads me at present to the tentative conclusion that we may well be witnessing the evolution in Yugoslavia of the basic institutional forms of government anticipated for an assumed vaguely and variously defined state of "full communism"—a theoretical stage of society's development achieved after the transition from socialism. Recent statements by Yugoslav officials and the existence of similar institutional forms in other socialist countries makes this a subject deserving further study and explanation.

What is the role of the republic under the communal system? Owing to the existing disparity in economic and natural resources, the republic acts today as a cushion between local needs and federal policy. At this stage of economic development, the republic has a vital coordinating role. Republican ordinances interpret federal law for the specific economic and social realities of the communes. The stress, as underlined in the Constitution, is on a uniform administrative system allowing for varying levels of economic development and social standards.

In view, however, of the projected development of the communal system, one might question the future role of the republics. The predominant role of the *opština* under the Constitution has, in theory, if not yet in fact, lessened the republic's importance. The squeeze on the republics is manifested in two directions: ". . . on the one hand, by the rights of the Federation and, on the other, by the rights of municipalities [communes] as basic autonomous units . . . The republic executive council and the republic administrative bodies have lost the right of control over the legality of municipal and district decisions enjoyed earlier." [1] In view of this de-emphasis of the republics, one can foresee, theoretically, the time when the commune and its subcommunal institutions could emerge as the ultimate administrative forms under the post-socialist stage of "full communism."

A uniform administrative system, the communal system, is the means by which political and social integration was expected to take place since 1963. Thus to the potential list of items that will be absent under the vaguely assumed and variously defined state of full communism must be added the republics, and at the head of the list. Though it is politically too explosive a matter to be actively discussed today, the commune offers an institutional means by which to ease out the republic gradually, while subrepublic autonomy is encouraged.

It must be emphasized that a fundamental change in approach evolved between 1956–1963 period, whose philosophy was manifested in the April 1963 Constitution, and secondly, the period which elapsed since the Constitution's adoption. The first period stressed an approach toward integration based upon institutional standardization and local administrative autonomy. Thus territorialization of the country developed with major powers and responsibilities, political, administrative, and economic, placed in the hands of local bodies directly responsible to local political authority under indirect federal control and supervision. This approach led, however, to a number of negative tendencies. As it was found during the initial postwar period that cultural self-determination without increased local administrative authority was meaningless so it is now realized that economic integration must precede further development of local autonomy and well before social integration can be expected to take place.

The philosophy underlying the evolution of the country between 1956 and 1963 was that each commune had the right, in theory, to expect a living standard comparable with the most advanced areas of the country. This implied that the earnings of the advanced North should be properly channeled to the South. Furthermore it was stipulated that economic

---

[1] Hamdija Cemerlic, "Relations between the Federation and Its Constituent Units in the Socialist Federal Republic of Yugoslavia," *Third Yugoslav-American Seminar* (Zadar, 1963), pp. 21, 23.

development must occur without significant interrepublic migration (in large part due to ethnic differences) which suggested by implication that an equal distribution of agricultural and industrial activities, proportional to population distribution, was necessary for each of the basic regional divisions of the country. This obviously was, if not impossible, certain to produce inefficiency.

The period since April, 1963, witnessed the gradual development of a new policy of decentralization which stipulated that each republic or commune should develop its economy in accordance with existing natural, financial, and local resources with only moderate and reasonable support from external (federal and republic) institutions. Federal investments (which are viewed as political) are to decrease. Local enterprises were given greater discretion in disposal of surplus and greater access to capital, independent of local political and administrative bodies. The new policy of restricting interregional capital transfers appears to be an improvement or a stimulus to reinvestment where both surplus and returns can be expected to be higher—in the North. The fund for financing the economic development of underdeveloped republics and regions will insure that capital continues to be made available, on a competitive basis, to the South.

One of the basic conclusions of the analysis was that classification of the cities by means of factor analysis, utilizing occupational and demographic variables, produced a regionalization of the country into the traditional north-south dichotomy which corresponds to the regions of traditional foreign domination. That is, despite economic development and increased urbanization, the cities have preserved their relative positions. The analysis of the communes and of housing quality produced the same conclusion. It is clear that the new economic reforms will only increase regional differences in economic development. This is a fundamental fact that must be realized and accepted within the country. But by stimulating the North to advance unimpeded now, the entire country will profit tomorrow. The viability of the State depends upon the incorporation of this philosophy into practice; there has been little evidence to indicate its acceptance to this date.

Journey-to-Work around Selected Cities

In April, 1957, the Federal Statistical Office, at the request of the Federal Planning Commission, made a special survey of daily migration or journey-to-work for seventy-five urban settlements ("urban" as defined by the Federal Statistical Office). Over 60 percent of the total labor force was included in the survey. This survey indicated that 16.3 percent of the actively employed population in Yugoslavia journeyed from their place of residence in an outlying surburban settlement to work in a central city and back each day. The corresponding figures for the individual republics were: Serbia, 18.8 percent; Croatia, 18.1 percent; Slovenia, 17.9 percent; Bosnia and Herzegovina, 25.4 percent; Macedonia, 3.8 percent; and Montenegro, 22.4 percent. One conclusion of the survey was that the larger the share or proportion of industry in a city's economy, in most cases, the larger was the number of people commuting to the city from its immediate hinterland. Table Eight indicated those cities that had the largest percent of their actively employed population engaged in industry.

Almost all of these cities have more than 30 percent of their total labor force commuting each day.

Utilizing the data available in the *Statistički bilten 101* of November, 1957, issued by the Federal Statistical Office, an attempt was made to create a simple model that would explain the spatial pattern of daily migration around selected urban centers and, in effect, suggest by implication the gravitational, tributary, or trade area of the central city. The following definition applies ". . . 'trade area,' is used to designate a more extended territory of city influence . . . a city's trade area may be defined . . . as 'the surrounding geographical territory economically tributary to a city and for which such city provides the chief market and financial center.' " [1] For each of the 48 central cities, the following information was provided:

> the name of the outlying center and the number of workers commuting to the central city each day;
> population of each outlying settlement in 1948 and 1953;
> each outlying town's agricultural labor force and the number of people actively engaged in nonagricultural activities.

Distance traveled could, of course, be computed, as the name of each outlying center was given.

After initial experimentation it was found that regression analysis of the commuting habits of several cities in Yugoslavia yields considerable information. By altering the number of independent variables nine different regressions were run for each selected city. Two regression combinations appeared to provide the best results. The first used the percent of the labor force in each outlying center which commutes as the dependent variable, while the independent variables were (1) population of the suburban town and (2) the percentage of the labor force engaged in agriculture. The second regression model used the same dependent variable and the same independent variables with the addition of two more independent variables. These were (1) distance from the central city and (2) total labor force of the outlying town.

The correlation coefficients for the second analysis were only slightly

---

[1] R. D. McKenzie, *The Metropolitan Community* (New York: McGraw-Hill, 1933) p. 84.

higher than for the first. This is best explained by two factors. First, labor force and total population are closely related so that the addition of labor force to the analysis did not in every case explain more than could be learned by considering population size alone. Secondly, distance from the central city to the outlying town does not appear to be equated usually with any of the other variables. Consequently, it explains little that was not already known. It is the quality of the means of transportation that is important. Subsequent study has shown that by simply estimating the "quality" of the means of transportation and assigning a number from 1 to 5, a significant improvement in the explained variance for larger cities occurs.

The regression coefficients for each of the cities selected for discussion here were as follows (see Table I-1 for explanation of each variable):

Zagreb
$$Y = 84.5901 + .0161X_1 - .0785X_2 - .3344X_3 - .1680X_4 \qquad (r^2 = .41)$$
Bor
$$Y = 41.3120 - .0201X_1 + .0090X_2 - .2627X_3 - .2435X_4 \qquad (r^2 = .98)$$
Niš
$$Y = 48.4572 - .0114X_1 + .0147X_2 - .3729X_3 - .0811X_4 \qquad (r^2 = .95)$$
Belgrade
$$Y = 19.1015 - .0055X_1 + .0044X_2 - .0634X_3 - .1626X_4 \qquad (r^2 = .47)$$

In an attempt to present the pattern of migration for selected cities the "expected" commuting value for each outlying town was subtracted from the "actual" or observed value. The difference or "residual" was then mapped; see Figures A-1, A-2, A-3, and A-4. In other words, in terms of the variables employed, which outlying centers had more or fewer people commuting to work in the central city each day than expected? Is the resulting pattern comprehensible in comparison with other known factors? Figures A-1 through A-4 present the "residuals from regression" for Zagreb, Belgrade, Bor, and Niš. In each case the resulting pattern appears logically to explain the flow of workers into the central city and, in fact, to suggest the actual tributary area of the central city itself.

The raw data, the expected values, and the residuals from regression for Zagreb are presented in Table I-1. The regression yielded a multiple correlation coefficient of .64. Distance was insignificant, as some suburbs close to, and some far from, the city exhibited negative residuals. The pattern of the residuals (see Figure A-1) does correspond with other information. Directly north of Zagreb, where there are large positive residuals, is the most densely populated area in the country. A railroad to this area has long provided an opportunity for laborers to commute to Zagreb's industrial plants. The town of Samobor, due west of Zagreb, was connected in 1940 by a new highway system which triggered increased commuting. The areas south and east of Zagreb lie for the most part on low swampy land of the Sava flood plain, where adequate transportation has never existed. Thus physical restraints and the quality of the transportation system appear to influence heavily the pattern of daily commuting to the central city. The regional structure presented by Figure A-1 conforms well with estimates of Zagreb's immediate tributary area.

Table I-1. Raw Data and Regression Output for Zagreb [1]

Multiple Correlation Coefficient $= .64$; $r^2 = .41$

Residual	$\hat{Y}$	Outlying town	Y	X_1	X_2	X_3	X_4
−14.9	48.9	Brdovec	34	703	367	44	20
+24.6	46.3	Donja Pušća	71	403	216	72	22
−.6	38.6	Donja Zdenčina	38	712	328	84	21
+44.0	55.9	Donja Stubica	100	839	427	15	21
−4.3	31.3	Dugo Selo	27	2074	933	29	21
−2.4	35.4	Galgovo	33	748	419	75	19
−12.4	39.4	Horvati	27	1191	618	39	16
−18.9	59.9	Klanjec	41	545	254	23	34
−9.2	51.2	Krapina	42	1653	643	7	42
−17.4	27.4	Jastrebarsko	10	2529	1089	23	27
−26.7	49.7	Sesvete	23	1115	556	21	12
+1.4	39.3	Strmec	41	477	268	89	11
+27.3	−3.3	Samobor	24	4665	1990	9	21
+2.0	14.9	Veliko Trgovišće	17	1149	779	69	23
−11.6	24.6	Vrbovec	13	1759	865	43	35
−17.7	35.7	Velika Gorica	18	2463	1030	17	11
+34.3	62.2	Zabok	97	466	226	21	27
+2.6	21.3	Zaprešić	24	2537	1136	36	16

[1] $\hat{Y}$ = expected percent of actively employed labor force that commutes daily.
Y = percent of active labor that commutes, observed values.
X_1 = population of outlying town.
X_2 = actively employed population of outlying town.
X_3 = percent of population engaged in agriculture.
X_4 = straight-line distance from outlying town to Zagreb.

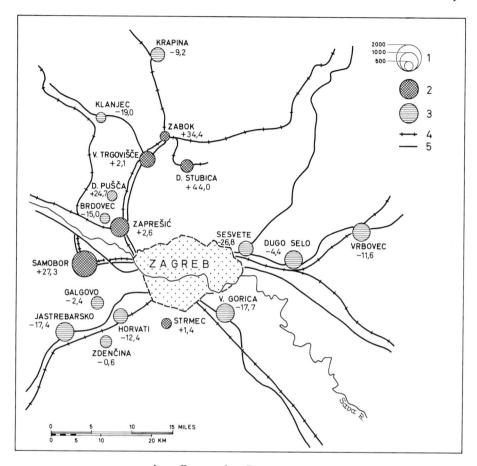

FIGURE A-1. Commuting Pattern around Zagreb.

Figure A-2 presents the commuting pattern for Bor, one of Yugoslavia's specialized mining centers. The multiple correlation coefficient was .99 and there were, of course, no large positive or negative residuals.

The negative residuals appear on a line running east-west south of the city. The largest positive residual is just to the north of the city in the town of Krivelj (−1.4). Approximately 15 percent of Bor's labor force commutes to work from this outlying area, which is one of the lowest figures for any of the cities analyzed. There is no single outstanding characteristic of the suburbs with respect to their residuals; however, the percentage of

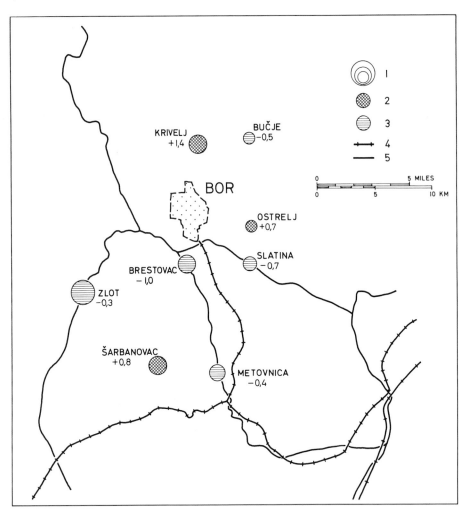

FIGURE A-2. Commuting Pattern around Bor.

agriculturally employed was generally higher in those cities which demon-
strated negative residuals.

Regression analysis for the city of Niš (Figure A-3) yields a pattern of
negative residuals to the west of the city, while towns with positive
residuals are strung along a north-south line through the city. The multiple
correlation coefficient was .97. The towns with negative residuals show
low commuter percentages and high percent of the population employed

in agriculture, while in towns with positive residuals the opposite is true. Distance does not appear to be a significant factor.

There is a well-defined pattern of negative residuals for Belgrade (see Figure A-4) to the west and east of the city with positive residuals generally lying on a line running northwest to southeast. The cities which exhibit the negative residuals have a higher percent employed in agriculture and a generally lower percentage commuting than the other cities in their immediate vicinity. However, the factor of agricultural employment

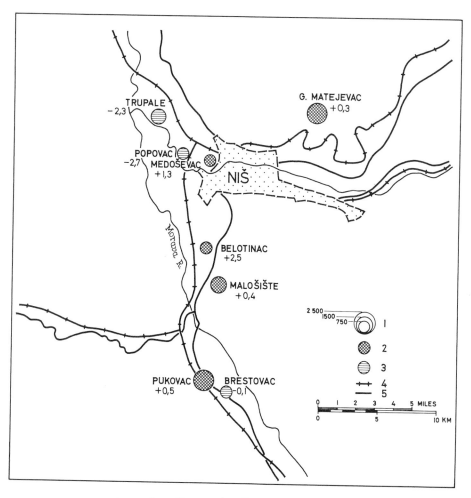

FIGURE A-3. Commuting Pattern around Niš.

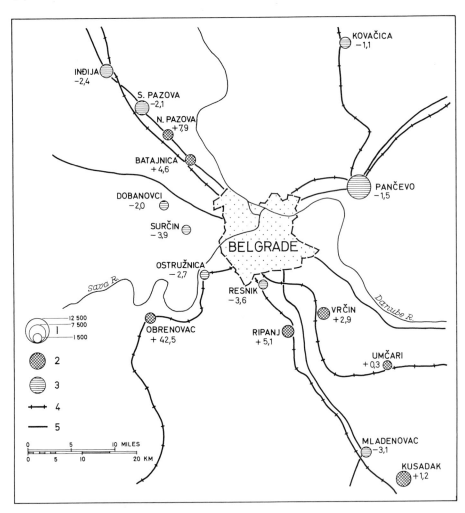

FIGURE A-4. Commuting Pattern around Belgrade.

does not seem to be as important as access or location since many of the
towns with low agricultural employment have both commuters and
negative residuals.

One major limitation of the statistics utilized for this analysis is that they
suggest that the commuters originated in the towns listed. In reality many
of the commuters resided long distances from central transport points,
which greatly increased the time spent in commuting each day.

For a discussion of radical change since 1957 among republics in the volume or intensity of daily journey-to-work see *Borba* (Zagreb), August 23, 1964. It appears the shift from centrally directed investments to the more decentralized administrative system contributed, along with improved transportation facilities which facilitated shorter travel periods, to a rapid increase in the number of commuters in Slovenia and Croatia relative to the South.

Though this is a topic of major importance, it is not possible to extend the discussion of it further at this point. The interested reader is referred to Muhibija Krešo, *Problematika dnevne migracije u N.R.B. i H.* (Sarajevo, 1961) and Stanko Žuljić, "O dnevnim kretanjima radne snage u Zagreb" *Geografski Glasnik* (Zagreb, 1957), pp. 135–147.

Varimax Factor Matrix for Republics

Table II-1. The Varimax Factor Matrix, Croatia

	Variable	Factor One	Factor Two	Factor Three	Factor Four
1	0–9	.81	.01	−.43	−.00
2	10–14	.43	.32	−.33	.21
3	15–19	−.45	.00	−.49	.38
4	20–24	.47	−.13	.58	−.01
5	25–34	.75	−.37	.25	−.03
6	35–49	−.69	−.31	.37	.10
7	50–64	−.94	.18	.03	−.13
8	Over 65	−.75	.37	.20	−.16
9	Population increase	−.07	.10	.20	.47
10	Agriculture and forestry	.08	.05	−.72	−.49
11	Construction	−.28	.81	.33	.00
12	Transportation	−.02	.96	−.08	−.09
13	Handicraft	−.22	−.08	.14	−.60
14	Utilities and housing administration	−.25	.13	−.00	.26
15	Cultural activities	−.18	.13	.80	.08
16	Industry	.10	−.57	−.20	.75
17	Commerce and entertainment	−.47	.26	.64	−.15
18	Social and state services	.12	.45	.27	−.39
19	Apartments completed in 1961	.52	−.15	.15	.68
20	Hard-surfaced streets	−.05	.04	.79	−.19
21	Population with radios	.04	−.75	.03	−.30
22	Construction and transportation	−.15	.95	.12	−.05
23	Handicraft and commerce	−.48	.14	.57	−.45
24	Cultural and social and state services	−.10	.25	.75	−.05
25	Construction, transportation, and utilities	−.18	.97	.12	−.01
26	Construction, transportation, utilities, and industry	.00	−.02	−.17	.95

Table II–2. The Varimax Factor Matrix, Serbia

	Variable	Factor One	Factor Two	Factor Three	Factor Four
1	0–9	.01	.93	.21	.11
2	10–14	.19	.70	.16	−.13
3	15–19	−.00	.72	−.46	.05
4	20–24	.22	.06	.72	.36
5	25–34	−.03	−.51	.72	.10
6	35–49	−.05	−.85	−.17	−.20
7	50–64	.06	−.69	−.70	−.05
8	Over 65	−.02	−.31	−.95	−.09
9	Population increase	−.68	−.17	.07	−.11
10	Agriculture and forestry	−.12	−.14	−.16	−.18
11	Construction	−.67	−.34	.04	.14
12	Transportation	.25	−.47	−.12	.35
13	Handicraft	−.12	.02	.22	.82
14	Utilities and housing administration	.03	−.15	.14	−.42
15	Cultural activities	−.80	−.04	.07	.13
16	Industry	.76	.24	.10	−.36
17	Commerce and entertainment	−.12	−.13	.19	.69
18	Social and state services	−.71	.08	−.09	−.27
19	Apartments completed in 1961	−.16	.05	.67	.02
20	Hard-surfaced streets	−.50	.27	.06	.01
21	Population with radios	.09	−.83	.06	−.14
22	Construction and transportation	−.46	−.56	−.02	.32
23	Handicraft and commerce	−.13	−.05	.24	.96
24	Cultural and social and state services	−.91	−.02	.01	.00
25	Construction, transportation, and utilities	−.43	−.57	.02	.18
26	Construction, transportation, utilities, and industry	.59	−.15	.13	−.29

Table II-3. THE VARIMAX FACTOR MATRIX, SLOVENIA

	Variable	Factor One	Factor Two	Factor Three
1	0–9	.98	−.15	−.07
2	10–14	.51	.00	.85
3	15–19	.62	.60	.48
4	20–24	−.02	−.99	.06
5	25–34	−.09	−.12	−.98
6	35–49	−.07	.66	−.73
7	50–64	−.94	−.30	.09
8	Over 65	−.89	.44	.05
9	Population increase	.00	.86	.50
10	Agriculture and forestry	.33	.83	.43
11	Construction	.83	.39	.38
12	Transportation	.19	.14	.96
13	Handicraft	−.28	.79	−.54
14	Utilities and housing administration	−.73	−.07	−.67
15	Cultural activities	−.81	−.49	−.30
16	Industry	.98	−.04	.15
17	Commerce and entertainment	−.91	.13	−.38
18	Social and state services	−.79	−.39	−.46
19	Apartments completed in 1961	−.03	−.82	−.55
20	Hard-surfaced streets	.74	−.18	−.64
21	Population with radios	.06	−.10	−.99
22	Construction and transportation	.47	.26	.84
23	Handicraft and commerce	−.74	.44	−.50
24	Cultural and social and state services	−.81	−.46	−.34
25	Construction, transportation, and utilities	.44	.28	.85
26	Construction, transportation, utilities, and industry	.87	.08	.46

Table II-4. The Varimax Factor Matrix, Bosnia and Herzegovina

	Variable	Factor One	Factor Two	Factor Three	Factor Four
1	0–9	.91	−.16	.33	−.13
2	10–14	−.11	.95	−.16	−.22
3	15–19	−.40	.83	−.35	.00
4	20–24	.29	−.95	.06	.09
5	25–34	.48	−.55	.52	.42
6	35–49	−.86	.31	−.35	.16
7	50–64	−.89	.11	−.36	−.22
8	Over 65	−.76	−.02	−.58	−.24
9	Population increase	−.78	.56	−.25	.02
10	Agriculture and forestry	.71	−.39	.19	.54
11	Construction	−.14	.94	.27	−.09
12	Transportation	.05	−.73	−.67	.07
13	Handicraft	−.85	.41	−.31	.03
14	Utilities and housing administration	−.88	−.00	−.41	.19
15	Cultural activities	−.90	.41	−.02	.01
16	Industry	.91	−.17	.34	.14
17	Commerce and entertainment	−.96	.23	.04	.06
18	Social and state services	−.92	−.25	.00	−.29
19	Apartments completed in 1961	.79	−.23	−.21	.51
20	Hard-surfaced streets	.15	−.27	.91	.23
21	Population with radios	−.06	−.19	.09	.97
22	Construction and transportation	−.09	−.04	−.99	.00
23	Handicraft and commerce	−.94	.30	−.08	.05
24	Cultural and social and state services	−.97	.19	−.01	−.09
25	Construction, transportation, and utilities	−.52	−.02	−.84	.10
26	Construction, transportation, utilities, and industry	.94	−.22	.13	.21

Table II-5. THE VARIMAX FACTOR MATRIX, MACEDONIA

	Variable	Factor One	Factor Two	Factor Three	Factor Four
1	0–9	.78	−.09	.54	−.16
2	10–14	.73	.12	.29	.56
3	15–19	.78	−.15	.32	.44
4	20–24	.97	−.18	.08	.09
5	25–34	.99	.08	−.03	−.02
6	35–49	.44	.75	−.14	.22
7	50–64	.28	−.22	−.10	.75
8	Over 65	−.03	−.11	.32	.81
9	Population increase	.40	−.25	.87	.09
10	Agriculture and forestry	.33	−.73	.26	.47
11	Construction	−.25	.34	−.77	−.29
12	Transportation	.15	−.16	−.92	.06
13	Handicraft	−.12	.96	−.06	−.04
14	Utilities and housing administration	.46	.45	.02	.75
15	Cultural activities	.16	.94	−.14	.13
16	Industry	.04	−.68	.66	.19
17	Commerce and entertainment	−.38	.76	−.44	−.16
18	Social and state services	.40	.07	−.11	−.85
19	Apartments completed in 1961	.44	.42	−.18	.07
20	Hard-surfaced streets	.57	.53	.40	−.30
21	Population with radios	.56	.11	−.51	−.14
22	Construction and transportation	−.09	.14	−.96	−.17
23	Handicraft and commerce	−.25	.91	−.24	−.10
24	Cultural and social and state services	.25	.91	−.16	−.09
25	Construction, transportation, and utilities	−.04	.20	−.97	−.07
26	Construction, transportation, utilities, and industry	−.00	−.75	−.41	.17

Factor Scores of Communes on Factors One, Two, and Four

Note: The communes are ordered according to their scores on Factor One. The ranks for Factors Two and Four are from the highest *negative* score while for Factor One they are from the highest *positive* score. Each commune is listed first followed by the district and republic in which it lies. The province of Kosovo-Metohija and the Republic of Montenegro do not have districts, therefore only the province (Kosmet) or the Republic (Montenegro) is given. The asterisks refer to urban communes; see Chapter Four for explanation.

Commune—District—Republic	Factor One Urbani- zation	Rank	Factor Two Relative Develop- ment	Rank	Factor Four Agri- culture	Rank
Novi Sad *—Novi Sad—Serbia	184.6365	1	−89.6201	1	−141.9192	1
Stari Grad *—Belgrade—Serbia	156.0981	2	−45.0523	14	−81.0606	8
Rijeka—Rijeka—Croatia	153.3239	3	−71.4630	4	−109.2395	4
Niš—Niš—Serbia	150.8812	4	−86.6699	2	−127.6170	2
Split—Split—Croatia	145.7906	5	−77.6742	3	−111.8000	3
Sarajevo Centar *—Sarajevo— Bosnia and Herzegovina	144.2663	6	−66.1962	5	−93.4371	7
Vračar *—Belgrade—Serbia	141.5491	7	−37.7061	25	−71.5444	11
Zvezdara *—Belgrade—Serbia	108.6906	8	−43.5715	18	−69.3500	14
Osijek—Osijek—Croatia	108.0744	9	−62.8554	6	−94.0320	6
Savski Venac *—Belgrade—Serbia	103.7636	10	−32.5037	32	−53.2602	21
Subotica—Subotica—Serbia	99.9211	11	−56.2745	7	−96.9045	5
Črnomerec *—Zagreb—Croatia	97.2727	12	−35.1332	28	−63.5417	16
Voždovac *—Belgrade—Serbia	91.2635	13	−41.3949	20	−62.0648	17
Centar *—Zagreb—Croatia	84.7828	14	−19.4782	70	−43.8512	36
Maksimir *—Zagreb—Croatia	81.2903	15	−31.8123	34	−56.0523	20
Zrenjanin—Zrenjanin—Serbia	79.5338	16	−44.6641	15	−72.4190	10
Trešnjevka *—Zagreb—Croatia	78.5670	17	−28.1408	41	−50.6297	23
Kragujevac—Kragujevac—Serbia	78.5591	18	−43.6509	17	−67.4513	15
Palilula *—Belgrade—Serbia	77.3464	19	−25.8348	47	−42.0850	40
Medveščak *—Zagreb—Croatia	77.0737	20	−15.5562	85	−35.3826	54
Zemun *—Belgrade—Serbia	76.4742	21	−33.4449	31	−47.6856	30
Pančevo—Pančevo—Serbia	74.2548	22	−47.1027	10	−70.3699	12
Čukarica *—Belgrade—Serbia	67.8771	23	−37.2795	26	−51.2563	22
Čakovec—Varaždin—Croatia	65.5045	24	−51.4382	8	−80.7241	9
Banja Luka—Banja Luka—Bosnia and Herzegovina	64.3643	25	−38.0301	24	−47.1302	31
Slavonski Brod—Osijek—Croatia	64.1967	26	−44.2236	16	−69.3609	13
Zadar—Split—Croatia	63.9807	27	−46.5373	11	−60.9029	18
Tuzla—Tuzla—Bosnia and Herzegovina	55.9253	28	−45.3662	13	−43.8798	35
Priština—Kosmet—Serbia	55.1980	29	−51.2643	9	−49.3486	26
Karlovac—Karlovac—Croatia	55.1670	30	−28.8267	38	−47.8734	29
Idadija *—Skopje—Macedonia	54.4034	31	−17.1001	77	−24.8312	74
Maribor Centar—Maribor— Slovenia	54.3635	32	−24.9671	50	−41.8322	43
Šibenik—Split—Croatia	52.2936	33	−36.8040	27	−49.9629	25
Zenica—Zenica—Bosnia and Herzegovina	51.7201	34	−45.9178	12	−43.8429	37
Vinkovci—Osijek—Croatia	51.5383	35	−39.2649	22	−57.3275	19
Titograd—Montenegro	51.0893	36	−34.4896	29	−42.0309	41
Sarajevo Novo—Sarajevo—Bosnia and Herzegovina	50.4638	37	−23.3444	55	−26.0431	68
Mostar—Mostar—Bosnia and Herzegovina	50.2285	38	−33.8700	30	−40.0583	45

Commune—District—Republic	Factor One Urbani- zation	Rank	Factor Two Relative Develop- ment	Rank	Factor Four Agri- culture	Rank
Varaždin—Varaždin—Croatia	49.7532	39	−30.8558	35	−48.4156	28
Trnje *—Zagreb—Croatia	49.1392	40	−14.5334	97	−25.3976	71
Pula—Pula—Croatia	49.1163	41	−21.7863	59	−31.0623	58
Sisak—Sisak—Croatia	47.6948	42	−30.3703	36	−50.4677	24
Leskovac—Leskovac—Serbia	45.8287	43	−30.1565	37	−42.1371	39
Ljubljana Center *—Ljubljana— Slovenia	44.7565	44	−4.9599	166	−16.7361	107
Ivanec—Varaždin—Croatia	42.3118	45	−42.6193	19	−38.5028	47
Ljubljana Vič Rudnik *— Ljubljana—Slovenia	42.2131	46	−13.8254	98	−27.8503	64
Kikinda—Zrenjanin—Serbia	41.9132	47	−28.6140	39	−46.2845	32
Kruševac—Kruševac—Serbia	38.7944	48	−22.5670	57	−34.8839	55
Požarevac—Požarevac—Serbia	38.6190	49	−24.4658	53	−40.9186	44
Kisela Voda *—Skopje—Macedonia	38.2623	50	−18.6462	73	−23.1796	82
Kraljevo—Kraljevo—Serbia	37.8458	51	−25.1583	49	−37.2295	48
Bitola—Bitola—Macedonia	37.2258	52	−19.3941	71	−25.7014	69
Valjevo—Valjevo—Serbia	36.6029	53	−24.8823	51	−37.2205	49
Pirot—Niš—Serbia	36.2190	54	−27.2626	44	−44.7649	33
Sabac—Šabac—Serbia	35.8903	55	−23.5098	54	−35.5881	53
Doboj—Doboj—Bosnia and Herzegovina	35.7939	56	−41.1705	21	−42.0018	42
Dubrovnik—Split—Croatia	35.6774	57	−14.8954	94	−30.2995	60
Slavonska Požega—Osijek—Croatia	35.5547	58	−27.2316	45	−44.3837	34
Celje—Celje—Slovenia	35.0678	59	−12.6055	107	−23.2269	81
Bjelovar—Bjelovar—Croatia	34.4164	60	−21.7492	61	−42.9926	38
Vukovar—Osijek—Croatia	34.2285	61	−22.6238	56	−36.5571	50
Čačak—Čačak—Serbia	33.2432	62	−18.9592	72	−27.2808	65
Bijeljina—Brčko—Bosnia and Herzegovina	32.3407	63	−38.4844	23	−48.8657	27
Peć—Kosmet—Serbia	31.2210	64	−31.8879	33	−33.7449	57
Ptuj—Maribor—Slovenia	30.1832	65	−21.2279	63	−36.2065	52
Koprivnica—Bjelovar—Croatia	29.2692	66	−20.3413	67	−39.5003	46
Sombor—Sombor—Serbia	29.1825	67	−12.3605	108	−24.4877	77
Loznica—Šabac—Serbia	28.1202	68	−28.4828	40	−34.6784	56
Nikšić—Montenegro	27.9285	69	−21.2743	62	−24.6384	75
Ljubljana Šiška *—Ljubljana— Slovenia	27.9130	70	−3.6595	184	−9.9580	143
Nova Gradiška—Osijek—Croatia	27.7420	71	−20.6845	66	−36.2991	51
Kale *—Skopje—Macedonia	26.7765	72	−21.7787	60	−22.1375	84
Kranj—Kranj—Slovenia	26.3501	73	−10.2810	125	−18.3763	98
Kosovska Mitrovica—Kosmet— Serbia	26.1889	74	−27.2206	46	−23.9311	80
Zaječar—Zaječar—Serbia	26.0611	75	−12.9269	103	−28.4593	63
Svetozarevo—Svetozarevo—Serbia	25.9851	76	−15.9855	83	−25.4277	70
Maribor Tabor—Maribor—Slovenia	24.6233	77	−6.9482	147	−13.9146	117

Commune—District—Republic	Factor One Urbani- zation	Rank	Factor Two Relative Develop- ment	Rank	Factor Four Agri- culture	Rank
Prizren—Kosmet—Serbia	24.3900	78	−27.8892	42	−26.9074	67
Derventa—Doboj—Bosnia and Herzegovina	24.1433	79	−25.3239	48	−25.2301	73
Vršac—Pančevo—Serbia	22.9109	80	−10.8865	120	−21.2326	88
Nova Gorica—Gorica—Slovenia	22.3917	81	−9.6452	127	−21.4611	86
Beli Manastir—Osijek—Croatia	22.2870	82	−17.3293	76	−30.8261	59
Brčko—Brčko—Bosnia and Herzegovina	22.1122	83	−27.4334	43	−29.2423	62
Murska Sobota—Maribor— Slovenia	21.9517	84	−9.0390	133	−24.1011	79
Novi Beograd *—Belgrade—Serbia	21.4624	85	−3.8639	178	−2.7814	201
Ljubljana Bežigrad *—Ljubljana— Slovenia	21.6068	86	−.6980	219	−3.4896	193
Bačka Palanka—Novi Sad—Serbia	20.8582	87	−15.4206	86	−25.3804	72
Prilep—Bitola—Macedonia	20.7703	88	−14.7254	96	−19.3828	93
Kumanovo—Kumanovo— Macedonia	20.0510	89	−16.1183	82	−16.9719	103
Virovitica—Bjelovar—Croatia	20.0404	90	−16.4056	80	−27.1362	66
Saat Kula *—Skopje—Macedonia	19.4256	91	−15.3982	87	−14.4704	114
Titovo Užice—Titovo Užice— Serbia	18.7529	92	−12.1431	109	−16.0715	112
Maribor Tezno—Maribor— Slovenia	18.4483	93	−7.4328	145	−13.7696	118
Bečej—Novi Sad—Serbia	18.3968	94	−9.2150	132	−21.8308	85
Novo Mesto—Novo Mesto— Slovenia	17.7030	95	−9.4119	130	−17.4931	102
Ljubljana Moste Polje *— Ljubljana—Slovenia	16.7824	96	−.9123	216	−4.9539	181
Prokuplje—Niš—Serbia	16.6507	97	−15.1874	89	−21.3446	87
Novi Pazar—Kraljevo—Serbia	16.2595	98	−24.5532	52	−24.5587	76
Djurdjevac—Bjelovar—Croatia	16.1536	99	−12.6292	106	−29.4617	61
Prijedor—Prijedor—Bosnia and Herzegovina	15.8769	100	−20.2754	68	−18.6529	96
Bor—Zaječar—Serbia	15.5595	101	−12.0048	111	−18.0070	99
Sremska Mitrovica—Sremska Mitrovica—Serbia	15.3771	102	−7.7714	143	−13.4453	121
Smederevo—Smederevo—Serbia	15.2579	103	−6.6303	150	−9.7578	145
Sinj—Split—Croatia	15.1003	104	−20.0762	69	−22.7966	83
Obrenovac *—Belgrade—Serbia	14.1718	105	−11.9742	112	−19.7407	92
Paraćin—Svetozarevo—Serbia	14.0958	106	−9.5912	128	−16.1736	111
Vrbas—Novi Sad—Serbia	14.0041	107	−8.8612	136	−13.0799	123
Knin—Split—Croatia	13.8155	108	−15.0069	92	−17.8006	101
Struga—Ohrid—Macedonia	13.6683	109	−16.5712	79	−14.2181	115
Krapina—Zagreb—Croatia	13.6656	110	−12.8716	104	−19.7834	90
Djakovo—Osijek—Croatia	13.2707	111	−12.8653	105	−20.9786	89

Commune—District—Republic	Factor One Urbani- zation	Rank	Factor Two Relative Develop- ment	Rank	Factor Four Agri- culture	Rank
Vranje—Vranje—Serbia	13.2521	112	−9.6612	126	−13.5224	120
Mladenovac—Smederevo—Serbia	12.2856	113	−9.0161	134	−16.5723	109
Zvornik—Tuzla—Bosnia and Herzegovina	12.2193	114	−21.9601	58	−24.3577	78
Gostivar—Tetovo—Macedonia	12.1511	115	−17.5627	75	−16.9687	104
Našice—Osijek—Croatia	11.9138	116	−11.0217	118	−16.9528	106
Djakovica—Kosmet—Serbia	11.8978	117	−18.0470	74	−16.2920	110
Bihać—Bihać—Bosnia and Herzegovina	11.5049	118	−14.9976	93	−11.1475	133
Stara Pazova—Sremska Mitrovica— Serbia	11.1974	119	−6.8523	149	−12.0975	128
Križevci—Bjelovar—Croatia	11.0354	120	−8.7885	138	−19.7673	91
Negotin—Zaječar—Serbia	10.7767	121	−5.4986	160	−17.8828	100
Uroševac—Kosmet—Serbia	10.7132	122	−20.9725	65	−18.6803	95
Smed. Palanka—Smederevo— Serbia	10.3519	123	−5.9769	155	−13.3211	122
Travnik—Zenica—Bosnia and Herzegovina	9.9213	124	−16.1951	81	−11.2735	132
Županja—Osijek—Croatia	9.8838	125	−11.0298	117	−16.9659	105
Gnjilane—Kosmet—Serbia	9.8422	126	−21.0446	64	−18.4883	97
Tetovo—Tetovo—Macedonia	9.7353	127	−11.1190	116	−10.2796	139
Ivangrad—Montenegro	9.3597	128	−11.5058	113	−10.9842	135
Knjaževac—Zaječar—Serbia	9.0548	129	−4.8558	168	−14.6227	113
Lazarevac—Valjevo—Serbia	8.8899	130	−10.7293	123	−13.6568	119
Titov Veles—Titov Veles— Macedonia	8.7603	131	−5.3739	161	−4.8228	183
Gospić—Karlovac—Croatia	8.6052	132	−6.4342	153	−10.3681	138
Imotski—Split—Croatia	8.5915	133	−13.5366	101	−16.6015	108
Bosanska Gradiška—Banja Luka— Bosnia and Herzegovina	8.4446	134	−16.8494	78	−18.8942	94
Pljevlje—Montenegro	8.3026	135	−13.4565	102	−12.6813	125
Kovin—Pančevo—Serbia	7.9838	136	−6.4869	151	−13.9397	116
Peščenica *—Zagreb—Croatia	7.5831	137	+3.1259	268	+3.1786	251
Zlatar Bistrica—Zagreb—Croatia	7.0441	138	−6.9159	148	−12.6683	126
Labin—Pula—Croatia	6.9798	139	−4.1411	177	−8.2713	154
Bijelo Polje—Montenegro	6.6378	140	−13.6624	100	−12.1726	127
Arandjelovac—Kragujevac— Serbia	6.2166	141	−4.9474	167	−9.0632	149
Samobor—Zagreb—Croatia	5.7922	142	−2.4740	194	−5.8033	172
Lukavac—Tuzla—Bosnia and Herzegovina	5.6941	143	−13.6698	99	−7.8228	156
Štip—Štip—Macedonia	5.6931	144	−5.8998	156	−4.3679	187
Aleksinac—Niš—Serbia	5.6805	145	−4.1957	176	−9.0893	148
Kurina—Sisak—Croatia	5.5919	146	−4.3276	172	−10.7377	136
Senta—Subotica—Serbia	5.4386	147	+1.0946	237	−5.0153	180

Commune—District—Republic	Factor One Urbani- zation	Rank	Factor Two Relative Develop- ment	Rank	Factor Four Agri- culture	Rank
Foča—Goražde—Bosnia and Herzegovina	5.4323	148	−15.9578	84	−10.5538	137
Daruvar—Bjelovar—Croatia	5.3233	149	−3.7678	182	−9.2324	147
Zabok—Zagreb—Croatia	5.3339	150	−3.6949	183	−9.0339	150
Kanjiža—Subotica—Serbia	5.0340	151	−1.9590	201	−10.1863	141
Odžaci—Sombor—Serbia	5.0318	152	−5.1967	164	−6.8663	163
Kula—Sombor—Serbia	4.9939	153	−2.2129	199	−5.2979	176
Apatin—Sombor—Serbia	4.9538	154	−2.4680	195	−5.2860	177
Ruma—Sremska Mitrovica— Serbia	4.7739	155	−1.3650	211	−3.9523	190
Kičevo—Ohrid—Macedonia	4.6507	156	−8.8712	135	−7.7039	157
Koper—Koper—Slovenia	4.1280	157	+1.3849	242	−.3036	215
Jastrebarsko—Zagreb—Croatia	4.0067	158	−3.8036	180	−11.9341	129
Ćuprija—Svetozarevo—Serbia	3.9860	159	−1.7829	205	−4.6692	185
Podravska Slatina—Osijek— Croatia	3.8349	160	−5.7278	157	−11.3495	131
Velika Gorica—Zagreb—Croatia	3.5870	161	−2.6953	192	−9.0339	151
Opatija—Rijeka—Croatia	3.4457	162	+5.0975	303	+3.9878	262
Jesenice—Kranj—Slovenia	3.3906	163	+4.0314	282	+3.0610	249
Novi Bečej—Zrenjanin—Serbia	3.3458	164	−1.8699	203	−7.2380	158
Žalec—Celje—Slovenia	2.9781	165	+1.1510	239	−1.8650	208
Kovačica—Pančevo—Serbia	2.9539	166	−1.6168	207	−8.7850	152
Ogulin—Karlovac—Croatia	2.9243	167	−3.4422	186	−3.2108	197
Ludbreg—Varaždin—Croatia	2.7418	168	−5.0095	165	−.1630	217
Radovljica—Kranj—Slovenia	2.5656	169	+4.1696	288	+2.5991	244
Konjic—Mostar—Bosnia and Herzegovina	2.5226	170	−9.3975	131	−4.8910	182
Duga Resa—Karlovac—Croatia	2.2525	171	−2.9743	190	−6.0193	168
Strumica—Štip—Macedonia	2.0904	172	−2.9357	191	−1.2093	209
Podujevo—Kosmet—Serbia	1.9757	173	−15.0307	91	−11.0300	134
Drniš—Split—Croatia	1.8964	174	−8.0273	140	−5.8709	171
Trebinje—Mostar—Bosnia and Herzegovina	1.8118	175	−.2420	227	+.2979	221
Bosanska Krupa—Bihać—Bosnia and Herzegovina	1.7154	176	−14.8228	95	−10.2644	140
Trstenik—Kruševac—Serbia	1.6994	177	−3.5691	185	−6.6237	165
Donja Stubica—Zagreb—Croatia	1.6827	178	−1.3237	213	−4.1698	188
Gračanica—Tuzla—Bosnia and Herzegovina	1.6668	179	−11.3201	115	−6.8199	164
Kočani—Štip—Macedonia	1.5757	180	−7.4730	144	−6.2458	166
Ub—Valjevo—Serbia	1.5048	181	−6.4770	152	−11.6630	130
Bačka Topola—Subotica—Serbia	1.2701	182	+1.3470	241	−4.5247	186
Šmarje pri Jelšah—Celje— Slovenia	1.2018	183	+1.5660	245	−3.3999	195
Domžale—Ljubljana—Slovenia	1.1713	184	+3.7744	276	+2.6784	245

Commune—District—Republic	Factor One Urbani- zation	Rank	Factor Two Relative Develop- ment	Rank	Factor Four Agri- culture	Rank
Prnjavor—Banja Luka—Bosnia and Herzegovina	1.1587	185	−15.0099	90	−13.0618	124
Vrbovec—Bjelovar—Croatia	.6402	186	−.5042	221	−9.8866	144
Livno—Livno—Bosnia and Herzegovina	.4159	187	−8.8210	137	−7.0893	160
Teslić—Doboj—Bosnia and Herzegovina	.4008	188	−15.2162	88	−7.0507	161
Gradačac—Brčko—Bosnia and Herzegovina	.1827	189	−11.3878	114	−9.5297	146
Alibunar—Pančevo—Serbia	.1165	190	−.4614	222	−6.1245	167
Bogatić—Šabac—Serbia	.1088	191	−4.2309	175	−10.0154	142
Brežice—Novo Mesto—Slovenia	.0971	192	+4.9269	299	+2.0019	239
Petrovac—Požarevac—Serbia	.0684	193	−.6961	220	−8.2669	155
Prijepolje—Titovo Užice—Serbia	.0643	194	−8.0374	139	−5.5473	173
Vučitrn—Kosmet—Serbia	.0493	195	−10.6199	124	−5.3192	175
Svilajnac—Svetozarevo—Serbia	−.0536	196	−.4350	224	−7.1869	159
Kakanj—Zenica—Bosnia and Herzegovina	−.0626	197	−11.0083	119	−.7133	212
Remetinec—Zagreb—Croatia	−.2311	198	+3.1048	267	+1.0409	228
Lipljan—Kosmet—Serbia	−.3337	199	−10.7691	121	−5.8761	170
Kučevo—Požarevac—Serbia	−.3359	200	−4.2434	173	−6.0179	169
Slovenska Bistrica—Maribor— Slovenia	−.3871	201	+1.8352	248	+.6551	224
Bujanovac—Vranje—Serbia	−.3979	202	−7.9807	141	−6.9509	162
Vlasotince—Leskovac—Serbia	−.8783	203	−3.7996	181	−3.7421	191
Požega—Titovo Užice—Serbia	−.8844	204	−1.1012	214	−2.9844	200
Žitište—Zrenjanin—Serbia	−.9609	205	+.1600	230	−5.3279	174
Žitkovac—Niš—Serbia	−1.0696	206	−.4462	223	−5.2767	178
Otočac—Karlovac—Croatia	−1.1123	207	−1.5504	209	−3.3661	196
Sanski Most—Prijedor—Bosnia and Herzegovina	−1.3630	208	−9.5907	129	−4.0403	189
Videm Krško—Novo Mesto— Slovenia	−1.3784	209	+4.0429	284	+1.9234	238
Ilidža—Sarajevo—Bosnia and Herzegovina	−1.5032	210	+2.7253	259	+7.7264	312
Kuršumlija—Niš—Serbia	−1.6922	211	−5.3488	162	−5.2081	179
Kosovska Kamenica—Kosmet— Serbia	−1.8056	212	−12.0652	110	−8.4357	153
Zavidovići—Zenica—Bosnia and Herzegovina	−1.8399	213	−7.7803	142	+.9536	227
Novi Marof—Varaždin—Croatia	−1.9058	214	−.4327	225	−2.9929	199
Metković—Split—Croatia	−1.9811	215	+2.9048	263	+3.6808	258
Valpovo—Osijek—Croatia	−2.0366	216	+2.9386	264	+1.0530	229
Zaprešić—Zagreb—Croatia	−2.1926	217	+3.2066	271	+1.5120	233
Bela Crkva—Pančevo—Serbia	−2.6696	218	+4.0517	285	+2.0410	240

Commune—District—Republic	Factor One Urbanization	Rank	Factor Two Relative Development	Rank	Factor Four Agriculture	Rank
Pakrac—Bjelovar—Croatia	−2.6731	219	+1.5447	243	−.0356	218
Škofja Loka—Kranj—Slovenia	−2.8738	220	+5.8769	319	+6.0874	291
Velika Palanka—Smederevo—Serbia	−2.9721	221	+2.7899	261	−.4568	213
Brus—Kruševac—Serbia	−2.9942	222	+1.6453	246	+3.5547	256
Benkovac—Split—Croatia	−3.0560	223	−5.5506	159	−3.2093	198
Aleksandrovac—Kruševac—Serbia	−3.1157	224	−1.5456	210	−3.5547	192
Babušnica—Niš—Serbia	−3.1241	225	−2.6918	193	−4.7015	184
Visoko—Sarajevo—Bosnia and Herzegovina	−3.2685	226	−1.3609	212	+4.2681	266
Ključ—Prijedor—Bosnia and Herzegovina	−3.2918	227	−10.7564	122	−2.4371	203
Jajce—Jajce—Bosnia and Herzegovina	−3.3033	228	−6.0815	154	+.4967	222
Bosanski Novi—Prijedor—Bosnia and Herzegovina	−3.5623	229	−4.3368	171	+.1533	219
Ohrid—Ohrid—Macedonia	−3.7940	230	+4.5953	295	+8.5991	325
Sjenica—Kraljevo—Serbia	−3.8423	231	−6.9757	146	−3.4833	194
Goražde—Goražde—Bosnia and Herzegovina	−3.9481	232	−2.2146	198	−3.4202	254
Maglaj—Doboj—Bosnia and Herzegovina	−3.9907	233	−4.2345	174	+2.2382	241
Gornji Milanovac—Čačak—Serbia	−4.1638	234	+2.9757	265	+.7789	226
Sečanj—Zrenjanin—Serbia	−4.2193	235	+2.4959	255	+.6604	225
Omiš—Split—Croatia	−4.5081	236	+3.2807	272	+4.9533	271
Ivanjica—Čačak—Serbia	−4.5297	237	−2.9808	189	−2.7043	202
Bajina Bašta—Titovo Užice—Serbia	−4.6634	238	−1.6987	206	−1.8866	207
Petrinja—Sisak—Croatia	−4.7415	239	+3.3886	275	+2.4139	243
Tolmin—Gorica—Slovenia	−4.9570	240	+6.8425	342	+4.9209	270
Topola—Kragujevac—Serbia	−5.0926	241	+2.9958	266	−2.1443	205
Svrljig—Niš—Serbia	−5.1361	242	+.8762	236	−1.9300	206
Bosanski Brod—Doboj—Bosnia and Herzegovina	−5.3300	243	+1.1094	238	+4.6049	268
Varvarin—Kruševac—Serbia	−5.3471	244	+1.5535	244	−2.2284	204
Raška—Kraljevo—Serbia	−5.4795	245	−.7169	218	+2.2507	242
Kriva Palanka—Kumanovo—Macedonia	−5.5371	246	−2.2671	197	+1.5584	234
Veliko Gradište—Požarevac—Serbia	−5.7004	247	+3.9150	280	−.9527	211
Glina—Sisak—Croatia	−5.7207	248	1.1727	247	−1.0248	210
Djorče Petrov—Skopje—Macedonia	−5.7262	249	−.0301	229	+5.1515	272
Žabalj—Novi Sad—Serbia	−6.0171	250	+4.2017	291	+3.2337	253
Ada—Subotica—Serbia	−6.1578	251	+7.4356	354	+5.5308	282

Commune—District—Republic	Factor One Urbani-zation	Rank	Factor Two Relative Develop-ment	Rank	Factor Four Agri-culture	Rank
Donji Miholjac—Osijek— Croatia	−6.2174	252	4.1719	289	1.6388	235
Sežana—Koper—Slovenia	−6.2926	253	9.4743	413	9.0896	337
Indjija—Sremska Mitrovica— Serbia	−6.3865	254	5.8233	316	6.9894	302
Cetinje—Montenegro	−6.3982	255	6.5692	335	7.9183	316
Grosuplje—Ljubljana—Slovenia	−6.5100	256	7.3034	348	7.2674	306
Istok—Kosmet—Serbia	−6.5769	257	−4.4487	170	−.4537	214
Bojevac—Zaječar—Serbia	−6.6013	258	4.1931	290	1.6555	236
Bar—Montenegro	−6.6292	259	4.1134	287	5.9892	285
Adjovščina—Gorica—Slovenia	−6.7748	260	7.8148	363	8.1246	319
Bela Palanka—Niš—Serbia	−7.0269	261	4.3782	293	3.6271	257
Ivanić-grad—Sisak—Croatia	−7.0731	262	5.7045	311	4.3799	267
Vladičin Han—Vranje—Serbia	−7.1298	263	2.3348	251	4.9292	269
Duvno—Livno—Bosnia and Herzegovina	−7.1513	264	−3.1028	187	.2221	220
Ravne na Koroškem—Maribor— Slovenia	−7.2597	265	6.4797	329	10.3973	361
Kamnik—Ljubljana—Slovenia	−7.3512	266	9.0013	398	10.9234	375
Lendava—Maribor—Slovenia	−7.3833	267	8.5757	388	7.1574	303
Šoštanj—Celje—Slovenia	−7.4227	268	6.4953	330	9.9677	342
Čapljina—Mostar—Bosnia and Herzegovina	−7.4491	269	4.0932	286	6.8795	300
Mrkonjić-grad—Jajce—Bosnia and Herzegovina	−7.5195	270	−3.8202	179	1.8504	237
Vitina—Kosmet—Serbia	−7.5743	271	−5.3398	163	−.2657	216
Trbovlje—Ljubljana—Slovenia	−7.6497	272	9.9619	429	12.6717	404
Delnice—Rijeka—Croatia	−7.8601	273	7.7733	361	11.5065	383
Postojna—Koper—Slovenia	−8.0027	274	9.7929	424	10.7290	367
Cazin—Bihać—Bosnia and Herzegovina	−8.0346	275	−4.6720	169	1.0839	230
Novska—Sisak—Croatia	−8.0942	276	5.7477	315	6.0105	287
Šid—Sremska Mitrovica—Serbia	−8.1025	277	7.1400	345	6.9401	301
Kavadarci—Titov Veles— Macedonia	−8.2312	278	5.0274	300	8.5590	324
Sokobanja—Niš—Serbia	−8.2378	279	5.5619	310	2.9689	248
Krajača—Belgrade—Serbia	−8.3501	280	5.8346	318	8.9939	334
Živinice—Tuzla—Bosnia and Herzegovina	−8.3714	281	−2.1265	200	6.7117	299
Kuzmin—Sremska Mitrovica— Serbia	−8.4399	282	4.4277	294	3.7336	259
Vladimirci—Šabac—Serbia	−8.5375	283	2.3513	252	.6392	223
Korčula—Split—Croatia	−8.5397	284	9.5303	416	9.7050	343
Resen—Ohrid—Macedonia	−8.5718	285	5.0320	301	6.6389	298
Nova Crnja—Zrenjanin—Serbia	−8.5761	286	5.8314	319	4.2517	265

Commune—District—Republic	Factor One Urbanization	Rank	Factor Two Relative Development	Rank	Factor Four Agriculture	Rank
Žabari—Požarevac—Serbia	−8.6590	287	5.4634	309	1.5063	232
Lopare—Tuzla—Bosnia and Herzegovina	−8.7425	288	−3.0496	188	1.4211	231
Garešnica—Bjelovar—Croatia	−8.9050	289	6.4957	331	3.8284	260
Knić—Kragujevac—Serbia	−8.9633	290	8.0286	370	7.8815	315
Sremski Karlovci—Novi Sad—Serbia	−9.1604	291	8.3173	382	10.0407	351
Bosanski Šamac—Brčko—Bosnia and Herzegovina	−9.1764	292	2.4975	256	5.4451	280
Lebane—Leskovac—Serbia	−9.2129	293	1.8398	249	3.4890	255
Tešanj—Doboj—Bosnia and Herzegovina	−9.2323	294	−.9350	215	5.4250	279
Priboj—Titovo Užice—Serbia	−9.2913	295	2.4009	253	7.5448	309
Srbica—Kosmet—Serbia	−9.2946	296	−2.3503	196	2.6980	246
Slunj—Karlovac—Croatia	−9.3024	297	.4063	232	3.1060	250
Tearce—Tetovo—Macedonia	−9.3496	298	2.7164	258	6.5011	295
Ljubuški—Mostar—Bosnia and Herzegovina	−9.3541	299	3.3421	273	5.3116	275
Despotovac—Svetozarevo—Serbia	−9.4033	300	4.5962	296	5.3590	276
Pazin—Pula—Croatia	−9.4121	301	6.2315	325	7.2291	305
Grocka—Belgrade—Serbia	−9.4772	302	5.3567	308	5.7283	284
Nova Varoš—Titovo Užice—Serbia	−9.4801	303	3.1626	269	8.0296	318
Kotor Varoš—Banja Luka—Bosnia and Herzegovina	−9.5715	304	−5.6537	158	2.8724	247
Sopot—Belgrade—Serbia	−9.5744	305	6.5619	334	6.0047	286
Kotor—Montenegro	−9.6084	306	11.2228	462	14.0860	429
Crikvenica—Rijeka—Croatia	−9.6104	307	10.4620	440	13.0344	410
Bugojno—Jajce—Bosnia and Herzegovina	−9.6640	308	3.3600	274	9.7357	345
Gornja Radgona—Maribor—Slovenia	−9.7152	309	9.7374	421	9.9632	349
Modrića—Doboj—Bosnia and Herzegovina	−9.7329	310	.8153	235	5.2139	274
Vareš—Sarajevo—Bosnia and Herzegovina	−9.9068	311	3.8689	277	11.8855	388
Suva Reka—Kosmet—Serbia	−10.0323	312	−1.5670	208	4.2202	264
Malo Crniće—Požarevac—Serbia	−10.0386	313	6.3849	326	3.1909	252
Srbobran—Novi Sad—Serbia	−10.1346	314	8.2630	381	7.2987	307
Sesvete—Zagreb—Croatia	−10.3021	315	8.6687	390	8.4727	321
Tutin—Kraljevo—Serbia	−10.3032	316	−1.9590	202	3.8799	261
Preševo—Vranje—Serbia	−10.3037	317	1.3407	240	6.0855	290
Herceg Novi—Montenegro	−10.3405	318	11.8000	475	15.4390	457
Batočina—Kragujevac—Serbia	−10.3482	319	8.0286	369	7.8815	314

Commune—District—Republic	Factor One Urbanization	Rank	Factor Two Relative Development	Rank	Factor Four Agriculture	Rank
Sevnica—Novo Mesto—Slovenia	−10.4150	320	9.6517	419	11.0084	379
Grdelica—Leskovac—Serbia	−10.4294	321	5.3230	307	8.6157	326
Zerovjane—Tetovo—Macedonia	−10.4567	322	.4992	233	4.0932	263
Ljutomer—Maribor—Slovenia	−10.4569	323	10.8274	450	11.5793	386
Saraorci—Smederevo—Serbia	−10.5801	324	7.3712	351	7.4693	308
Srebrenik—Tuzla—Bosnia and Herzegovina	−10.6513	325	−.9112	217	6.5621	297
Srebrenica—Tuzla—Bosnia and Herzegovina	−10.6801	326	−1.7983	204	5.2006	273
Hrastnik—Ljubljana—Slovenia	−10.7498	327	11.1903	461	14.6310	444
Ljubovija—Šabac—Serbia	−10.7977	328	2.7643	260	6.2732	293
Surčin—Belgrade—Serbia	−10.8370	329	7.4312	353	10.2491	355
Orahovac—Kosmet—Serbia	−10.8878	330	−.1415	228	6.0840	289
Bač—Novi Sad—Serbia	−10.9055	331	6.5726	336	7.9288	317
Višegrad—Goražde—Bosnia and Herzegovina	−10.9123	332	2.8176	262	9.4526	340
Laktaši—Banja Luka—Bosnia and Herzegovina	−10.9845	333	2.4915	254	5.3867	278
Trogir—Split—Croatia	−11.0390	334	7.8809	366	11.9870	389
Gazdin Han—Niš—Serbia	−11.0860	335	5.2878	306	5.6124	283
Slovenske Konjice—Celje—Slovenia	−11.1152	336	9.7413	422	12.5776	401
Mala Krsna—Smederevo—Serbia	−11.2786	337	6.8004	340	7.5742	310
Vrnjačka Banja—Kraljevo—Serbia	−11.3046	338	9.0790	400	11.7074	387
Temerin—Novi Sad—Serbia	−11.3055	339	9.4484	411	11.5293	384
Sivac—Sombor—Serbia	−11.3489	340	7.9948	368	9.0823	336
Mionica—Valjevo—Serbia	−11.3531	341	5.9820	322	5.3772	277
Vlasina Okruglica—Vranje—Serbia	−11.3837	342	9.3315	407	14.6241	442
Dečani—Kosmet—Serbia	−11.4872	343	2.2921	250	6.5006	294
Čoka—Zrenjanin—Serbia	−11.5495	344	9.0980	401	9.1119	338
Drvar—Bihać—Bosnia and Herzegovina	−11.5659	345	7.6132	357	12.9200	407
Klina—Kosmet—Serbia	−11.5734	346	.5839	234	6.0633	288
Perlez—Zrenjanin—Serbia	−11.6074	347	8.2620	380	8.7858	331
Lištica—Mostar—Bosnia and Herzegovina	−11.6288	348	4.0382	283	8.4923	323
Ormož—Maribor—Slovenia	−11.6943	349	9.7501	423	10.3158	357
Velika Drenova—Kruševac—Serbia	−11.7016	350	7.1102	344	6.1577	292
Kočevje—Ljubljana—Slovenia	−11.7092	351	10.2424	435	14.8912	448
Bosanska Dubica—Prijedor—Bosnia and Herzegovina	−11.7257	352	4.6491	297	8.8445	333
Vrginmost—Karlovac—Croatia	−11.7275	353	5.7236	312	7.7813	313

Commune—District—Republic	Factor One Urbani- zation	Rank	Factor Two Relative Develop- ment	Rank	Factor Four Agri- culture	Rank
Čazma—Bjelovar—Croatia	−11.7368	354	8.2543	379	6.5229	296
Grubišno Polje—Bjelovar— Croatia	−11.7742	355	8.4198	384	7.6597	311
Sveti Nikola—Štip—Macedonia	−11.9442	356	4.7406	298	9.0039	335
Ilijaš—Sarajevo—Bosnia and Herzegovina	−12.1283	357	6.0979	324	13.9244	426
Danilovgrad—Montenegro	−12.2144	358	9.1807	404	13.5704	418
Dimitrovgrad—Niš—Serbia	−12.2665	359	9.8716	425	10.3489	359
Velika Kladuša—Bihać—Bosnia and Herzegovina	−12.3427	360	−.3265	226	5.4872	281
Rogatica—Goražde—Bosnia and Herzegovina	−12.3546	361	2.5670	257	8.7563	330
Idrija—Gorica—Slovenia	−12.3609	362	10.7197	448	13.2708	411
Lajkovac—Valjevo—Serbia	−12.4240	363	8.7581	395	11.0850	380
Guča—Čačak—Serbia	−12.4268	364	5.9114	320	7.1779	304
Blace—Niš—Serbia	−12.4476	365	6.4498	327	8.4789	322
Orahovica—Osijek—Croatia	−12.5399	366	8.2472	378	10.4737	364
Doljevac—Niš—Serbia	−12.5465	367	7.7542	360	11.4453	382
Žitoradja—Niš—Serbia	−12.5907	368	5.9256	321	8.8406	332
Litija—Ljubljana—Slovenia	−12.6068	369	10.9532	453	14.0560	428
Surdulica—Vranje—Serbia	−12.6373	370	7.5979	356	12.5524	400
Črnomelj—Novo Mesto— Slovenia	−12.6987	371	11.1354	459	13.5437	417
Krupanj—Šabac—Serbia	−12.7035	372	4.2463	292	8.1844	320
Novi Kneževac—Zrenjanin— Serbia	−12.7159	373	10.6067	444	10.8745	371
Šentjur pri Celju—Celje— Slovenia	−12.9166	374	11.1761	460	12.9352	408
Radlje ob Dravi—Maribor— Slovenia	−12.9257	375	9.5569	417	14.0356	427
Medvedja—Leskovac—Serbia	−13.0345	376	4.0229	281	8.6601	327
Vučje—Leskovac—Serbia	−13.0437	377	6.6963	337	10.3284	358
Bački Petrovac—Novi Sad— Serbia	−13.1153	378	11.4475	468	12.5821	402
Stragari—Kragujevac—Serbia	−13.1347	379	9.1329	402	9.1964	339
Radoviš—Štip—Macedonia	−13.2312	380	5.1928	304	10.2474	354
Ljig—Valjevo—Serbia	−13.2330	381	8.7539	394	9.9088	348
Trebnje—Novo Mesto—Slovenia	−13.2412	382	10.8912	451	12.9531	409
Mali Idjoš—Subotica—Serbia	−13.2634	383	11.0008	457	12.0655	390
Plandište—Pančevo—Serbia	−13.2714	384	8.9335	396	10.6662	366
Novi Travnik—Zenica—Bosnia and Herzegovina	−13.3153	385	7.8642	365	16.0398	468
Brestovac—Leskovac—Serbia	−13.3443	386	7.7938	362	10.4547	362
Kalesije—Tuzla—Bosnia and Herzegovina	−13.3595	387	.3608	231	8.6847	328

Commune—District—Republic	Factor One Urbani- zation	Rank	Factor Two Relative Develop- ment	Rank	Factor Four Agri- culture	Rank
Dvor—Sisak—Croatia	−13.4370	388	6.7711	338	10.7847	369
Poreč—Pula—Croatia	−13.6062	389	9.5180	415	11.2238	381
Zagorje ob Savi—Ljubljana— Slovenia	−13.6949	390	11.8557	478	10.5398	480
Osečina—Valjevo—Serbia	−13.6551	391	6.9072	343	8.7059	329
Zelina—Zagreb—Croatia	−13.7297	392	10.9983	456	9.9876	350
Kolari—Smederevo—Serbia	−13.7424	393	8.6979	392	9.7203	344
Merošina—Niš—Serbia	−13.7846	394	7.2754	347	9.8750	347
Ozalj—Karlovac—Croatia	−13.7999	395	9.6839	420	10.9102	374
Kostajnica—Sisak—Croatia	−13.8965	396	10.0537	432	12.5035	398
Hodžići—Sarajevo—Bosnia and Herzegovina	−13.9434	397	8.9513	397	16.7640	485
Ražanj—Kruševac—Serbia	−13.9868	398	9.5653	418	10.2325	353
Brač—Split—Croatia	−13.9959	399	12.5857	495	15.2833	452
Bosilegrad—Vranje—Serbia	−14.0545	400	9.2959	405	12.2944	396
Bojnik—Leskovac—Serbia	−14.0696	401	7.4109	352	10.2898	356
Bezdan—Sombor—Serbia	−14.0879	402	11.5206	470	13.7092	421
Vlasenica—Tuzla—Bosnia and Herzegovina	−14.1987	403	3.1841	270	10.8043	370
Prnjavor—Šabac—Serbia	−14.2085	404	7.6495	358	9.8192	346
Rovinj—Pula—Croatia	−14.2148	405	11.5838	473	15.4584	458
Vrhnika—Ljubljana—Slovenia	−14.2649	406	14.2277	541	18.2744	512
Sipovo—Jajce—Bosnia and Herzegovina	−14.3390	407	6.4659	328	14.3694	438
Cajetina—Titovo Užice—Serbia	−14.3491	408	8.1030	371	10.9662	377
Bosanski Petrovac—Bihać— Bosnia and Herzegovina	−14.3743	409	7.1965	346	12.5171	399
Cerknica—Ljubljana—Slovenia	−14.4101	410	13.3266	515	16.2781	471
Srbac—Banja Luka—Bosnia and Herzegovina	−14.4772	411	5.7236	313	9.9620	341
Beltinci—Maribor—Slovenia	−14.4826	412	12.3553	489	14.5719	440
Arilje—Titovo Užice—Serbia	−14.5157	413	8.2445	377	10.8793	372
Pećinci—Sremska Mitrovica— Serbia	−14.5295	414	9.4422	410	10.8895	373
Bratunac—Tuzla—Bosnia and Herzegovina	−14.5475	415	3.8714	278	10.9413	376
Ugljevik—Brčko—Bosnia and Herzegovina	−14.5570	416	3.8860	279	10.3809	360
Orašje—Brčko—Bosnia and Herzegovina	−14.6089	417	6.5299	333	10.4586	363
Kosjerić—Titovo Užice—Serbia	−14.6363	418	8.1030	372	10.9662	378
Dolneni—Bitola—Macedonia	−14.6988	419	6.7992	339	10.5238	365
Koceljevo—Šabac—Serbia	−14.6991	420	8.2324	376	10.1936	352
Slovenj Gradec—Maribor— Slovenia	−14.7637	421	11.4028	466	16.0481	469

Commune—District—Republic	Factor One Urbanization	Rank	Factor Two Relative Development	Rank	Factor Four Agriculture	Rank
Kladovo—Zaječar—Serbia	−14.7858	422	9.3156	406	12.1808	395
Titel—Novi Sad—Serbia	−14.8454	423	11.4033	467	13.7463	423
Brod—Ohrid—Macedonia	−14.8638	424	8.5560	387	13.7698	424
Odžak—Doboj—Bosnia and Herzegovina	−15.0062	425	5.7288	314	10.7447	368
Dugo Selo—Zagreb—Croatia	−15.0064	426	12.8236	504	14.4138	439
Mozirje—Celje—Slovenia	−15.0732	427	11.9361	480	15.4234	456
Gračac—Karlovac—Croatia	−15.1269	428	9.9519	428	14.1292	431
Dragaš—Kosmet—Serbia	−15.1685	429	7.3167	349	14.1500	432
Ivanjska—Banja Luka—Bosnia and Herzegovina	−15.1792	430	6.5208	332	13.3928	413
Lenart—Maribor—Slovenia	−15.2153	431	11.5417	471	13.2988	412
Delčevo—Štip—Macedonia	−15.2196	432	7.5635	355	13.4088	414
Ljubija—Prijedor—Bosnia and Herzegovina	−15.2995	433	6.8015	341	14.2072	435
Barajevo—Belgrade—Serbia	−15.3608	434	10.6081	446	12.1047	393
Krk—Rijeka—Croatia	−15.3631	435	13.8066	532	14.9054	449
Plav—Montenegro	−15.5570	436	7.9327	367	13.9186	425
Ilirska Bistrica—Koper—Slovenia	−15.5749	437	13.3773	517	16.7258	484
Nevesinje—Mostar—Bosnia and Herzegovina	−15.5897	438	7.6760	359	12.0909	392
Djevdjelija—Titov Veles—Macedonia	−15.6031	439	12.2835	487	17.2371	492
Rača—Kragujevac—Serbia	−15.6524	440	12.6145	498	13.6320	419
Kačanik—Kosmet—Serbia	−15.6577	441	5.9894	323	13.4313	415
Demir Hisar—Bitola—Macedonia	−15.7348	442	10.1541	434	14.3533	437
Stolac—Mostar—Bosnia and Herzegovina	−15.8070	443	9.4756	414	13.6485	420
Ulcinj—Montenegro	−15.8858	444	9.8867	426	15.8582	463
Titova Korenica—Karlovac—Croatia	−15.9013	445	10.3421	438	14.1725	433
Piran—Koper—Slovenia	−15.9520	446	14.5702	544	19.9288	533
Bajmok—Subotica—Serbia	−16.0653	447	12.5057	492	14.8014	446
Grude—Mostar—Bosnia and Herzegovina	−16.0909	448	9.0220	399	12.5941	403
Ribnica—Ljubljana—Slovenia	−16.1254	449	14.7113	549	18.6902	515
Veliki Šiljegovac—Kruševac—Serbia	−16.1461	450	10.6077	445	12.3415	397
Bileća—Mostar—Bosnia and Herzegovina	−16.1550	451	11.5020	469	16.4797	476
Leposavić—Kosmet—Serbia	−16.1567	452	7.8341	364	14.2047	434
Pale—Sarajevo—Bosnia and Herzegovina	−16.1634	453	9.4579	412	16.5966	482
Debar—Ohrid—Macedonia	−16.2092	454	9.9925	431	17.3217	495
Glogovac—Kosmet—Serbia	−16.2172	455	5.2798	305	12.1320	394

Commune—District—Republic	Factor One Urbanization	Rank	Factor Two Relative Development	Rank	Factor Four Agriculture	Rank
Mališevo—Kosmet—Serbia	−16.2399	456	5.0821	302	11.5295	385
Resavica—Svetozarevo—Serbia	−16.2620	457	10.9802	454	16.5185	478
Azanja—Smederevo—Serbia	−16.3457	458	11.2480	464	12.8655	406
Veliko Laole—Požarevac—Serbia	−16.4808	459	10.5512	443	12.0902	391
Negotino—Titov Veles—Macedonia	−16.5307	460	10.4344	439	15.9516	465
Novo Selo—Štip—Macedonia	−16.5328	461	8.3808	383	13.5184	416
Stara Moravica—Subotica—Serbia	−16.5741	462	13.4691	518	15.3981	454
Vitez—Zenica—Bosnia and Herzegovina	−16.6598	463	9.8869	427	17.9228	504
Banovići—Tuzla—Bosnia and Herzegovina	−16.7055	464	8.2026	374	17.9896	506
Tržič—Kranj—Slovenia	−16.7605	465	15.3819	566	20.3452	539
Golubac—Požarevac—Serbia	−16.7826	466	11.8446	477	13.7340	422
Kolašin—Montenegro	−16.8983	467	12.0632	484	17.3832	496
Petrovac—Skopje—Macedonia	−16.9279	468	9.3677	408	14.8044	447
Makarska—Split—Croatia	−17.0543	469	14.7554	551	18.9810	521
Laško—Celje—Slovenia	−17.0610	470	14.0463	536	18.4483	513
Jabukovac—Zaječar—Serbia	−17.1079	471	10.7451	449	12.7097	405
Mrčajevci—Čačak—Serbia	−17.1257	472	11.9873	482	14.6284	443
Mali Lošinj—Rijeka—Croatia	−17.1912	473	15.0299	560	18.8692	519
Minićevo—Zaječar—Serbia	−17.2265	474	13.6845	525	14.0917	430
Klanjec—Zagreb—Croatia	−17.2359	475	12.8592	506	15.8878	464
Probištip—Štip—Macedonia	−17.2564	476	10.4678	441	16.5890	481
Glamoč—Livno—Bosnia and Herzegovnia	−17.2620	477	9.1789	403	15.2722	450
Lipkovo—Kumanovo—Macedonia	−17.3327	478	7.3333	350	14.2828	436
Stanišić—Sombor—Serbia	−17.3736	479	11.9462	481	16.6451	483
Vogošća—Sarajevo—Bosnia and Herzegovina	−17.3844	480	13.6184	523	21.0675	555
Irig—Sremska Mitrovica—Serbia	−17.3859	481	13.2448	512	17.1143	490
Donji Vakuf—Jajce—Bosnia and Herzegovina	−17.3977	482	9.3765	409	17.5649	498
Sokolac—Sarajevo—Bosnia and Herzegovina	−17.4623	483	8.6923	391	15.7908	462
Berovo—Štip—Macedonia	−17.4758	484	12.3514	488	17.1769	491
Vitanovac—Kraljevo—Serbia	−17.5427	485	11.8839	479	15.5003	459
Senj—Rijeka—Croatia	−17.5604	486	13.4976	519	19.7347	529
Kiseljak—Sarajevo—Bosnia and Herzegovina	−17.5675	487	10.3048	437	17.6766	500
Crna Trava—Leskovac—Serbia	−17.5813	488	13.1435	510	18.8410	518
Popovac—Svetozarevo—Serbia	−17.6083	489	12.2025	486	16.0094	467
Hvar—Split—Croatia	−17.6184	490	15.1619	562	17.9408	505

Commune—District—Republic	Factor One Urbanization	Rank	Factor Two Relative Development	Rank	Factor Four Agriculture	Rank
Uljma—Pančevo—Serbia	−17.7503	491	13.3083	514	16.0836	470
Staro Nagoričane—Kumanovo— Macedonia	−17.8147	492	9.9819	430	14.6116	441
Ćićevac—Kruševac—Serbia	−17.8285	493	14.0333	535	17.7785	501
Logatec—Ljubljana—Slovenia	−17.9345	494	15.6386	572	20.5175	542
Platičevo—Sremska Mitrovica—Serbia	−17.9484	495	12.6068	497	17.2751	494
Kratovo—Kumanovo— Macedonia	−17.9579	496	10.2710	436	16.4842	477
Salaš—Zaječar—Serbia	−17.9913	497	13.8014	531	15.2802	451
Kamenica—Valjevo—Serbia	−17.9915	498	11.8210	476	14.7670	445
Stapar—Sombor—Serbia	−18.1197	499	14.2976	543	17.2432	493
Omarska—Prijedor—Bosnia and Herzegovina	−18.2151	500	8.7326	393	15.7429	460
Dračevo—Skopje—Macedonia	−18.2358	501	10.0828	433	16.4788	475
Biograd—Split—Croatia	−18.2965	502	12.7498	500	17.8030	502
Žagubica—Požarevac—Serbia	−18.3217	503	12.4690	491	15.3062	453
Beočin—Novi Sad—Serbia	−18.3968	504	14.5702	545	19.4334	525
Čelinac—Banja Luka—Bosnia and Herzegovina	−18.4127	505	8.6499	389	16.4437	474
Zablaće—Čačak—Serbia	−18.5581	506	12.9884	507	16.8701	486
Rudo—Goražde—Bosnia and Herzegovina	−18.5794	507	10.4876	442	17.1015	489
Mavrovo—Tetovo—Macedonia	−18.6587	508	12.6019	496	20.5583	544
Orašec—Kumanovo—Macedonia	−18.6792	509	10.6904	447	15.7836	461
Prozor—Mostar—Macedonia	−18.7242	510	8.2241	375	15.9972	466
Gornji Vakuf—Jajce—Bosnia and Herzegovina	−18.8374	511	8.4831	386	17.5426	497
Posušje—Mostar—Bosnia and Herzegovina	−18.8480	512	10.9055	452	16.5309	479
Žepče—Zenica—Bosnia and Herzegovina	−18.9309	513	10.9845	455	19.6562	528
Vinica—Štip—Macedonia	−18.9648	514	11.3439	465	17.8293	503
Bulušić—Svetozarevo—Serbia	−18.9920	515	13.3707	516	16.3470	473
Bronzani Majdan—Banja Luka— Bosnia and Herzegovina	−19.0630	516	8.1033	373	15.4221	455
Krupa na Vrbasu—Banja Luka— Bosnia and Herzegovina	−19.2245	517	8.4478	385	16.3469	472
Čantavir—Subotica—Serbia	−19.2524	518	14.9770	556	18.7080	516
Izola—Koper—Slovenia	−19.2562	519	16.3213	580	22.6476	574
Kupres—Livno—Bosnia and Herzegovina	−19.2795	520	13.7240	529	22.0893	569
Gacko—Mostar—Bosnia and Herzegovina	−19.4450	521	12.4292	490	18.1946	510
Brza Palanka—Zaječar—Serbia	−19.4862	522	13.3063	513	16.8852	487

Commune—District—Republic	Factor One Urbani- zation	Rank	Factor Two Relative Develop- ment	Rank	Factor Four Agri- culture	Rank
Pag—Rijeka—Croatia	−19.5157	523	16.1651	577	22.3800	572
Opovo—Pančevo—Serbia	−19.5277	524	14.6513	547	18.1581	509
Breza—Sarajevo—Bosnia and Herzegovina	−19.5592	525	12.5567	494	21.4522	564
Rožaj—Montenegro	−19.5793	526	11.0850	458	18.9305	520
Čitluk—Mostar—Bosnia and Herzegovina	−19.7650	527	12.8173	503	18.0806	508
Topokani—Bitola—Macedonia	−19.8334	528	11.5536	472	17.5924	499
Majdanpek—Požarevac—Serbia	−19.8483	529	13.6267	524	19.8124	531
Rekavac—Svetozarevo—Serbia	−19.8705	530	14.8612	553	18.0497	507
Olovo—Sarajevo—Bosnia and Herzegovina	−19.9593	531	11.2436	463	20.7726	549
Volujac—Šabac—Serbia	−20.0092	532	12.7899	501	17.0093	488
Vranjska Banja—Vranje—Serbia	−20.0310	533	13.0167	509	18.8254	517
Ušće—Kraljevo—Serbia	−20.3098	534	12.5296	493	18.5811	514
Trgovište—Vranje—Serbia	−20.3814	535	11.9918	483	18.2629	511
Medvode—Ljubljana—Slovenia	−20.5201	536	17.6053	593	23.7145	588
Lučani—Čačak—Serbia	−20.5669	537	15.4902	568	21.3685	560
Obrovac—Split—Croatia	−20.7118	538	12.1663	485	19.5623	526
Krivogaštani—Bitola—Macedonia	−20.7174	539	13.6005	522	19.4181	524
Belčišta—Ohrid—Macedonia	−20.7227	540	14.2644	542	20.5267	543
Kukurečani—Bitolj—Macedonia	−20.8319	541	12.9952	508	19.3172	523
Mačvanska Mitrovica—Sremska Mitrovica—Serbia	−20.8352	542	15.3403	565	20.3333	538
Busovača—Zenica—Bosnia and Herzegovina	−20.8526	543	13.1595	511	21.8030	566
Buzet—Pula—Croatia	−20.9903	544	15.9580	574	20.5781	546
Bosanko Grahovo—Livno— Bosnia and Herzegovina	−20.9927	545	14.0505	537	20.6329	547
Zjum—Kosmet—Serbia	−21.0538	546	12.6260	499	19.9038	532
Kalna—Zaječar—Serbia	−21.0556	547	14.7420	550	19.7617	530
Vrbovsko—Karlovac—Croatia	−21.0836	548	16.9921	587	22.9109	576
Buje—Pula—Croatia	−21.1259	549	16.0691	576	20.9831	551
Donji Lapac—Karlovac—Croatia	−21.2211	550	14.9957	557	21.0717	556
Rab—Rijeka—Croatia	−21.2524	551	17.0699	589	23.1098	580
Mali Zvornik—Šabac—Serbia	−21.2556	552	14.1585	538	21.4211	563
Bistrica—Bitola—Macedonia	−21.3733	553	14.1772	540	20.2308	534
Vasilevo—Štip—Macedonia	−21.3744	554	12.8025	502	19.5884	527
Bogdanci—Titov Veles— Macedonia	−21.3912	555	15.5124	570	21.1197	557
Orlane—Kosmet—Serbia	−21.5028	556	11.5950	474	19.0783	522
Jablanica—Mostar—Bosnia and Herzegovina	−21.5070	557	14.8693	554	23.2787	583
Petrovci Šalovci—Maribor— Slovenia	−21.5366	558	17.7914	595	22.1581	571

Commune—District—Republic	Factor One Urbani- zation	Rank	Factor Two Relative Develop- ment	Rank	Factor Four Agri- culture	Rank
Kremna—Titovo Užice—Serbia	−21.5536	559	15.2516	564	21.3801	561
Vrgorac—Split—Croatia	−21.5927	560	15.1769	563	20.5733	545
Bunar—Svetozarevo—Serbia	−21.5965	561	16.0592	575	20.4259	541
Kladanj—Tuzla—Bosnia and Herzegovina	−21.6762	562	12.8465	505	22.5702	573
Štrpce—Kosmet—Serbia	−21.6754	563	13.7612	530	21.3440	559
Mariovo—Bitola—Macedonia	−21.7114	564	13.8700	534	20.3274	536
Novaci—Bitola—Macedonia	−21.7195	565	13.6915	526	20.3092	535
Veliki Kupci—Kruševac—Serbia	−21.7241	566	15.1364	561	20.8681	550
Donji Milanovac—Zaječar— Serbia	−21.8060	567	14.8147	552	20.6953	548
Umag—Pula—Croatia	−21.8663	568	17.4737	592	23.9141	591
Vis—Split—Croatia	−21.8712	569	18.1195	599	23.7329	589
Pranjani—Čačak—Serbia	−21.8994	570	15.3933	567	20.3320	537
Kalinovik—Sarajevo—Bosnia and Herzegovina	−21.9192	571	13.8160	533	20.9972	553
Kruševo—Bitola—Macedonia	−21.9287	572	16.2427	579	22.8158	575
Čaška—Titov Veles—Macedonia	−21.9738	573	14.6693	548	20.9914	552
Čajniče—Goražde—Bosnia and Herzegovina	−22.0335	574	13.5129	520	21.0308	554
Vojnić—Karlovac—Croatia	−22.0814	575	15.4986	569	21.2695	558
Sarakince—Tetovo—Macedonia	−22.1966	576	13.5314	521	20.4242	540
Rudnik—Čačak—Serbia	−22.2793	577	16.4098	583	22.1494	570
Trnovo—Sarajevo—Bosnia and Herzegovina	−22.3562	578	13.7203	528	21.8885	567
Hrpelje—Koper—Slovenia	−22.4790	579	17.8524	597	23.3235	585
Žitni Potok—Niš—Serbia	−22.5141	580	15.6321	571	21.6990	565
Lušci Palanka—Prijedor—Bosnia and Herzegovina	−22.5316	581	13.7043	527	21.4138	562
Dravograd—Maribor—Slovenia	−22.5998	582	17.8984	598	24.7606	598
Zubin Potok—Kosmet—Serbia	−22.6131	583	15.0123	558	21.9430	568
Tivat—Montenegro	−22.7188	584	19.0710	606	25.9568	604
Valandovo—Titov Veles— Macedonia	−22.7612	585	16.4331	584	23.1624	582
Metlika—Novo Mesto—Slovenia	−22.8548	586	18.5589	604	24.4674	595
Mojkovac—Montenegro	−22.9108	587	16.3333	581	24.2657	593
Fojnica—Sarajevo—Bosnia and Herzegovina	−22.9144	588	14.1692	539	23.3738	587
Plužine—Montenegro	−23.1272	589	16.3828	582	23.0372	579
Gradsko—Titov Veles— Macedonia	−23.5136	590	16.5192	586	23.2855	584
Dihovo—Bitola—Macedonia	−23.6131	591	17.2732	590	24.0931	592
Šehovići—Tuzla—Bosnia and Herzegovina	−23.6576	592	14.6294	546	22.9145	577
Kosel—Ohrid—Macedonia	−23.7406	593	16.4588	585	24.4817	596

Commune—District—Republic	*Factor One Urbani- zation*	*Rank*	*Factor Two Relative Develop- ment*	*Rank*	*Factor Four Agri- culture*	*Rank*
Vlase—Vranje—Serbia	−23.7554	594	16.2068	578	23.0367	578
Novo Brdo—Kosmet—Serbia	−23.7884	595	15.0195	559	23.1124	581
Čabar—Rijeka—Croatia	−23.9408	596	18.1580	600	25.7841	601
Bosanska Kostajnica—Prijedor— Bosnia and Herzegovina	−24.0636	597	17.0145	588	24.3052	594
Krepoljin—Požarevac—Serbia	−24.0957	598	17.2896	591	23.3403	586
Han Pijesak—Sarajevo—Bosnia and Herzegovina	−24.2306	599	15.9082	573	25.5964	599
Šavnik—Montenegro	−24.3757	600	17.7614	594	24.6558	597
Skender Vakuf—Banja Luka— Bosnia and Herzegovina	−24.4416	601	14.9483	555	23.7728	590
Žabljak—Montenegro	−24.7816	602	18.4890	603	25.7634	600
Pehčevo—Štip—Macedonia	−24.8689	603	18.6863	605	25.8826	602
Budva—Montenegro	−24.9224	604	19.7159	609	27.1963	608
Bogomila—Titov Veles— Macedonia	−25.0274	605	18.2792	601	26.1135	605
Kreševo—Sarajevo—Bosnia and Herzegovina	−25.1155	606	17.8276	596	26.4361	606
Devići—Čačak—Serbia	−25.8276	607	18.4131	602	25.9179	603
Ljubinje—Mostar—Bosnia and Herzegovina	−26.0860	608	19.2932	608	26.8574	607
Konopište—Titov Veles— Macedonia	−26.1487	609	19.2782	607	27.3570	609
Novigrad—Pula—Croatia	−27.4629	610	21.1670	610	29.3295	610
Lastovo—Split—Croatia	−28.4650	611	22.2481	611	30.6716	611

Selected Bibliography

Sources on Yugoslav Planning, Politics,
and Administration

Mihajlo Aleksić, "Unapredjenje saobraćaja i razvoj privrede zaostalih područja," *Ekonomist* (Belgrade: No. 2, 1962).

Phillis Auty, "Building a New Yugoslavia," *Fabian Society—Research Series* (London: No. 165, 1954).

Vladimir Bakarić, "Aktuelni problemi izgradnje našeg privrednog sistema" (Zagreb: Biblioteka Ekonomskog pregleda, 1963).

Miho Barada, "*Hrvatski vlasteoski feudalizam*" (Zagreb: Jugoslavenska akademija znanosti i umjetnosti, No. 44, 1952).

Rudolf Bičanić, "La Concurrence Socialiste en Yougoslavie," *Archives de l'Institut de Science Economique Appliquée* (Paris: Vol. 9, No. 3, 1956).

223

———— "Economic Growth under Centralized and Decentralized Planning in Yugoslavia—A Case Study," *Economic Development and Cultural Change* (Chicago: Vol. 6, No. 1, 1957).

———— "Interaction of Macro and Micro-Economic Decisions in Yugoslavia, 1954–1957," *Value and Plan in Eastern Europe* (Berkeley: University of California Press, Russian and East European Studies, 1960).

———— "O monocentričnom i policentričnom planiranju," *Ekonomski pregled* (Zagreb: No. 6–7, 1963).

———— "Tri koncepcije ruralnog planiranja," *Sociologija sela* (Zagreb: No. 5–6, 1964).

CHARLES E. BIDWELL, "Language, Dialect, and Nationality in Yugoslavia," *Human Relations* (Vol. 15, No. 3, 1962).

SRETEN BJELIČIĆ, *Communal System in Yugoslavia* (Belgrade: "Jugoslavija," 1961).

C. BOBROWSKI, *La Yugoslavie Socialiste* (Paris: Librairie A. Colin, 1956).

DUSAN ČALIĆ, *Izgradnja industrije u FNRJ* (Zagreb: "Kultura," 1957).

NIKOLA ČOBELJIĆ, *Politika i metodi privrednog razvoja Jugoslavije* (Belgrade: Ekonomska biblioteka, 1959).

JOVAN CVIJIĆ, "The Zones of Civilization of the Balkan Peninsula," *Geographical Review* (Vol. V, No. 6, 1918).

S. DAPČEVIĆ-KUČAR, D. GORUPIĆ, R. LANG, M. MESARIĆ, I. PERIŠIN, J. SIROTKOVIĆ, i V. STIPETIĆ, "O nekim problemima privrednog sistema," *Ekonomski pregled* (Zagreb: No. 3–5, 1963).

EVGENI DIMITROV, "Position of the Republics in the Federal System of Yugoslavia," *Selected Problems of Social Sciences and Humanities* (Skopje: Papers from the Yugoslav-American Colloquium, Ohrid, 1963).

JOVAN DJORDJEVIĆ and NAJDAN PEŠIĆ, "The Communal Self-Government System in Yugoslavia," *International Social Science Journal* (Vol. XIII, No. 3, 1961).

F. DVORNIK, *The Slavs—Their Early History and Civilization* (Boston: American Academy of Arts and Sciences, 1956).

JACK C. FISHER, "Political Decision: A Factor in the Changing Agricultural Geography of Yugoslavia," *Journal of Geography* (November, 1960).

———— *The Continuity of Urban Patterns under Socialism: The Yugoslav Experience* (Syracuse University: PhD Dissertation, 1961).

———— *Stari planovi Zagreba* (Zagreb: City Planning Commission, 1961).

———— "Planning the City of Socialist Man," *Journal of the American Institute of Planners* (November, 1962).

———— "Urban Analysis: A Case Study of Zagreb, Yugoslavia," *Annals of the Association of American Geographers* (September, 1963).

———— "A Need for Regional Planning," *Naši razgledi* (Ljubljana: January 11, 1964).

———— "The Reconstruction of Skopje," *Journal of the American Institute of Planners* (February, 1964).

———— "The Yugoslav Commune," *World Politics* (April, 1964).

———— "The Structure of Planning in Poland and Yugoslavia," *Proceedings of the 1964 Annual Conference of the American Institute of Planners* (Washington: American Institute of Planners, 1965).

———— and ZYGMUNT PIORO, MILOŠ SAVIĆ, "Socialist City Planning: A Reexamination," *Journal of the American Institute of Planners* (February, 1965).

F. GAŠPAROVIĆ, B. PETROVIĆ, and S. ŽULJIĆ, "Regionalno prostorno planiranje," *I Kongres Saveza društava urbanista Jugoslavije* (Belgrade, 1957).

LEO GERŠKOVIĆ, "Selo—grad i regionalno planiranje," *Komuna* (Belgrade: No. 1, 1958).

LEON GERŠKOVIĆ, *Social and Economic System in Yugoslavia* (Belgrade: 1959).

GOJKO GRDŽIĆ, "Neki problemi teorije razvoja nerazvijenih prodručja," *Ekonomist* (Belgrade: No. 2, 1955).

ALEKSANDAR GRLIČKOV, "Metodi finansiranja razvitka nerazvijenih područja u FNRJ," *Ekonomist* (Belgrade: No. 1–2, 1958).

A. HEIDBORN, *Droit Public et Administratif de l'Empire Ottoman* (Wien-Leipzig, 1908).

TOUSSAINT HOCEVAR, *Slovenia's Role in Yugoslav Economy* (Columbus, Ohio: Slovenian Research Center, 1964).

———— *The Structure of the Slovenian Economy, 1848–1963* (New York: Studia Slovenica, V, 1965).

GEORGE W. HOFFMAN, "Yugoslavia in Transition: Industrial Expansion and Resource Bases," *Economic Geography* (Vol. XXXII, No. 4, 1956).

—— "Yugoslavia; Changing Character of Rural Life and Rural Economy," *American Slavic and East European Review* (Vol. XVIII, No. 4, 1959).

—— and FRED W. NEAL, *Yugoslavia and the New Communism* (New York: The Twentieth Century Fund, 1962).

JACOB B. HOPTNER, *Yugoslavia in Crisis, 1939–1941* (New York: Columbia University Press, 1962).

BRANKO HORVAT, "The Characteristics of Yugoslav Economic Development," *Socialist Thought and Practice* (June, 1961).

—— *Ekonomska teorija planske privrede* (Belgrade: "Kultura," 1961).

ALEXANDER T. HRISTOV, *Origin and Development of Public Self-Management Institutions in Yugoslavia* (JPRS: 11898, December 21, 1961).

BRANISLAV IVANOVIĆ, "Nov način odredjivanja odstojanja izmedju više dimenzioniranih statističkih skupova sa primenom u problemu klasifikacije srezova FNRJ prema stepenu ekonomske razvijenosti," *Statistička revija* (Belgrade: No. 1–2, 1957).

—— "Predvidjanja utjecaja investicija na budući porast ekonomske razvijenosti regionalnih jedinica," *Statistička revija* (Belgrade: No. 1–2, 1959).

CHARLES JELAVICH, "Nikola P. Pašić Greater Serbia or Yugoslavia," *Journal of Central European Affairs* (July, 1951).

—— *The Balkans in Transition* (Berkeley: University of California Press, 1963).

BORIVOJ JELIĆ, "Sistem planiranja u jugoslavenskoj privredi," *Ekonomska biblioteka Saveza ekonomista Jugoslavije* (Belgrade: No. 17, 1962).

D. JOSIPOVIĆ, "Mesne i stambene zajednice u sistemu društvenog samoupravljanja komuna," *Nova administracija* (Belgrade: No. 11, 1960).

A. JOVANOVIĆ, "Političko teritorijalne promene u periodu 1945–1960 godine," *Nova administracija* (Belgrade: No. 2, 1960).

R. A. KANN, *The Multinational Empire: Nationalism and National Reform in the Habsburg Monarchy, 1848–1918* (New York: Columbia University Press, 1950).

EDVARD KARDELJ, "Ustavni odnosi socijalističkih društveno-ekonomskih odnosa i društvenog samoupravljanja," *Ustavni sistem SFRJ* (Belgrade: "Komunist," 1963).

ROBERT J. KERNER (editor), *Yugoslavia* (Berkeley: University of California Press, 1949).

Z. KOSTELSKI, *The Yugoslavs: The History of the Yugoslavs and Their States to the Creation of Yugoslavia* (New York: Philosophical Library, 1952).

BRANKO KUBOVIĆ, "O privrednoj snazi naših kotareva i gradova," *Ekonomski pregled* (Zagreb: No. 7, 1954).

—— "Razvoj privredno nerazvijenih područja Jugoslavije," *Informationi bilten* (Belgrade: April, 1958).

—— and others, *Economic Planning in Yugoslavia* (Belgrade: Federal Planning Commission, 1959).

—— *Analitička metoda utvrdjivanja stupnja teritorijalne privredne razvijenosti* (Zagreb: PhD Dissertation, Ekonomski fakultet u Zagrebu, 1960).

—— *Regionalni aspekt privrednog razvitka Jugoslavije* (Zagreb: "Ekonomski pregled," 1961).

—— and V. TRIČKOVIĆ, *National and Regional Planning in Yugoslavia* (Belgrade: Federal Planning Commission, 1961).

IVO J. LEDERER, *Yugoslavia at the Paris Peace Conference* (New Haven: Yale University Press, 1963).

FITZROY MACLEAN, *The Heretic: The Life and Times of Josip Broz-Tito* (New York: Harper, 1957).

MILOŠ MACURA, *Stanovništvo kao činilac privrednog razvoja Jugoslavije* (Belgrade: Ekonomska biblioteka, No. 7, 1958).

CHARLES P. MCVICKER, *Titoism, Pattern for International Communism* (New York: St. Martin's Press, 1957).

V. MEDENICA, "Sistem raspodele nacionalnog dohodka u uslovima radničkog i društvenog samoupravljanja Jugoslavije," *Finansije* (Belgrade: No. 7–8, 1961).

ANTON MELIK, *Jugoslavija* (Ljubljana: Državna založba Slovenije, 1958).

K. MIHAJLOVIĆ, R. STOJANOVIĆ, D. TODOROVIĆ, B. KUBOVIĆ, B. ČOLANOVIĆ, M. MLADENOVIĆ, I. VINSKI, B. HORVAT, R. UVALIĆ, U. AMBROŽIĆ-POČKAR, I. KREŠIĆ, *Problemi regionalnog privrednog razvoja* (Belgrade: Ekonomska biblioteka 18, 1962).

MIHAJLO MITROVIĆ (editor), *Gradovi i naselja u Srbiji* (Belgrade: Urban-istički zavod N. R. Srbije, 1963).

ZDRAVKO MLINAR, "Aspekti sociološke definicije komune," *Naše teme* (Zagreb: No. 2, 1962).

KREŠO MUHIBIJA, *Problematika dnevne migracije u N.R. Bosni i Hercegovini* (Sarajevo: "Veselin Masleša," 1961).

PAUL F. MYERS and A. A. CAMPBELL, *The Population of Yugoslavia* (Washington: U.S. Bureau of the Census, International Population Statistics Report, 1954).

F. W. NEAL, *Titoism in Action: Reforms after 1948* (Berkeley: University of California Press, 1958).

NENAD NENADOVIĆ, "Socijalistički razmještaj proizvodnih snaga, *"Ekonomist* (Belgrade: No. 3–4, 1951).

VLADIMIR NENADOVIĆ, "O regionalnom prostornom planiranju," *Socijalna politika* (Belgrade: No. 2, 1959).

G. OSTROGORSKY, *History of the Byzantine State* (Oxford, 1956).

B. PETROVIĆ and S. ŽULJIĆ, "Regional Space Planning in Yugoslavia," *Community Development* (Rome: No. 1, 1958).

RUDE PETROVIĆ, *Prostorna determinacija teritorijalnih jedinica u komunalnom sistemu Jugoslavije* (Sarajevo: Ekonomski Institut Univerziteta u Sarajevu, No. 1, 1962).

—— *Prostorne relacije u komunalnom sistemu FNRJ* (Zagreb: Ekonomski fakultet u Zagrebu, 1960/61).

MILENTIJE POPOVIĆ, "Jedinstvo privrednog sistema—samoupravljanje—planiranje," *Ustavni sistem SFRJ* (Belgrade: "Komunist," 1963).

I. PUCIĆ, *Pregled administrativne podjele područja N.R. Hrvatske kroz posljednjih 100 godina* (Zagreb, 1955).

EUGEN PUSIĆ, *Lokalna zajednica* (Zagreb: Biblioteka udžbenici 9, 1963).

VLADIMIR RAŠKOVIĆ, "O uticaju medjusobnih odnosa privrednih i društvenih faktora na razmještaj proizvodnih snaga," *Ekonomski analizi Ekonomskog fakulteta* (Belgrade: No. 1, 1955).

ŽELJKO RIJAVEC, "Upotreba nacionalnog dohodka pri analizi privredne razvijenosti teritorija," *Ekonomski pregled* (Zagreb: No. 10, 1958).

VELJKO ROGIĆ and STANKO ŽULJIĆ, *Geography of Yugoslavia* (J.P.R.S. 11327, 1961).

Veljko Rogic, "Geografski osnovi naseg promorstva," *Zbornik radova IV Kongresa Jugoslavenskih geografa* (Belgrade, 1955).

——"Geografski osnovi stoćarskih veza Like i Dalmacije," *Zbornik radova Kasicne gimnazije* (Zagreb, 1956).

—— "Problem izbora i primjena metoda za odredjivanje geografskih medja nasih gradova," *Zbornik radova V Kongresa Jugoslovenskih geografa* (Titograd, 1958).

——"Fizionomika i funkcionalna regionalizacija Hrvatske," *Zbornik radova Jugoslovenskih geografa* (Ljubljana, 1961).

—— "Regionalizacija naseg primorja," *Zbornik radova VII Jugoslavenskih geografa* (Zagreb, 1964).

Zygmunt Rybicki, "Problems de l'évolution des organes administratifs des Etats socialistes après la Deuxieme Guerre mondiale," *Revue internationale des sciences administratives* (Paris: No. 2, 1960).

Savezni zavod za statistiku, *Dnevna migracija zaposlenog osoblja* (Belgrade: Statistički bilten 101, 1957).

—— *Gradjevinarstvo 1959* (Belgrade: Statistički bilten 195, 1961).

—— *Prethodni rezultati popisa stanovništva od 31 Marta 1961 godine* (Belgrade: Statistički bilten 223, 1962).

—— *Privredno statistički presek komuna Jugoslavije u 1960 godini* (Belgrade: Studije, analize i prikazi, No. 14, 1962).

—— *Privredno statistički presek komuna Jugoslavije u 1961 godini* (Belgrade: Studije, analize i prikazi, No. 17, 1963).

—— *Statistički godišnjak SFRJ* (Belgrade: appearing each year).

Savezni zavod za urbanizam i komunalna i stambena Pitanja, *Usmeravanje gradskog razvoja* (Belgrade: Dokumentacija broj 2, 1961).

—— *Planiranje razvoja velikih gradova u Jugoslaviji* (Belgrade: Dokumentacija broj 3, 1961).

—— *Regionalno prostorno planiranje* (Belgrade, 1962).

—— *Stambena zajednica kao predmet prostornog planiranja* (Belgrade, 1962).

The Constitution of the Socialist Federal Republic of Yugoslavia (Belgrade: Secretariat for Information of the Federal Executive Council, 1963).

H. Seton-Watson, *East European Revolution* (London: 3rd edition, 1956).

Jakov Sirotković, *Novi privredni sistem FNRJ* (Zagreb, 1954).

———— *Problemi privrednog planiranja u Jugoslaviji* (Zagreb: "Naprijed," 1961).

———— *Odnosi u nivou razvijenosti komuna i politika pomaganja nerazvijenih područja* (Zagreb: Ekonomski fakultet u Zagrebu, 1962).

———— *Privredni sistem i društveno planiranje* (Zagreb: Biblioteka udžbenici, 12, 1964).

BERISLAV SREBRIĆ, "Osnovne komponente razmještaja poslijeratne industrije Jugoslavije," *Ekonomist* (Belgrade: No. 3, 1957).

———— "Regionalni aspekt privrednog razvitka Jugoslavije," *Ekonomist* (Belgrade: No. 4, 1961).

JOSIP ŠTAHAN, "Teritorijalni aspekt privrednog razvoja FNRJ," *Ekonomski pregled* (Zagreb: No. 1–2, 1956).

JANEZ STANOVNIK, "O nekim problemima teorije planiranja ekonomskog razvoja u nerazvijenim zemljama," *Medjunarodni problemi* (Belgrade: No. 2, 1957).

———— *Historical Roots of the Problems of Economic Underdevelopment* (J.P.R.S., 7565, 1961).

R. STOJANOVIĆ, *Teorija privrednog razvoja u socijalizmu* (Belgrade: "Naučna knjiga," 1961).

A. SUĆESKA, "Neke osobenosti turske lokalne uprave u Bosni XVIII stoljeća," *Zbornik Pravnog fakulteta u Zagrebu* (Zagreb: No. 3–4, 1962).

MIJALKO TODOROVIĆ, *Problemi privrednog planiranja u Jugoslaviji* (Belgrade, 1959).

A Handbook of Public Administration (New York: United Nations, 1961).

IVO VINSKI, *Procjena nacionalnog bogatstva po područjima Jugoslavije* (Zagreb: Ekonomski Institut, 1959).

———— *Kretanje fiksnih fondova Jugoslavije 1947–62* (Zagreb: Ekonomski Institut, 1963).

DOLFE VOGELNIK, "Ka pitanju klasifikacije srezova FNRJ prema stepenu ekonomske razvijenosti," *Statistička revija* (Belgrade: No. 2, 1957).

———— *Urbanizacija kao odraz privrednog razvoja FNRJ* (Belgrade: Ekonomska biblioteka, No. 13, 1961).

W. S. VUCINICH, "The Yugoslav Lands in the Ottoman Period: Postwar Marxist Interpretations of Indigenous and Ottoman Institutions," *Journal of Modern History* (September, 1955).

D. Vukašinović i M. Vujadinović, "Uloga srezova u sistemu komunalne samouprave," *Nova administracija* (Belgrade: No. 9, 1961).

Svetozar Vukmanović-Tempo, "Delovanje sistema raspodele i planiranja na privredna kretanja i razvoj Jugoslavije," *Naša stvarnost* (Belgrade: No. 6, 1962).

Benjamin Ward, "Workers' Management in Yugoslavia," *The Journal of Political Economy* (Vol. LXV, No. 5, 1957).

Albert Waterston, *Planning in Yugoslavia* (Baltimore: The Economic Development Institute, 1962).

Robert L. Wolff, *The Balkans in Our Times* (Cambridge: Harvard University Press, 1956).

Zavod za unapredjenje komunalne delatnosti N.R. Srbije, *Gradsko stanovništvo N.R. Srbije kao predmet planiranja* (Belgrade, 1962).

—— *Osnovni principi sistema samofinanciranja u komunalnim delatnostima u gradovima N.R. Srbije* (Belgrade, 1961).

—— *Problematika prostornog planiranja i zadaci komuna u vezi sa Zakonom o urbanističkom i regionalnom prostornom planiranju* (Belgrade, 1962).

Stanko Žuljić, "Potreba izgradnje željezničke veze Split- dolina Bosne," *Problem povezivanja srednje Dalmacije sa dolinom Bosne* (Split: Privredna komora kotara, 1958).

—— "Porast gradskog stanovištva N.R. Hrvatske," *Geografski glasnik* (Zagreb: Vol. XXII, 1960).

—— "Stanovništvo N.R. Hrvatske godine 1961," *Geografski glasnik* (Zagreb: Vol. XXIII, 1961).

—— "Prilog poznavinju strukture teritorija N.R. Hrvatske i tendencija razvitka," *Geografski glasnik* (Zagreb: Vol. XXIV, 1962).

—— "Položaj kao faktor gospodarske structure Jugoslavije," *Geografski glasnik* (Zagreb: Vol. XXVI, 1964).

—— "Suvremeni problemi razvoja Zagreba," *Zbornik radova VII kongresa geografa Jugoslavije* (Zagreb, 1964).

Josip Županov, "O problemima sociološke definicije komune," *Naše teme* (Zagreb: No. 2, 1962).

Explanation of Selected Terms

A.P.   Abbreviation for *Autonomna Pokrajina* (Autonomous Province of ——); official name for regions of Vojvodina and Kosovo and Metohija. Kosovo and Metohija is often referred to as Kosmet.

Albanians   The largest national minority in Yugoslavia; officially the expression for these people is *Šiptari* which refers only to Albanians within the Yugoslav state, not those in Albania.

Banovina   Historically the "ban" in Croatia was the highest authority representing the king throughout eight centuries. During the interwar period, the term *Banovina* was the name given to the provinces.

Belgrade   In Serbo-Croatian: *Beograd* (white city).

Beograd   In English: Belgrade.

Bitola   City in southern Macedonia; in Serbo-Croatian: *Bitolj*.

Bosna i Hercegovina   South Slavic expression for Bosnia and Herzegovina.

Bosnia and Herzegovina   One of the six Yugoslav republics.

Capodistria   Italian name for the town of Koper in Slovenia; in Serbo-
    Croatian: *Kopar*.
Constantinople   Earlier term for Istanbul; other terms were *Byzantium*
    and *Carigrad*.
Crna Gora   South Slavic expression for Montenegro.
Croatia   One of the six republics; in Serbo-Croatian: *Hrvatska*.

Dalmacija   South Slavic expression for Dalmatia.
Dalmatia   Croatian province along the central Adriatic coast, including
    most of the islands; in South Slavic languages: *Dalmacija*.
Danube River   In Serbo-Croatian: *Dunav*.
Dinaric Mountains   Series of mountain ranges spreading from the Kupa
    River in the Northwest to the Albanian frontier in the South,
    separating Pannonian area of the country from the Littoral; in
    Serbo-Croatian: *Dinarske planine* or simply *Dinaridi*.
društveni plan   Annual economic plan prepared separately by all territorial
    units; the national plan is prepared by the Federal Planning Com-
    mission in Belgrade.

Fiume   Italian name for the city of Rijeka, in general use during the
    Austro-Hungarian period and during the interwar period when
    Rijeka was annexed by Italy.
F.N.R.J.   Abbreviation for: *Federativna Narodna Republika Jugoslavija*
    (Federal People's Republic of Yugoslavia); official name of the
    state for the period 1946–1963.
Fond za stambenu izgradnju   Fund for Housing Construction; agency at
    the communal and district level, concerned with housing policy and
    finance.

grad   Town or city; in two cases (Belgrade and Zagreb) the term *grad*
    means also an administrative unit composed of many communes,
    corresponding in rank to district (*srez* or *kotar*).

Hrvatska   Serbo-Croatian term for Croatia.

Istria   Italian for Istra; *Istria* is a peninsula in the northern Adriatic area,
    located mostly within the Croatian Republic, except for the extreme

northwestern section around Koper, which is included within Slovenia.

Jugoslavija   South Slavic spelling for Yugoslavia (*jug* = south, *Slavija* = land of the Slavs), meaning a state of the South Slavs. Technically the Bulgarians are also considered South Slavs although Bulgaria is not part of Yugoslavia.

komuna   Yugoslav expression for commune, which corresponds to the term *opština* (Serbian) or *općina* (Croatian). Technically the use of the word *komuna* suggests the meaning of a socioeconomic unit rather than only an administrative unit.

Koper   Slovenian coastal town; Serbo-Croatian spelling: *Kopar;* Italian: *Capodistria.*

kotar   Croatian expression for district; in Serbian: *srez.*

Kosmet   Abbreviation for *Kosovo i Metohija.*

Kosovo i Metohija   Autonomous province in the southwestern part of the Socialist Republic of Serbia having a large Albanian composition.

League of the Communists of Yugoslavia   *Savez Komunista Jugoslavije.*

Macedonia   One of the six Yugoslav republics; in south Slavic languages: *Makedonija.*

Macedonian language   Similar to Bulgarian as Croatian is to Serbian. Established as a literary language only after the Second World War which involved a series of distinct steps to distinguish Macedonian from Bulgarian.

Magyars   Hungarians; in South Slavic: *Madjari*

Makedonija   Macedonia.

master plan   *Urbanistički plan* or *generalni urbanistički plan.*

mesna zajednica   "Local community," a self-governing community of citizens corresponding in urban areas to neighborhood units. In 1963 these units were extended to both urban and rural communes and represent in theory a subcommunal structure designed to secure the participation of local citizens in activities most directly related to their daily needs.

Montenegro   One of the six Yugoslav republics; in south Slavic languages: *Crna Gora.*

Moslems   Religious group in Yugoslavia composed of Albanians, Turks, and Yugoslavs. For the Slavic groups the term "Moslem" denotes an expression of nationality and refers to that part of the population (for the most part in Bosnia) which do not declare themselves either Serbs or Croatians. During the Second World War the Moslems of Bosnia were treated as Croatians. After the war the term "Moslem" was again introduced to denote the more general meaning of "Yugoslav," rather than either Serb or Croatian.

N.D.H.   Abbreviation for *Nezavisna Država Hrvatska* (Independent State of Croatia) which existed as a formally independent state during the war period, 1941–1945.

N.R.   Abbreviation for *Narodna Republika* (People's Republic of ——). Official designation of the republics during 1946–1963.

općina   Croatian expression for commune.

opština   Serbian expression for commune.

Savez Komunista Jugoslavije   League of the Communists of Yugoslavia (the Communist Party).

Savezni zavod za statistiku   Federal Statistical Office.

Savezni zavod za urbanizam i komunalna i stambena pitanja   Federal Office for Town Planning, Housing, and Communal Affairs.

Savez Sindikata Jugoslavije   Trade Union Association of Yugoslavia.

selo   Village in the meaning of a rural settlement.

Serbia proper   Territory of the Republic of Serbia excluding Vojvodina and Kosovo and Metohija; in Serbo-Croatian: *uža Srbija.*

Serbo-Croatian or Croato-Serbian   Officially treated as one language under existing linguistic agreement in Yugoslavia with one common grammar and dictionary. Both the Serbs and Croatians continue, however, to use specific expressions. The most significant difference is the use of the Cyrillic alphabet by the Serbs and the Latin alphabet by the Croatians. Though the dominant language for Yugoslavia, it has been specifically adopted only in the Army.

S.F.R.J.   Abbreviation for *Socijalistička Federativna Republika Jugo-slavija* (Socialist Federal Republic of Yugoslavia); official designation for the state as of the 1963 Constitution.

Skopje   Macedonian spelling for the capital of Macedonia.

Skoplje   Serbo-Croatian spelling for Skopje.

Skupština   Assembly.

Slavonija   Northeastern part of Croatia; in English: Slavonia.

Slovenija   One of six Yugoslav republics; in English: Slovenia.

Socialist Alliance of Working People   *Socijalistički savez radnog naroda Jugoslavije;* mass political organization organized territorially under the leadership of the League of the Communists.

S.R.   Abbreviation for *Socijalistička Republika;* official designation for each of the six republics since the April 1963 Constitution.

Srbija   One of the six Yugoslav republics; in English: Serbia.

srez   Serbian expression for district.

stambena zajednica   Term used prior to 1963 for *mesna zajednica* (local association).

Titograd   Postwar capital of Montenegro; the traditional capital was Cetinje but this was replaced because of its isolated site. The former name for the town on the site of Titograd was Podgorica. Tito is the only contemporary Yugoslav leader whose name has been given to towns and cities; Titograd, Titov Veles, Titovo Užice and Titova Korenica. The former towns of Rankovićevo and Kardel-jevo returned after 1948 to their former names: Kraljevo and Ploče.

Trade Union Association of Yugoslavia   *Savez Sindikata Jugoslavije.*

urbanistički plan   Master plan.

Vojvodina   Autonomous Province in the northeastern part of Yugoslavia forming part of the Socialist Republic of Serbia. Serbs are the largest ethnic group in the region but besides Croatians and small numbers of other Yugoslavs there are large numbers of ethnic minorities: Magyars, Rumanians, Slovaks, and others.

Zavod za plan   Economic planning offices at the federal level (*Savezni zavod za privredno planiranje*); at the level of the republics (*Re-*

publički zavod za planiranje); at the district level (*Zavod za priv-redno planiranje kotara* or *sreza*), and at the communal level (*Zavod za plan opštine*).

Zemun One commune forming the city of Belgrade (population in 1961 was 75,000); until 1918 and during the period 1941–1944 it repre-sented the eastern point of Croatia. It was incorporated into the city of Belgrade after the war and is connected with Belgrade proper by Novi Beograd.

Index